D0175278

ADDITIONAL ADVANCE PRAISE FOR

BRAVO COMPANY

"*Bravo Company* is not your average book about the military or men at war. The book, brilliantly told through the lens of one company, perfectly captures the true cost of the decades-long war in Afghanistan. We meet young men who dreamed of life and adventure in the US Army, only to be broken physically and mentally by the toll of combat. For anyone who ever wanted to know about the cost of war, this is the book."

—Ron Nixon, global investigations editor, Associated Press

"The men of *Bravo Company* are captivating, raw, salty—and above all real. Ben Kesling knows of what he writes and does us a service to bring home their stories of war and the battles afterward."

—Quil Lawrence, NPR correspondent and
former bureau chief in Baghdad and Kabul

"If you want to understand the fingerprints of American military culture and the terrible human consequences of bad policy decisions, this excellent book by Ben Kesling is the way."

—Kori Schake, director of foreign and defense policy
at the American Enterprise Institute

"In *Bravo Company*, Ben Kesling searingly transports readers first into the lush valley at the heart of President Barack Obama's surge, where paratroopers saddled with an unsustainable mission rolled the dice with every step they took, and then into their lives back home as they wrestle with grievous injuries and the loss of friends in a war America ultimately lost."

—Wesley Morgan, author of *The Hardest Place: The American
Military Adrift in Afghanistan's Pech Valley*

BRAVO COMPANY

BRAVO COMPANY

★ ★ ★

AN AFGHANISTAN DEPLOYMENT AND ITS AFTERMATH

★ ★ ★

BEN KESLING

NORTHERN PLAINS
PUBLIC LIBRARY
Ault, Colorado

ABRAMS PRESS, NEW YORK

Copyright © 2022 Ben Kesling

Jacket © 2022 Abrams

Published in 2022 by Abrams Press, an imprint of ABRAMS. All rights reserved. No portion of this book may be reproduced, stored in a retrieval system, or transmitted in any form or by any means, mechanical, electronic, photocopying, recording, or otherwise, without written permission from the publisher.

Library of Congress Control Number: 2022933888

ISBN: 978-1-4197-5115-8
eISBN: 978-1-64700-140-7

Printed and bound in the United States
10 9 8 7 6 5 4 3 2 1

Abrams books are available at special discounts when purchased in quantity for premiums and promotions as well as fundraising or educational use. Special editions can also be created to specification. For details, contact specialsales@abramsbooks.com or the address below.

Abrams Press® is a registered trademark of Harry N. Abrams, Inc.

ABRAMS The Art of Books
195 Broadway, New York, NY 10007
abramsbooks.com

For Kate, Gus, Lewis, and Alice. And Mara.

CONTENTS

LEAVING AFGHANISTAN BEHIND

It's annoying that ten years after losing his legs in Afghanistan, Alex Jauregui still loses them.

Jauregui—"Sergeant J" to the men of Bravo Company—was swimming in a creek near his house a while back, and damned if one of his prosthetics didn't come off in the water. Those things go straight to the bottom, they're all carbon fiber and metal. He should have known better, but he wasn't wearing a sleeve over his stump, so the prosthetic just slipped off when it got wet. *Bloop!* To the bottom.

Really the only time he wears a sleeve like he's supposed to is when he's doing something like skydiving. A leg could come off pretty easily up there in the air, and good luck finding it after that.

When J's not losing his legs, he's breaking them. He broke his foot the other day, snapped the carbon fiber. He's got a passel of legs, so he can get by on spares if he needs to, but that's like driving a car around on one of those tiny spare tires, the donut. It just isn't right.

After he lost that leg in the creek and cracked a foot, he was down to spares. It's no good trying to get new ones from the local VA hospital—it can take weeks to get a new leg, sometimes more than a month. It takes even longer to fine-tune it and get it properly adjusted. It's not the local VA's fault, there's only so much demand for new legs out there where he lives in Woodland, California, away from a big city like LA.

So in times like that J just goes ahead and books a trip direct to Walter Reed, where the prosthetic clinic gets things done quickly. That place is the premier spot for veterans to get new limbs. Jeez, it's like a factory show-room for fake legs. A couple of days there and he gets new legs, sleeves, liners. Everything.

When he first left Walter Reed, years ago, he had five sets of legs: pri-maries and spares and swimming legs and some fancy blades for running. But running hurts his back like hell, so the blades didn't get a lot of use.

Some adjustments he can do himself, little tweaks here and there, but for major adjustments he goes to the VA. Every time he gets a new pair of shoes, the tiny difference in soles will throw off his balance, and he has to get a tune-up so he doesn't trip all over the place.

And man, you can forget about dress shoes—those things call for a complete overhaul. Nowadays he rarely wears anything but his regular old work shoes with a suit—when he has to wear a suit. Maybe it's worth going through the tune-up hassle to wear dress shoes with a tuxedo, but how often does a guy need a tux?

As far as shoes go, he does miss the pleasure of caring about them. He was once a sneakerhead. He'd spring for the latest, greatest models. Jordans. But not now. A few years ago he dropped a couple hundred dollars on a new pair of basketball sneakers, real sharp. But he tripped and fell and that carbon-fiber foot of his ripped right through the shoe.

Fuuuuck, he said to himself. *I'm going to Ross.*

And so he went to the discount clothing store for some beaters. He gets utilitarian shoes now. He buys them at Ross and wears them until the sole is gone.

* * *

Nowadays, being with his family gives J peace, yes, but a different kind of peace came for him with the bees. It started with seventy-five hives a few years ago, in 2015. When he first got his bees, he was hardly prepared. He'd jump if a bee landed on his hand. But he's got 1,200 hives now.

The apiary business—beekeeping—is a dream now that he's out of the Army.

The Army *was* his dream, a career as an infantryman his plan, but once his legs were taken off by a booby trap in Afghanistan he had to shift gears. For a fellow like Jauregui, the loss of his legs was just an unfortunate byproduct of his choice of profession, so he dealt with it.

He's out there in California now, him and his wife and their three kids. Out where farmers have to rent truckloads of bees to pollinate their crops. It's mostly almond-tree orchards. Pollination is done the old-fashioned way, with bees flying flower to flower. People keep approaching him about starting a honey business, but he's focused on pollination.

For a pollination job, he moves a few hundred crates of beehives out to a farm, then comes and picks up those crates a few weeks later once the bees have done their thing and returned to their hives, sated and happy. After he got started in the business, a nonprofit gave him a forklift adapted for a man with carbon-fiber feet instead of flesh and blood. That lets him really make time when loading and unloading hives.

No joke, though, business is stressful out there in California. There are assholes who will sneak into the fields and steal your bees if you're not careful. It's not like you can brand a bee's rump the way you can with cattle. But it's no combat zone—it's a dream life. And now he spends his days tending the pollination cycle, among the gnarled branches of almond trees that have been arranged into militarily precise rows. It's a good setup.

Sergeant J had a few deployments, fought the Taliban, and was forced to leave Afghanistan and never return. And in late 2021, like almost every other Afghanistan veteran, Sergeant J watched the news as the Taliban retook province after province. As the Taliban consolidated their gains. As the Taliban officially defeated the American juggernaut.

He had watched, perplexed, months earlier as negotiations for peace ramped up. He wanted peace—he wasn't against having talks with the Taliban. After all, peace does come. But he was confused and frustrated that the United States was unmooring itself, forcing the Afghan government at the time to release Taliban prisoners. *That's not the way things should be done,* he remembers thinking.

Some veterans were furious about the end of the war, that their sacrifices and efforts were seemingly erased. Not Sergeant J. Yes, he was mad about the way the withdrawal happened, how America seemed to turn tail and run at the very end. He was mad that the United States abandoned the place and jacked it all up at the end. What a mess.

But his time in uniform and what he did as an individual entity in the American military system was not degraded. The war effort, writ large, is beyond his scope to think about and out of his hands to direct or influence. But what he did as a soldier, what the men around him did: He knows that and can consider it often. And it brings him pride.

"We were there to do a job, and we did a job," he says.

Some days they did a fine job of it, and other days the Taliban did better. Some days the US Army might kill the bad guys while befriending and assisting civilians. Other days, a soldier like Sergeant Alex Jauregui might step on a bomb that blows off both legs. It's just the ebb and flow of war. And the withdrawal from Afghanistan, well, that's much the same thing writ large.

Sergeant J can have a bee land on his hand now, no sweat. Sometimes hundreds crawl all over him. No big deal. He's happy to be at the center of all these tiny creatures struggling to live, to thrive, and to find their life's purpose.

They take a lot of attention, too, the bees. He can't just let them alone or things quickly go south. They die off or get sick. It's nerve-racking because the tiniest problem with the hive can cause the bees to up and leave, just like that. Sometimes mites get in there and feast on the bees themselves, ruining a hive. There are so many variables when you're a beekeeper. It's so delicate. And in the end, it can be just luck that wrecks things or makes things work.

The bees gave J an appreciation for the business of daily caretaking, making constant checks and adjustments, attuning to the smallest signals of distress that portend larger disaster. But sometimes a colony will just up and leave the hive, never to return, and he'll have no idea what screwed everything up or what he could have done differently. All he knows is he probably made a mistake and now they're gone.

PART I

BEFORE

CHAPTER 1

COUNTRY SONGS

Back in 2008, Sergeant Allen Thomas of Bravo Company was a soldier so focused on training and his men, he didn't have time for a girlfriend. Then he met Danica Savic.

Every military base is next to a town, and every town has strip clubs, tattoo parlors, and bars that every soldier knows. The Cadillac Ranch in Fayetteville, North Carolina, the town's "Favorite Country Club" according to a sign posted out front, was one of those. For Fort Bragg, home of the 82nd Airborne Division, the line dancing and two-step lessons at the Cadillac Ranch were a perpetual draw for paratroopers, though often the first step was getting way too drunk and the second was getting thrown out.

Danica was friends with a bartender at the Ranch, and she hung out there pretty regularly. That's how she met a few of the soldiers in Allen's squad. At five foot one inch tall, Danica was a foot shorter than Allen, a six-foot-three infantryman who, when he wasn't in uniform, sometimes liked to wear a dirty Coors Light baseball cap tipped back on his head so he seemed another inch taller. She was a brunette white girl with family roots in Indiana. He was a Black guy with roots in suburban Washington, DC. Danica's smile was bigger than her, something that doesn't always come through in photos but took center stage in person. Her bright white smile and dark eyes, combined with a square jaw, made her seem larger than her small stature first suggested.

She became close to Specialist Jason Johnston, one of Allen's squadmates. Johnston was one of those guys who men from Bravo all seemed to know. He was magnetic—always the center of every group, drawing people together. He was a guy who could make memories.

Johnston was from Albion, New York, a damn fine guy who loved being everyone's friend about as much as he loved being a paratrooper. He had never graduated from high school, but got his GED before joining the Army in 2006. He loved country music, cowboy hats, singing, and heading out to dance. He also took the opportunity to be goofy and make people smile whenever the situation called for it, thus he was the ideal character to make introductions. A senior NCO, or noncommissioned officer, from the company remembers that Johnston was a hellion, one of the few men who could be depended on to get into trouble at the Cadillac Ranch.

One night, a handful of Bravo Company soldiers and others ended up at Allen's house, and Johnston introduced Allen to Danica. She was twenty, he was twenty-four. She was intrigued by Allen, this huge guy whose smile filled the room and who played guitar and loved country music. That was how the two of them first connected. They both loved the kind of music that was hard to find on the radio back then, Jason Isbell or the Drive-By Truckers. Texas country.

That night they first met, Allen played his acoustic six-string. What was it, maybe a Taylor? She can't remember which one he played because he had a few of them anyway. But she would never forget Allen playing guitar while Jason sang the Tim McGraw song "If You're Reading This."

> *So lay me down*
> *In that open field out on the edge of town*

It's a song about a soldier who's killed on deployment.

* * *

Allen Thomas had always been able to light up a room with that winsome smile of his. That's probably the perfect word to describe his smile, "winsome"—a sort of effervescent perfection of joy. He'd had that smile even as a kid in Rockville, Maryland, where he went to Rockville High School, one of the smallest in the county. There, Allen was everybody's pal, his longtime close friend Patrick Exon remembered. He was outgoing, he was happy.

Allen was a year behind Patrick in school, and they bonded through music. They played in the jazz band together, the symphony, too, and the marching band. Patrick on the trombone and Allen on the saxophone. Allen was an anomaly, though, because he also played football. That was easy enough to mix when Allen was on the JV team—no conflict with the halftime show—but when he made the varsity squad, he had to figure out a way to do both things he loved. So he'd play football the first half of the game, rush over to grab his sax, and then march in the halftime show while still in his uniform and pads.

Once they had their driver's licenses, Patrick and Allen really bonded. They were both raised by strict families, so they balanced the need to break free from their parents while at the same time not doing anything that would get them into real trouble and disappoint their folks. They transgressed, but not too much.

Allen had a job at a local ice rink and loved to skate, so Patrick would visit him and take some laps when he could. They were that way through school, confident friends. In an old prom photo they posed in a group looking tough yet casual. Allen wore an outfit custom-made for a cocky teenager in the early 2000s: a black dress shirt with white banker's collar and cuffs and a black-and-white tie. His smile was held in check by a look of seriousness and purpose.

After graduation, Allen went off to Bowie State for college, and Patrick went to community college before heading to Ohio State. They still talked to each other while at school and took time to hang out when they were home in Maryland for vacations. Allen soon realized college wasn't for him. His dad was a veteran, he was athletic, and college wasn't working, so off he went to join the Army.

* * *

Patrick went to Allen's boot camp graduation and occasionally went to Fort Bragg to visit Allen once he was stationed there. Even though Patrick had no interest in the Army, he remained close to Allen and watched his friend grow and change, becoming a soldier.

Allen first arrived at the 82nd Airborne in August of 2004. He was grumpy about it, remembered Dave Abt, who was already in the unit, and who over time would become one of Allen's best friends. Allen was pissed off because he'd washed out of Special Forces training. He'd signed up for what's known as an 18X contract, which fast-tracks a recruit into the Green Beret pipeline. But Allen had faltered somewhere along the way and failed a training cycle.

The Green Beret pipeline in the Army—just like the SEAL pipeline in the Navy—routinely spits people out along the way. Special operations training consists of a selection phase followed by month after month of grueling physical and mental training. Some guys can't handle the mental fatigue involved, some can't hack it academically, and some break themselves physically—even something as simple as a twisted ankle can mean the end of the road for an aspiring Green Beret.

But those contracts are a helluva way for recruiters to get soldiers into the Army. By promising a shot at becoming a Green Beret, a skilled recruiter can coax a potential recruit into the military despite the reality that a kid fresh out of high school will have a tough time making it through the intense training. Imagine if a university recruiter promised a studious high school graduate a fast-track into a PhD program. That sounds great, but a young student doesn't have the foundational skills, knowledge, or mental preparation that comes from getting bachelor's and master's degrees first. Nobody would just throw a high schooler into a PhD pipeline, but the Army happily does a similar thing with the 18X contracts.

They do it because, in part, recruits are, indeed, able to succeed and go on to have great careers. Those 18X contracts do yield Green Berets. A cynic would say the military offers these contracts because when an enlistee washes out of the pipeline, the Army has on its hands a young soldier who still has years on their contract and who can be sent wherever the Army needs them. And since many of these recruits get through boot camp and jump school before they wash out, they are often prime fodder to plug gaps in Airborne units' rosters.

Allen washed out and the system spat him into Bravo Company (which was then part of the Third Battalion, 325th Regiment). He showed up listening to hip-hop and rock, wearing baggy pants and long T-shirts, and would get yelled at for not having his pants pulled all the way up, Dave remembered. Allen was clearly a guy from the outskirts of Washington, DC, rather than someone steeped in a culture of country music and North Carolina.

As a team leader, Dave outranked Allen and sometimes made him mop floors and do the usual shit new guys have to do in the barracks.

Dave was over six feet tall and two hundred pounds, and he remembers that since he and Allen were both big guys, they were always sizing each other up. Even though Dave was Allen's team leader they'd scrap during physical training, roughing each other up a little bit more than what might be considered roughhousing in good fun. They didn't really bond until the week Dave and some other specialists conscripted Allen to be their designated driver.

The 82nd is made up of three brigades of infantry, with about four thousand people in each one. The division also has an air support brigade, an artillery brigade, and a sustainment brigade that deals with logistics. They even have their own band made up of musicians who are uniformed soldiers. At any given moment, there's always a brigade from the 82nd division that's on two-hour recall, which means nobody from the unit can be more than two hours from being in uniform and ready to go in case there's an international incident. Because of this, the 82nd is known as America's 9-1-1.

Though their brigade was on recall, Dave and three other guys were set to go to Winston-Salem to see a concert. They wanted to drink beers and possibly even spend the night there. But Winston-Salem was just beyond their two-hour recall perimeter, and that required them to get special permission from an officer.

There was no way they were asking for permission.

So Dave decided they should do the responsible thing—at least the responsible thing in a young soldier's eyes: They should force somebody to go with them and stay sober so they could race back and make it just in time if they were recalled. The important thing was to be able to get back and be in formation, they could always sober up later. They were violating regulations, but they were also covering their asses. Allen was the driver they picked. They told him, yeah, sure, everything was totally fine—this was normal and within regulations. All good! The way things are always done. So he went as their designated driver.

At the Jack Ingram and Pat Green concert, everyone but Allen got good and drunk and had a great time. Allen, the sober driver, even got to meet Jack Ingram after the post-show fan meet-and-greet. They stayed the night and made it back the next day with no problem, and nobody got in trouble. Allen even admitted the next day to Dave that the music was OK.

The next weekend, that same tour came rumbling back through North Carolina, so Dave and the three other specialists decided to do it all over again. Allen was again pressed into service. Same thing: beers and music and a fan meet-and-greet.

These artists, they meet hundreds—probably thousands—of people over the course of a week. They give out autographs and take photos and go through the motions. But this time, when Allen stepped up to say hello to Jack Ingram, the star said, "Hey, Allen, welcome back to my second show in North Carolina."

That was the day Dave remembers he and Allen really became friends. And, he says, that was the day Allen transformed from a kid who grew up on the far reaches of suburban Washington, DC, to a guy who truly lived in North Carolina. Allen started liking the country artists Dave liked, and, man, did Allen have a great singing voice when they'd go to karaoke bars. He sounded like Darius Rucker, the Hootie and the Blowfish lead singer who later became a country star.

* * *

Fort Bragg, where Allen Thomas was stationed, was named for Braxton Bragg, a veteran of the Second Seminole War and Mexican War who was so patriotic that he decided to turn his back on his country and become a Confederate general in the Civil War. The infantry has a bulky portion of its presence on bases in the South, and despite efforts to make it otherwise, the 82nd Airborne Division was steeped in the hushpuppy-and-vinegar-sauce ethos of the region. Chattanooga and Chickamauga and the Stars and Bars were woven into the fabric of so many bases, including the one where Bravo Company stacked its rifles when they were not on deployment. It was in those bottoms and hollers of the South that a sizable portion of the nation's pride was trained, whence they were deployed to combat zones and whither they returned. And the high and lonesome sounds of the Old South permeated the soul of the US Army contrary to, or sometimes because of, the efforts to root it out. Fort Benning, Fort Campbell, Fort Hood—there was even a Fort Lee in Virginia named after the ultimate symbol of the Lost Cause, Robert E. Lee himself.

Deep in the marrow of that tradition was the God-given right to wallow in loss and tragedy and for a man to make his own goddamn way, thank you very much. And since infantrymen soaked in the marinade of the South, they either had their already stubborn ways reinforced or slowly had it seep into their very selves.

That southern tradition is the tradition of country music. It's guitar ballads about misery and sadness, partying and drinking, and, most importantly, nostalgic snapshots of the past. Nostalgia, that longing for a past that never really was, is one of things the South can do very well, and it's something country music can conjure up better than most any other kind. A weekend in Fayetteville, North Carolina, was like living in a Waylon Jennings fever dream, with guys getting drunk and into fights and arrested and hitting on strippers before heading off to Bible study on Sunday (or at least telling themselves they'd be going to church if they were back home with their folks and weren't so goddamn hungover).

The old Saturday-night and Sunday-morning country song was alive and well in the hearts and actions of paratroopers across the land. And there was always the nostalgia. There was the getting drunk and talking about the last deployment or maybe that deployment years ago in the Old Army days, before everything got soft and the fucking pussies took over. And the most delicious part of a country song, its nougat center, is the way it empowers an individual to wallow in his own misery or broken-up relationship or whatever feeling that he happens to be feeling.

The deep-fried southern connection with a soundtrack of country music was dyed in the deepest tint of Lost Cause nostalgia that affects troops from North, South, East, and West because it was everywhere in the Army. It was the mindset that allows self-pitying to combine with self-reliance, whiskey, and fistfights to yield a combustible byproduct. It yielded America's soldiers.

The culture of the Army began to shift in the waning years of the Wars on Terror. Don't Ask, Don't Tell was dropped, allowing gay and lesbian soldiers to openly serve in the military, combat roles opened up to women, and the military shifted to acknowledge pervasive race issues, including rethinking whether bases should be named after Confederate generals.

But in the mid-2000s, that shift was still years away. The Army still barred open homosexuality, prohibited women from serving across combat roles, and had a casual racism that often didn't even seem like racism to many of those who trafficked in it.

In the Vietnam movie *Full Metal Jacket*, the Black infantryman has the nickname "Eightball," and at one point the character Animal Mother goes on a rant filled with racist profanities, hurled as apparent jokes, that draws a head-shaking laugh from Eightball. He doesn't appear to take offense because, as he says, the white man who's insulting him is the finest machine gunner around when the fighting starts and that's what really matters. When Allen Thomas began his career in the military there was still that sort of joking around—but was it joking? It was hard to tell.

Allen Thomas didn't speak much about how his race affected his life in the Army. At some point, though, he did get a nickname that would stick with him. Someone started calling him "Toby," the name LeVar Burton's character from *Roots* is given when he is enslaved in America. Despite its origin, Allen embraced the nickname, took it on, and ran with it. He'd also go to parties in a fake blond mullet and wear a shirt that said "Pure White Trash," ever the joker, grabbing what might have been negative attention and amplifying it to make it his own. He was supremely comfortable with himself, so he was seemingly able to absorb anything that came his way. Seemingly.

* * *

Dave and Allen were soon pals, drinking and cavorting as infantrymen do.

"What does the infantry do?" Dave asked. "They stay up all night drinking beer, then go running in the morning."

And that's what they did. And as Allen grew as a person, he also grew as a soldier, shedding his bitterness about not making Special Forces and turning into a damn fine paratrooper. Some soldiers are always trying to get into the Special Forces, thinking that there's no other real option but to go that route. Civilians, too, may not understand the gradations and differences in Army units and how they're used. The Green Berets might be likened to a Ferrari, a high-performance vehicle that everyone knows and admires for its prowess and performance. But a Ferrari isn't always what's needed. Hell, a Ferrari is rarely needed when you're on the road. Sometimes you need a Mack truck that can drive all day and night, run over anything in its way, and do it with a "Fuck you" attitude. Well, that's the 82nd Airborne. And just as a Mack truck driver eventually realizes their hulking vehicle is more beautiful in its own way than a sleek Ferrari, so, too, do paratroopers come to see the sublime beauty of their battering ram of a unit.

In the 82nd, Allen was always happy, even when things were shitty and nobody else was happy. Even when they were in the field or stuck doing some crap duty, cleaning floors or picking up cigarette butts around the company area, Allen was all smiles and jokes. He became a grenadier, the guy who has an M203 grenade launcher attached to the bottom of his M4 rifle for added firepower when needed. The stumpy tube under the rifle's main barrel launches 40mm grenades that look like gigantic bullets, arcing through the air just slow enough that a grenadier can keep his eye on the round as it sails away from him on its trajectory of destruction.

It was right around Thanksgiving of that year when Dave and Allen were playing in a pickup football game at a church lot along with a local reporter for the *Fayetteville Observer*. That reporter found out the unit they were with and told them they could expect to get called up on December 5 for a deployment to Iraq. Sure enough, when December 5 rolled around, they were told to be ready to leave for Iraq. The reporter knew long before they did that they'd be headed to combat.

They were told that they were to deploy in a couple of days to boost security for the forthcoming Iraqi elections. Someone had called America's 9-1-1—it just took some time for the call to get properly routed to the men who had to do the fighting.

* * *

Dave and Allen, among the rest of their battalion, were sent on their first Bravo Company deployment in December of 2004. They were attached to the First Battalion, Ninth Cavalry Regiment, a unit that once rode around on horses but in modern times rode around on tanks and Bradley Fighting Vehicles, machines with tracks instead of tires that can hold nearly a dozen soldiers and fire 25mm Bushmaster cannons. They deployed for four months in Iraq and saw some combat and firefights, but nothing too brutal. No deaths. Some Purple Hearts. Allen received one of them. Somebody threw a grenade at his squad and he was a little too close to where it landed. He took some shrapnel, but nothing major.

That's the way Dave describes it, as "nothing major." Allen didn't talk much about that Purple Heart, but he received a combat wound nonetheless. A grenade exploded close enough to him to cause him to be hurt. Even if the injuries appeared to be slight, it was a wound.

The injury Dave really remembers from that deployment in Iraq was when one of the other soldiers was shot by an insurgent. By chance, the insurgent's bullet hit the grenade loaded in the M203 grenade launcher mounted on the soldier's rifle. It didn't set off the grenade, thank God, but instead ricocheted down and glanced off the guy's penis.

Dave remembers it because the guy went to the medic, got his dick bandaged up, and then went running around the squad bay showing people his member, all wrapped up like a piggie in a blanket. A few days later the guy again went running around the squad bay hollering with delight because he'd just been able to get an erection, and now he was certain the machinery was still fully functioning.

All in all, that deployment didn't seem to have any lasting impact on the guys from that old Bravo Company. Allen didn't seem to have been affected by his relatively minor wound, Dave said. They came home after about four months, went through a more than yearlong workup, and were rechristened as Bravo Company, Second Battalion, 508th Regiment, or the 2-508. Then they were sent off in January 2007 on a fifteen-month deployment to Ghazni in eastern Afghanistan.

Now *that* was a helluva long slog of a deployment, one that ultimately left many Bravo Company veterans salty. For Allen Thomas and Dave

Abt, it meant their platoon was stationed about one hundred kilometers south of the rest of the company, partnered with some Afghan police forces and patrolling all the time. There were some firefights for his platoon, Dave remembers, but it wasn't gnarly. It was mostly fifteen months of a daily grind.

Patrol. Stand guard duty. Sleep.

Oh, and Dave had to listen to Allen try to learn how to play guitar.

A guy in the platoon played in a metal band, and he'd brought along his guitar. A few months into the deployment, Allen decided he wanted to learn. Dave remembers ten months of bad guitar. It still makes his head hurt thinking of Allen trying to learn that thing.

Then they all came home. It was a boring year and a half. But Allen Thomas had metamorphosed from a whiny Special Forces dropout into a soldier with two deployments and legitimate combat experience. He was the real deal.

* * *

Another real deal in the unit was Rob Musil, a frenetic guy with a wiry frame and a loud mouth—one of those guys who could talk about anything for any amount of time.

At age nineteen, Musil—pronounced "muscle"—had joined the Army. Having been steeped in an Evangelical Christian worldview, the Army was for him a higher calling, an extension of God's good and ultimate desire to use America for righteousness in the world.

Musil was devout as a kid. He almost made a career as a pastor but detoured off the seminary path to join the Army. Heck, in his youth he had won the Martin Luther Award as the guy most likely to work in the church. Something called him to service of some kind, but he chose military service. Once in the Army, Musil started to realize a few things, started to change, to grab onto the Army ethos as his philosophy. The Army's morality became his morality, his religion.

"I accepted a long time ago that this job is to conduct violence," he said. "I'm OK with it, and I'm going to be OK with it for the rest of my life."

Musil had a craggy face and a shaggy smile. Even when freshly shaven it seemed like his face had—or ought to have had—a bit of a stubble. He was not a huge guy, though he was lean and muscular, a specimen that makes an outside observer realize that it's not a bodybuilder's physique that makes a prime soldier. Instead, it's the stringy bastard who doesn't have to carry all that bulk of useless muscle around who often makes the best fighter. Musil didn't have massive thighs, but they popped with muscle from running and hiking and hauling and carrying. He had the body of a person who could just keep going, and when unburdened by the weight of a pack he nearly bounced around, lacking any outside force to act upon him as a paperweight atop a sheaf always ready to scatter.

Once in the Army and all through boot camp, Musil squared the reality of violence with the notion that he was a force for good across the globe. American violence could bring American values and, by extension, the righteousness of the Kingdom of God, which was woven through Evangelical culture right into the fabric of the American flag, or so he thought. The Army and the Church: partners in the creation of a better world.

Musil was on the 2005 deployment to Iraq, the same one where Allen Thomas was hit—but not too bad—by a grenade. It was Musil's first deployment, too, the first in a very long series of deployments over nearly two decades to come. Musil moved at a million miles an hour, but he wasn't frantic—he was wild with the sheer here-ness of the moment. From his first days in the Army, Musil burned with an immediate need to find Truth with a capital *T*, and to find it as soon as possible. It pushed him to the edge of control. A seeker on steroids. The very quality that allowed him to achieve excellence as a soldier was also what made him burn like a comet, always in danger of simply flaming out.

One day Musil's weapons squad was walking down Haifa Street in Baghdad to replace another platoon that had been in position when some asshole from that platoon started heckling them. Musil was just a new soldier fresh from boot camp. He was an ammo bearer, which is a glorified pack mule, but even then he was Rob Musil—ever-confident in himself, his mission, and his righteousness. So he decided he'd be the only person to talk back to the jerk who was heckling them, the jerk named Allen Thomas.

Pretty soon Musil was surrounded by combat veterans from the other platoon who got in his face, calling him a "cherry" and asking him if he had something else to say to them. *Go on, say something, you fucking cherry.*

Ah, yes, cherry: it was and might always remain the Army's standard-issue insult from a wizened soldier to someone who has no experience, a perfectly crafted putdown that rankled everyone who was still a virgin to combat. It was a hell of a way for a bunch of soldiers on patrol in a combat zone to be acting, getting into a pissing contest in the middle of Baghdad. But that was how Musil met Allen Thomas.

CHAPTER 2

MAC, THE HARD-ASS

Right before the end of the fifteen-month slog of a deployment, back in 2007, Bravo Company picked up a new first sergeant, Donald McAlister. Now, that dude was a hard-ass, Dave Abt remembers. He wanted to do things by the book. The bottoms of every soldier's trousers had to be bloused, perfectly tucked into the tops of their boots. Gear had to be worn on flak jackets just so, with no special tweaks or changes for personal preference. The Army decided how things should be worn, goddammit, not some pissant private. First Sergeant seemed a jerk and an asshole and nobody really liked him. When they got back to the United States and got ready to start working up for their next deployment, he got even worse than he had been in-country.

Donald "Mac" McAlister grew up in Ponchatoula, Louisiana, and was saturated with the tradition of military service. His grandpa had been a Navy salvage diver in World War II. His uncle Mike was a recon Marine who did two tours in Vietnam—but he killed himself when Mac was a kid, so Mac really didn't know him too well. Mac's uncle "Junior" did twenty years in the Marines, got out as a gunnery sergeant, and was probably the hardest motherfucker Mac ever knew. Mac himself was born in 1973 when his dad was nineteen. Pops got drafted and went to Marine boot camp but never deployed because of Vietnam drawdowns.

So Mac was preprogrammed to go into the Marine Corps. He was around all those old Marines and thought they were the best. But then as a kid he saw the movie *The Longest Day* with John Wayne and Henry Fonda as 82nd Airborne paratroopers. It changed his mind. Suddenly he wanted to be an Airborne soldier.

Soldier or Marine, whatever may come, Mac was ready because he'd been imbued with the rough-and-tumble. His mom and dad got divorced when he was in high school, and he was expelled for fistfights his freshman year. All the tumult landed him on a five-year plan, meaning he graduated at age nineteen instead of eighteen. It would have been easy for him to do like so many other guys from his hometown and just forget about school, but the draw of becoming a paratrooper pushed him to finish up and get that degree.

John Wayne, man, he was so cool in that uniform! Henry Fonda!

If *The Longest Day* hadn't sealed Mac's fate to become a soldier, his rap sheet did. As a senior in high school, he got probation for smashing mailboxes. The Marine recruiter didn't want to talk to him because the Marines don't recruit so much as decide whether they'll let you in. But the Army recruiter was always looking to make quota, especially for the infantry, because what dumb son of a bitch wants to join the Army infantry? As soon as that recruiter heard Mac was interested in jumping out of airplanes, well, he ushered the young John Wayne wannabe right in.

For Mac, it was the best thing that had ever happened to him. He went to Army basic training and then on to Airborne school. He always got a perfect score on the physical fitness test, which involved running and sit-ups and push-ups. He looked good in uniform and was a physical stud, a low-slung smile affixed to a jaw that looked like it could take a punch and a set of hands sturdy enough to deliver a few licks of their own. He looked like a soldier ought to look, so the Old Guard recruited him.

It was 1992 and there wasn't any war going on and nothing big on the horizon, so there really were only two places a new soldier with dreams of glory and honor wanted to go, at least as far as Mac remembers it: the Ranger Regiment or the Old Guard.

Ranger Regiment are the guys who parachute in and blow stuff up, seize airfields and kick ass. They're considered special operators and are known throughout the Army for their prowess. Plus, there's always great training. Even when there are no official wars going on, they seem to get to do fun stuff like get plenty of ammo to shoot at ranges and time to jump out of airplanes. They might even deploy real quick for some action in a place like Somalia or Grenada while the rest of the Army is sitting around like a bunch of lumps on a log, waiting for a big war so they can get into the action.

And there was the Old Guard. Based in Washington, DC, they do the official spit-and-polish ceremonial stuff for the Army, including funerals at Arlington. When you see pictures of soldiers at the Tomb of the Unknown Soldier or doing twenty-one-gun salutes, that's the Old Guard.

Mac didn't know anything about the unit at the time, but one of the Old Guard recruiters showed him some photos of the hot chicks a guy could meet in the nation's capital.

"I'm this podunk dude from Louisiana," Mac said. He was awed by the heretofore unknown potential for getting laid in DC.

Mac went to DC, and it ended up setting the tone for the rest of his Army career.

Back then, a guy could still raise a little hell on the weekends in DC, so the boys of the Old Guard would sometimes get into punch-ups with the Marines, who had their own honor guard based at the Marine barracks at Eighth and I. Trading some fisticuffs with Marines, now, that's a hoot!

The Old Guard also spends about as much time polishing their boots and burnishing the brass on their uniforms as they do serving in ceremonies. It was aggravating as hell, all that spit and polish, but it meant Mac glistened and gleamed for official events, including funerals. Everything had to be just so.

"For me, it was so good as a young soldier to do funerals in Arlington because I got to see what it was about when we buried a guy," Mac said. "It wasn't about him, it was about the family."

And Mac realized quickly that he was sometimes the last soldier the family would see. It meant that the way Donald McAlister performed was the thing the family would remember about the Army. If you thought about it, in the hush of those ceremonies he *was* the Army, its very embodiment.

At that time, the Old Guard was vacuuming up guys with combat experience so at ceremonies they'd have dudes with plenty of ribbons shining and medals tinkling on their dress uniforms. Mac's first platoon sergeant had a Bronze Star with a combat "V" for valor. His squad leader had already done seventeen years in the Army. He learned the spit and polish but also started drinking deep from the well of combat glory before he'd had the opportunity to pursue it himself. He learned discipline. He learned what death meant. He learned to punch Marines.

After that, he reenlisted and headed for a spell to a unit in Hawaii. Then September 11, 2001, happened. By that time Mac understood well the reputation of the 82nd, and so he finagled a way to get himself there.

* * *

Mac was a senior staff sergeant in the 82nd when the invasion of Iraq kicked off in 2003.

His company had pushed into the country at the beginning of it all with hours-long firefights against the Fedayeen—Saddam's commandos. There were also patrols and raids aplenty. Then, months into that deployment, Mac had a supremely shitty day.

It was October 8, 2003, and he was sitting in his hooch, playing *NCAA Football* on a PlayStation. He was crushing a fellow staff sergeant, extending the video game dynasty of his beloved LSU Tigers, when they had to pause midgame so they could go out in some Humvees to check on soldiers out on posts around the area.

Mac gathered up his small team, including a local interpreter who went by the name "Fred." As far as interpreters go, Fred was one of the good ones, Mac remembers. Soldiers can wax nostalgic about many things, interpreters included. To hear some veterans talk about it, every local who worked alongside soldiers was worthy of everlasting love and trust. The truth is interpreters are like any other group of people in this world: Some are good and some are bad and most are just OK. And a few of the bastards would steal your wallet if you weren't paying attention.

Mac, like any soldier who worked with different interpreters over time, realized a good number of them weren't trustworthy and were more interested in what Uncle Sam could do for them than in doing their job well.

Fred, though, he was top-notch. He was an Iraqi Christian, a minority in the country, and his children were all girls, Mac remembers Fred telling him. Mac is the first to admit that he wasn't the type of soldier who'd go hang out and drink tea with the "terps" just to be a nice guy. That, in fact, is something Mac would never, ever do if he had his druthers. But he talked to Fred in the quiet times they'd have together during that deployment about what life was like for Iraqis under Saddam, how after Desert Storm things got far worse. Fred told Mac about his hopes and dreams for his daughters to get an education, to find equality in a very unequal world. Fred told him why he'd started working for the Americans as an interpreter. He wanted Al Qaeda and extremism rooted out, wanted to embrace the promise of reform that came with the toppling of Saddam. Fred didn't ever wheedle Mac, didn't ask him for favors or for letters of recommendation he could later use to try and get an American visa.

When Mac looked Fred in the eyes, he could see sincerity and integrity, not greed. Mac liked the guy, trusted him, which wasn't exactly de rigueur for the Louisianan.

Fred might have been the best interpreter Mac ever had. And he loaded up in the Humvee next to Mac that day.

This was back when the Humvees had no armor, no doors, no back. They were glorified Jeeps, really. Open-air. Mac was in the back of one that day, sitting next to his interpreter. As they drove out to check on some soldiers, a blast came from underneath and everything went into slow motion for him. Even though it only took a second or two, to him it seemed like half a minute for the explosion and then for everything to settle. He'd been thrown ten feet or more, and the Humvee had been flipped over.

A piece of shrapnel went right through Fred, he was dead before anyone could do anything for him. The chunk of metal that hit him likely killed him in an instant.

Right away, Mac knew that he'd been hit in the face with something, couldn't see out of his right eye. He started groping around for his rifle and then reached up and touched his face. His hand came away covered in blood. He looked over at a fellow soldier who stared back at him bug-eyed and said, "Mac, you're gonna make it."

It's never good when a dude tells you something like that, because they're probably thinking the exact opposite.

Then Mac saw his cammies were soaked with blood.

"Oh shit," he said, but nobody could understand him because his lip had been split clean in half and flubbered around when he tried to talk. He had a hole in the skin on his forehead, so his skull shined through underneath.

Mac blacked out for a while and was a real asshole to the guys who tried to help him, they told him later. He thrashed around so much that the medic who tried to inject him with morphine missed Mac and accidentally jabbed himself instead. "He was stoned as a motherfucker," Mac remembers, laughing.

Fred had been killed, and the driver was injured as well. They got Mac on a medevac and then flew him to Landstuhl, a base in Germany with excellent surgical facilities. Once he got there the docs immediately said they'd have to pluck his right eye out because there was shrapnel in it.

"The nurse was like, 'You need to be prepared: You're not going to look the same again,'" Mac remembers. *Fucking thanks, lady. What an insightful prognosis*, he thought to himself.

But one of the docs in Germany had a pal at Walter Reed back in the States—an ocular surgeon named, no kidding, Dr. Dick—and ol' Dr. Dick said he could probably save the eye if they got Mac back home. It's crazy how one phone call, one random doctor who just happened to know another, could keep the bastards from plucking out a guy's eye.

Mac later found out that his colonel had taken care of Fred's family, found a way to get them visas for the neighboring country of Jordan. Maybe his daughters would have a better life.

Mac spent two months at Walter Reed National Military Medical Center in Washington, DC. Dr. Dick saved his eye. More important than the eye, he got back his prized talisman that he had carried tucked in his body armor on patrol after patrol. Not long before that explosion, Mac and his team had been going house to house, and at this one place his team found—inexplicably—a box full of the ugliest, shittiest bright-green hats emblazoned with the logo of the heavy-metal band Metallica.

Mac had always been a metalhead, and Metallica was his favorite band, so the guys grabbed one of those horrible hats and gave it to him. They all signed it for him, and he kept it tucked into his body armor on every single patrol. He had it on him during that patrol when he got blown up.

The medics had to cut off Mac's body armor and uniform before shipping him to the hospital, but his team made sure they recovered the hat from his gear and held on to it, then shipped it back to him in the States so he could have it with him while he recovered at Walter Reed. More than Army medics, Defense Department surgeons, or high-tech body armor, it was the occult power of the Metallica hat—let's be honest—that prevented Mac from dying or losing any limbs or eyes. One day, Mac swears he is going to show that hat to the guys in Metallica and let them comprehend the power they hold over life and death. Who cares about luck or anything else when you have Metallica to ward off evil.

That was a shitty end to a deployment, yes. At the same time, he got that sweet hat, so—in the end—it was a wash.

* * *

People think it's combat trauma that causes PTSD, or post-traumatic stress disorder. Getting blown up or injured. Yet Mac's god-awful experience didn't really do anything to him long term, he says. (Yet when he talks about Fred his voice gets a faraway sound to it for a bit.)

Of course, it did something at the most basic physical level. His face looked different after all the plastic surgeries, and he still tweezered out little pieces of shrapnel from of his head every so often when they worked their way to the surface, like plucking ingrown hairs made of steel.

Yes, sure it did that. But he never got nightmares or woke up in cold sweats because of that explosion. In many ways, the explosion was good, because it made him a better NCO. It canceled any feelings of being bulletproof and made him double down on training and doing everything just right to avoid that sort of thing in the future. It made him want to train his units so they wouldn't experience what he had. Not every trooper has a magic Metallica hat to save their ass.

The recurring pain and trauma, the stuff that keeps Mac up at night, none of that is related to the explosion. That all came later with the loss of friends, the death of buddies. It's kinda funny, he'll say: It's not the stuff that happened to *him* that keeps him up at night. It's the explosions that happened to other people that ended up fucking with him.

In the years since the invasion Mac used the lessons he learned at the Old Guard and from getting blown up to make himself a by-the-book sergeant whose only job was to train soldiers and lead them to be successful in combat and not get killed if they could avoid it.

That was his mindset when Mac picked up with Bravo Company in 2007 and became a first sergeant. What his troops didn't know was that it had taken years of lessons learned and of real, hard-nosed soldiering for him to become such a grade-A asshole of a first sergeant. He didn't have time for any whininess from the troops because he had to train them to not get blown up like he'd been blown up in Iraq. He had to train them to have the gusto of the 82nd and the spit and polish of the Old Guard, to bring that discipline to combat operations. Once he was at Bravo as the first sergeant, the top enlisted guy, he was ready to build himself a company.

* * *

Mac already had a decent run of it in the Army by this point. He was good at being a leader, great at being a soldier, and excellent at being an asshole.

In April 2008, Bravo Company was salty as hell, having just come off a fifteen-month deployment to Afghanistan. Dave Abt remembers the damn Army pulled them out of country on the last day of April so the Department of Defense wouldn't be on the hook for paying them yet another month of combat pay. It's a common thing for deployments to finish up at the end of the month for just that reason. If troops spend just the first day of the month in a combat zone, they're due a passel of extra pay, and the bean counters are loath for that to happen.

For some of the men from Bravo, it had been difficult. During their fifteen months in Afghanistan, they were out in Ghazni province, where a good number of the company had gotten into firefights.

Iraq and its "surge" had gotten all the attention while Bravo was up on a mountain in remote Afghanistan. Back home everyone was arguing about Iraq and President George Bush, and the war in Afghanistan was pretty much forgotten.

During that deployment, some of the men of Bravo Company were stop-lossed, which meant guys weren't allowed to go home as they'd been promised. For some troops, it meant not only their time on deployment was being extended but also their time in the Army. Troops whose contracts said it was time for them to become civilians were forced to extend their service in this so-called volunteer army. The deployment crept from a year to fifteen months, and when the men finally returned, they were worn out and pissed off.

It was around this time that Secretary of Defense Robert Gates told reporters that one of the biggest threats to the military was wearing it out through overuse. Gates went so far as to call stop-lossing units a practice that was "breaking faith" with troops. Gates argued that these wars were no longer extraordinary circumstances, that they had become routine (which is one hell of a thing for them to have become), and that stop-losses put unnecessary wear and tear on the troops. Gates also wanted to stop sending guys on immediately consecutive deployments, especially when the deployments lasted up to fifteen months, meaning a soldier might miss two Christmases, or two of a kid's birthdays, if the timing was particularly bad.

"Back then guys were used to coming back from deployment and going on another one," Mac said.

Gates wanted to avoid having companies like Bravo go through ungodly long deployments, then turn around and do it all again. He wanted this not only for the health and well-being of the individual soldier but also for the chances of strategic success in the wars in Iraq and Afghanistan. Fatigued, pissed-off soldiers won't fight well for Uncle Sam if they're busy being furious with Uncle Sam. It was a nice sentiment from the SecDef. Too bad Bravo Company had already been stop-lossed.

* * *

First Sergeant McAlister had joined Bravo mid-tour in Afghanistan. He returned to the United States with them and then stayed on. Mac was slated to keep staying on through the next deployment.

In places like Great Britain, it's not uncommon for guys to join a unit and stick with it for life. Not in the United States. While military units may appear to remain constant, the component parts are always in flux. Men might spend many years in the same unit, but it's more common for them to just stick around for three years, maybe five years, before moving on. The United States sees it as a way to distribute experience throughout the system and to keep troops fresh by sending them across the country and across the globe to routinely join new units.

What that means, in essence, is that once a unit comes back from a deployment to war, soldiers scatter and new ones join. The unit becomes a nearly new entity, not unlike Theseus's ship on the Mediterranean Sea.

In 2008, one thing connected all these soldiers, old and new: They were men. Years later the military started opening up more jobs to women, things like infantry, the Rangers, Special Forces. But for Bravo Company at the time, combat arms were the province of men. Occasionally, female soldiers had a chance to prove their mettle in combat, to fight alongside men, but that typically happened when a logistics unit or similar outfit got caught up in combat. The opportunity was rare. About the only place a woman was accepted in combat then was as a pilot. The infantry, and Airborne units especially, were bastions of chauvinism and machismo, with nary a woman in sight.

In the immediate days after deployment, once all the gear was accounted for—all the radios and rifles and night vision goggles and bayonets and pistols and binoculars—just about everyone went on post-deployment leave, to visit family or go on vacation, and the unit was hollowed out for about a month. Guys who signed up for short-term contracts often want to just get out of the Army, so they left to become civilians. If they did their jobs passably, they got honorably discharged and went about their lives. Bravo Company had plenty of guys who were stop-lossed and got stuck fighting in what they felt was a forgotten war. They were ready to get their paperwork finished and get out.

For the senior noncommissioned and the officers, it was a different cycle altogether. By virtue of their leadership positions, they would all be shuffled around, rotated to different units, moved to different bases—across the country or even around the world—or slotted into different positions in the chain of command.

After everyone went on leave to celebrate returning home in one piece, after that brief and beautiful post-deployment afterglow, just like clockwork the workup for the next deployment began. Because of the post-deployment shuffle, Bravo Company was suddenly populated with a whole crop of new troops fresh from boot camp. They showed up devoid of any meaningful experience, ignorant of what was to come, and bereft of even a single battle patch.

Units like the 82nd Airborne retain their core identity even as the component parts are swapped out regularly. A lot of that unit continuity was provided by lower-level troops who have one deployment under their belts and are stuck with a particular unit for a second deployment before they're eligible to get out. Those guys also know what it was like to get hazed and want their good goddamn comeuppance by hazing the next crop of new guys. NCOs also frequently stick around and take on greater leadership positions. Squad leaders move up to be platoon sergeants. A platoon sergeant moves up to be first sergeant. And it's those enlisted who have the responsibility to uphold training, tradition, and the ethos of the organization. Guys like Mac provide the continuity for units like Bravo Company and—to hear them tell it—the continuity for the whole damn Army.

A gravelly voiced lifelong soldier, Mac didn't have time for anybody who couldn't hack it. He was old-school all the way. For starters, Mac never gave a shit about where they were deploying or even why. His job was to get the troops trained and to use them to fight once they were in-country.

"I guess for me as a ground soldier, I never looked at the end state because that's a strategic thing, you know?" he said.

So Mac focused on the here and now and didn't have time for guys who couldn't keep up. In May of 2008, Bravo started training for their next combat deployment—already scheduled for Iraq.

They started with the most basic of things. They marched twenty miles with a full pack. They went to the rifle range for M4 rifle marksmanship, then they formed fire teams of four guys all able to shoot at the same target and run toward it in a coordinated way, hitting the plastic cutouts of bad guys downrange without accidentally shooting one another as they moved.

As the unit worked to come together again—after the return, the brief hibernation, the reshuffle—the unit also faced the constant tug of entropy that pulls troops out of the unit and into schools for weeks at a time to earn credentials for specific tasks. Some had to go to the Army's driver's education to get their Humvee licenses. Some were sent to sniper school. Some went to become EMTs. And since they're paratroopers, there was the pain in the ass that was getting jump qualified and staying qualified.

An Airborne soldier didn't just get his jump wings and that was that. He was required to parachute out of airplanes regularly to make sure he still knew what he was doing. He also got a bonus in his paycheck when he was jump qualified, so all those 82nd troopers needed to remain current on their jumps for the sake of Uncle Sam's readiness, but also because they wanted to get paid.

Every couple of months, soldiers had to take a few days out of their preparation for deployment to jump out of an airplane. It was a headache for commanders to plan around but it had to be done, even if the unit was deploying to Iraq and walking around in the desert for a year with no parachutes in sight.

* * *

It's a well-understood truth in the military that the most miserable and difficult training ties troops together. Troops say with a misery-filled laugh that if it ain't rainin', then you aren't trainin'. Soldiers revel—after the fact—in detailing the worst parts of their training cycles. Nobody talks about the balmy spring day they went on a leisurely hike with their platoon, they remember the god-awful forced march in the middle of winter. Nobody is happy while they're at boot camp, but just about everyone *looks back* on boot camp with a laugh and a shake of the head. It is equally a truism that troops are going to bitch and moan every step of the way of that very training as they're going through it.

For many of the men of Bravo Company, the unit—remnants of those who had been on previous deployments and the guys who had just been added—really only came together through the biggest misery of all training evolutions: the dreaded Observation Point 13.

OP 13 is a standard training exercise at Fort Bragg that paratroopers are required to go through to be considered fully qualified to deploy. It involves days of staying out on the range no matter the weather to practice coordinated assaults on everything from buildings to bunker complexes and trenches.

Bravo went through it in the depth of winter, but since it's North Carolina, it wasn't quite cold enough to snow. The sky just sort of dropped freezing rain all day long. And thanks to the nearby ocean, there was ample precipitation. Many soldiers consider OP 13 the most miserable of Army ranges. One junior soldier, Dave Huff, who was there for the workup called it the "Trail of Tears."

Dave Huff was only one of the Huffs in the company. His brother, Jonathan, was the other. Dave was known as the "evil Huff," because of his surlier nature. But he was also known as the Huff with good hair. Even a decade after the deployment, Dave had impeccable hair. It was a dark, voluminous coif that refused to move no matter how late the hour, how many cocktails had been drunk, or how many times his massive laugh had been uncorked—likely at one of his own quips. Dave had long been the type of guy who says something to a reporter and then follows it up with an elbow to the guy's ribs and a reminder that what he just said was a helluva quote and probably should be included in whatever story the reporter's writing. Hell, it probably should be the headline!

Huff remembers heading up to one target after it had been raining non-stop. He was supposed to jump into a bunker and clear it with a grenade and his rifle. But he hesitated. One of the senior troops who was grading his performance asked him, "Soldier, what's the delay?"

"It's flooded," he remembered saying. "If there's enemy in there, they've already drowned."

The misery wasn't just designed to teach them how to soldier, it was also designed to glue them together with hardship and strain. On those cold, rainy days at places like OP 13, the troops of Bravo Company recognized they were working with the men around them, focusing in large part on becoming proficient in the infantry tactics they'd need wherever they might go. In some ways that universal training is training to endure suffering and to trust the men on either side of you.

Dave Abt remembered times that Bravo Company would head to a field exercise around the same time as other companies and then Bravo would just stay out in the field, spending days longer out there camped out while other units went back to the barracks. It gave them a chip on their shoulder, knowing that they were out there doing more, being more miserable, being more soldierly than everyone else.

Many times when units go out into the field for a training exercise, they hike or get trucked miles into the wilderness or out on some corner of a sprawling base. Sometimes, though, a unit will encamp in a training area within sight of the barracks and battalion headquarters building. That provides a special dose of grumbling.

"Nothing's more miserable than staying in the woods when you can see your bedroom window," Dave Abt said.

CHAPTER 3

CAPTAIN AMERICA

Mac was trying to deal with getting ready for a deployment, and the last thing he needed was to break in a new officer. Captain Adam Armstrong joined Mac and Bravo Company in 2009, mid-workup for their slated deployment to Iraq. As soon as he took over the company he seemed to the troops like he was, as they say, "in it to win it."

Being "in it to win it" is no compliment from enlisted guys who have little time for officers and even less for one like Armstrong. He seemed the picture-perfect cookie-cutter officer to the men of Bravo Company, a freshly groomed, regulation-loving smarty-pants who they assumed hoped to get through this command, then move along with his career and leave them all behind.

When an officer is in it to win it, they don't give a shit about the troops, all they care about is getting a good evaluation report and moving on to the next unit and up to the next rank. Naive officers don't really know the ins and outs of tactics and training, according to most soldiers. It's the senior enlisted, like Mac, who run the show.

This new Armstrong guy was coming into a salty company effectively run by a hard-as-nails first sergeant, and in the eyes of the men of Bravo Company he was someone to be shunned whenever possible, mocked at every opportunity, laughed at regularly, and avoided at all costs.

In other words, Armstrong was facing attitudes from the junior enlisted as standard-issue as the very uniforms they were wearing. Those junior guys knew only what the senior guys told them: An officer exists in a different realm, apart from them. An officer is somebody they only needed to deal with for one deployment before forgetting him, because an officer will sure as shit forget about them. The junior enlisted, like all junior enlisted across the US military, took these messages to heart.

When Armstrong took command, he did go through the motions and spout the expected speech from a new guy, talking about how the troops were now part of his family and blah blah blah, all the rote stuff a new CO says to his unit. This guy was such a flag-waving, apple-for-the-teacher, gleaming-smile suck-up that the junior enlisted had the perfect name for him: Captain America.

Armstrong sure could look like a goofball when he was in a jocular mood. His puckish smile and dimples were charming. Tall and lean, he was a marathon runner at heart and could do laps around just about anyone. He was so committed to running that he washed out of his first attempt at Ranger school because he couldn't ace the push-ups. Since then, Armstrong bulked up enough to complete any physical task assigned to him, but he still kept that runner's build. He could certainly be serious, and when he locked on that officer scowl, a soldier knew he meant business. But he also had that grin that belied his God-granted good nature. That smile wasn't going to win him any beauty contests, but he had the face of someone you want to trust.

He grew up in Chardon, Ohio, an area in the northeast of the state best known for its booming maple syrup industry. His grandfather was a soldier in World War II, a mechanic who served in Africa, the Middle East, and Europe. Granddad was burned so badly during the Ardennes campaign that he had to spend time in the hospital over there, then back at home. Armstrong had an idea from a young age what combat injuries did to a man, knew how they lingered for years, shaped a person. He also knew what the Army meant, the challenges and legacies it created, the unbreakable bonds it forged.

Armstrong idolized his grandfather. His dad was a big military history buff. His uncle had gone to Vietnam. As a first-grader Armstrong decided that he wanted to enlist in the Army. His parents—both school administrators—asked him whether maybe college might be a better idea instead. Mostly they humored him, because this enlistment stuff was probably a passing fancy, but those school administrators got concerned the kid might not grow out of the playing-Army phase of life. Then one day his old man was watching West Point football on TV.

"Look, Adam, if you go to this school, you can do college and— *and*—you'll be an Army officer," he said.

Armstrong was in. It sounded good—what did he need to do? Well, step one was prep to play for Army's football team. With his build, he could be the kicker. Except he ended up stinking at kicking a football. What now?

His dad said he guessed Adam just needed to do well at everything to cover his bases. So he worked on everything. In middle school he went to the library and checked out a test-prep book with a West Point questionnaire in it, a checklist of stuff a kid might think about accomplishing to make his or her academy application better.

And Adam Armstrong set about checking off every box he could.

By the time he was in high school and ready to apply to West Point, Armstrong had ticked off the athletics boxes by running track and cross country. He checked off National Honor Society, student council, senior class president. He was a trombonist, so he added jazz band, pep band, marching band, and symphonic band. He took all the AP classes he could. He sat for the ACT and SAT twice each to bump his scores up.

When he was working on his congressional appointment—chasing one from a senator and one from a congressman just to be safe—West Point had already relented and given him a conditional acceptance based on everything he'd done. All he had to do was get that appointment, which he did.

Adam accepted his West Point appointment, which is, of course, a pipeline to an Army career. But many West Pointers don't become lifers. They do their time in uniform and get out after maybe a decade, sometimes less. Armstrong thought he would be one of those guys—he hadn't yet embraced his fate. (His younger brother, Alex, would take a different route, attending Ohio State before becoming an Army infantry officer, too.) Adam went to West Point expecting to be a computer science major, planned on being a signals officer, in charge of radio equipment, propagating sine waves, total dork stuff and not what the typical infantry officer is interested in. Compared with infantry, a signals officer is a whole other branch on the tree of evolution for an Army officer.

In that first year, Armstrong ditched computer science as a major and switched to physics. He had great grades in physics his first semester. The only problem was those amazing physics grades all but fell into his lap because West Point used the exact same textbook as his high school AP class. He took damn near the same tests and everything. On the final exam he got 597 out of 600 points. He must be a whiz!

"It turns out that after the first class, which you already took, physics turns out to be hard," he said. "Really hard."

It wasn't the best way to have chosen a major, and the next three years were a painful academic trudge. Since it was West Point, with its onerous honor code, the handful of physics majors couldn't even rely on each other the way they might have at a normal college. They couldn't help each other with homework or anything for fear of violating the code, so Armstrong studied in monk-like, cloistered misery.

On the athletics end of life, he ran marathons for Army and notched three sub-three-hour races. One of his coaches was an armor officer, so Armstrong started thinking he might become a tanker.

Adam was also still dating the girlfriend he'd met in high school, Kim. He knew early on that nothing was going to get between him and West Point, and he told her as much, but they kept dating anyhow. They stayed together once he made it to the Academy. She went to Kent State, which was much more fun than the US Military Academy, that's for sure. It made him mad that she went to a fun college while he was stuck sitting under some desk lamp in his starchy uniform, learning about quantum mechanics. She told him it was his own fault: He'd made his choice and now he had to march with it.

He had a bunch of the hang-ups of a young guy wired too tight who didn't yet realize there's more to life than the parade ground. As college progressed, Adam fell deeper in love with Kim, but she was skeptical the skinny cadet was ready for commitment. She told him again and again, Don't even think about proposing, we're not ready for it yet. But he recognized true love and professed as much.

Nope. No way. Don't do it, she said. So he waited.

During senior year, as part of standard training, Armstrong went down to Fort Hood in Texas for a month. There they made him a temporary platoon leader for a mechanized infantry unit. He was, no kidding, leading an Army unit.

Here was this cadet put in charge of a real-life infantry unit where he got to be out there in the woods when the unit donned gas masks as instructors pumped tear gas into the trenches. He oversaw a few live-fire exercises on the range. Well, to say he "oversaw" some ranges is a stretch. He was just sort of there as a figurehead, a platonic form of "officer" at the top of the roster.

Armstrong wasn't even allowed to shoot some of the bigger weapons himself because he hadn't qualified on them. Mostly—because of the permanently hierarchical structure of the Army—the platoon sergeant just needed some officer to say "OK" when it was time to blow something up. But still, Armstrong got a taste of what the infantry was like. After that trip, he was sold on the infantry. It was amazing. He'd come a long way from wanting to be a signals officer.

Back in those days, cadets got to choose their jobs in the Army based on their standing in the class. The top man or woman picked whatever they wanted. Some of those top jobs were in military intelligence, engineers, and infantry. The "goat"—a traditional term for the last in the class—got whatever was left, and in the middle was everyone else, hoping what they wanted would still be available when it was their turn to choose. Maybe if you did abysmally you'd get stuck with some crap job like adjutant, a glorified secretary.

The year Armstrong graduated, it seemed like the entire football team became low-altitude missile defense officers, he remembers.

It was the same thing for the base a new officer headed to. The top cadet would walk up to the front of the room where there was a board plastered with Post-it notes, each with a base name written on it. Grab the best of what's left and off you go! The Army has some bases in objectively wonderful places, like Hawaii. And it's got bases in the middle of nowhere, like Fort Leonard Wood in Missouri. A cadet isn't necessarily looking for the prettiest base in the world, though. Maybe Kentucky or North Carolina was the best choice to get a guy to an infantry unit getting ready to deploy to Iraq or Afghanistan. For many West Pointers, no number of Hawaiian beaches would make up for missing a deployment to a combat zone.

Armstrong was in a good enough position in his class that he got what he wanted: infantry. And he had wanted to go to Germany, but he chose a stateside base instead. It was one of the first compromises he'd make with Kim, who wasn't asking for much, considering she'd stuck with him this long. They weren't married then, but he knew she was The One. And she—unbeknownst to him—was now ready for him to pop the question.

Right after graduation she joined Adam and his family on a trip to New Hampshire. One day the two of them were on a drive home from the mall and she was kind of sad. He asked her why.

"Well, I thought you might have proposed on that vacation," she said.

It boggled his mind, and he had nothing to say. She had been so vociferous in her protestations that this was news to him. He didn't tell her he'd already bought a ring and had a grand plan to propose when they were back in their hometown, hoping he wasn't acting contrary to her wishes.

Soon enough, they were home, so Armstrong launched his grand plan. He put on a banana costume. His brother wore a gorilla suit. They planned on ambushing her in the produce section of the local Giant Eagle grocery for him to ask her the big question, but the West Point graduate botched their reconnaissance. They lost track of her and didn't catch up until she was in the parking lot. It wasn't exactly a girl's dream proposal in the making.

Still, they salvaged the operation. They chased her down, and Armstrong got down on a knee in that banana suit while his brother stood there holding a sign that said, "Adam will go bananas if you marry him."

Good Lord, if she would say yes to *that*, she must be The One.

She said yes.

So the young officer with a young fiancée chose infantry and Fort Carson in Colorado for his first base.

Now that they were slated to be married, he and Kim thought he'd do a couple deployments, maybe with the Fourth Infantry Division, with which he'd be based, then try and get a teaching gig at West Point to finish out the required five-year contract.

Whatever Armstrong and Kim thought they had decided, Adam Armstrong was as predestined as a Calvinist to be a lifer. He was yet still young enough to think he had free will to leave after a few years, though.

When he got to Fort Carson, he was assigned to the First Battalion, 503rd Infantry Regiment, the 1-503, part of a brigade that was, at that very moment, deployed to Ramadi, Iraq. It wouldn't have been a big deal for Armstrong to show up to Fort Carson and do this or that task until the brigade came back home. But he didn't want to wait: He'd been playing Army his whole life and now it was time to do it for real. He emailed a battalion commander from the unit and the guy was happy to have an officer begging to come to Iraq. The lieutenant colonel told him, Hell yeah, come on out and meet us.

But first, he had to get married. He and Kim dashed to the El Paso County courthouse in Colorado Springs to see the Justice of the Peace and get hitched. An apparent shotgun wedding isn't an unusual maneuver for soldiers and shouldn't be misconstrued. Many times, couples will have weddings planned out, then a deployment gets quickly announced or some new orders get cut and they need to tie the knot so they're legal. That's what Kim and Adam did, saving their proper church wedding at the Chardon United Methodist Church for later in the year, 2006. (Their honeymoon would come a year after that, sandwiched by deployments to Iraq.)

Within just weeks of joining 1-503, Armstrong caught an Army flight to Kuwait. A battalion staff officer had figured out a way to get him from there to Ramadi. He arrived with a mere forty-five days left in the deployment.

Everybody he passed at the battalion HQ looked at him like he was crazy, wondering what the hell a new guy was doing showing up as they were packing up to go home. But the battalion commander knew what a young lieutenant needed: experience. He needed experience of any kind and every kind, and that's why they prioritized getting him boots on the ground in Ramadi. The CO told him to find a platoon or a squad with a mission that day and to fill some gap, any gap, in their roster. If he had to stand in for some PFC, or private first class, who couldn't go out, then he'd stand in for the PFC. If they needed somebody up in a vehicle's turret behind a machine gun, well, Lieutenant Armstrong was their man. He was instructed to then come back, rest a day, find another unit going out, and do it all over again. There was no better way to learn how the real Army works.

On his first mission, part of a company's patrol, one of the patrol's .50-caliber gunners shot at a vehicle laden with explosives and the whole damn car blew up. That was Armstrong's first mission out of the wire. Next mission, an enemy sniper shot a soldier in the leg, and Armstrong had to lead a convoy of vehicles to get the guy back to base and to the hospital. By the time those forty-five days were up, Armstrong had earned a combat patch, his Combat Infantryman Badge, and all the other stuff boot lieutenants don't have when they arrive at their first units.

So when Armstrong got back to Fort Carson, he strutted around. He wore his Combat Infantryman Badge and combat patch on his right sleeve for all to see. Other lieutenants looked at him with eyes agog and said, No way, it's impossible for this guy to have already had a deployment.

This fast-track scheme positioned him well for greater leadership roles in the battalion. He became an executive officer in a company—with experience—for that same unit's next deployment back to Ramadi for fifteen months. Armstrong doesn't have much to say about that deployment because he wasn't in command. His job, as executive officer, was to tinker with the machinery of the unit, so to speak. He moved people here and there, paid attention to spreadsheets, strategized about how to fill gaps. He kept his head down and did his best. Meanwhile, some men were killed, some were wounded, and operations happened.

That's often the life of an executive officer. And when you spend a career in the Army, there are entire combat deployments that don't really register, or if they do, they are relatively minuscule and weightless, almost as nothing compared with others.

* * *

By the time 2008 rolled around and Armstrong took over Bravo Company, he'd already had two previous deployments, one as a platoon leader and the other as an executive officer, and he'd seen combat and death. But he still looked like a pain-in-the-ass noob to Mac.

To be fair to all the troops who made fun of him for being a lifer, by the time he took over Bravo, Armstrong himself knew full well he was, indeed, a lifer. After those two combat deployments, Armstrong had grown a liking for the infantry and for the Army. He gave in to his fate, certain he'd do at least twenty years in the Army, probably more.

He and Kim had planned out having their first child around his likely Army career. The way he figured it, if they did it right, the oldest would be en route to high school around the time he was hitting the twenty-year retirement mark. Might as well mark that child-rearing timeline down in one of those green, cloth-covered notebooks that every officer in the military seems to have in their pocket, ready to whip out to note down something-or-other using a Rite in the Rain pen.

As a captain he thought he'd be able to perfectly calculate retirement dates and procreation timelines. It was yet another of the delusions an Army lifer must have in the natural course of affairs. But nothing remains on schedule in the Army despite best efforts. Back then Armstrong wasn't figuring there'd ever be a chance for him to get battalion command or brigade command, he was simply too young to imagine that being something he'd do, even though it would *have to happen* for him to remain in for a career. That stuff was a million miles away and out of the realm of imagination for him.

* * *

Armstrong wanted to make sure this new company of his was ready for anything. And that meant they had to train with absolute efficiency. He cared about the troops, so he had to train them to peak performance, tune them like a carburetor in a race car. It wasn't long before Armstrong started to realize that training the troops is not all efficiency and economy. It's art as well as science. He realized it when Mac took Armstrong aside and let him know that the platoon sergeants thought this West Point guy was just trying to climb the ladder and didn't really give two shits about them.

As far as the Captain America thing went, well, Armstrong knew commanders got crummy nicknames. But when Mac took him aside to talk, the two started forging a bond, something that would be tried and tested and strained and strengthened over the coming years. Mac wanted Armstrong to know that the troops needed to see another side of him. Mac knew that they were in it together and they had to be a team.

Mac went about demonstrating his zeal in the only way he knew how. He knew what it was like to get fucked up in combat—he'd seen it happen to other guys, and it had happened to him. Now he was a first sergeant, the top enlisted guy for an infantry company, and so his job was to make sure it didn't happen to his guys.

That's why Mac was Mac, and, goddammit, his job was to get these guys trained up. He knew he didn't have time to slow down, or let up, or take time to think about all the injuries and pain he'd seen and experienced himself.

While it sucked for the boys that Bravo and all the rest of 2-508 who had just gotten back from a ballbreaker of a deployment to Afghanistan, where they were stop-lossed and had to stay fifteen months, there wasn't time for sympathy. They had to turn around and get ready for another deployment. They'd run through exercises like rifle ranges and practice assaults again and again and again to make sure they weren't squandering any opportunity. Mac was the one who had to keep pushing and moving forward. But he could be a real dick.

Jason Johnston, the guy who was everybody's friend and had introduced Danica to Allen, had some funky issue with the skin on his face so he couldn't shave, Sergeant Major Bert Puckett remembered. Johnston had a chit (a note) from the doctor that allowed him an exception to the shaving rules. He was growing a beard—a beard in an American infantry unit! Mac couldn't have that unprofessional-looking shit in his unit, so he told Johnston, Don't wear a uniform, just show up to formation in civilian gear. Poor bastard didn't look the part, so Mac sidelined him.

Puckett walked by one day and saw Johnston, who he thought was some bearded civilian in civvy clothes, and asked him what the fuck he was doing in the battalion area. He got the story and, with a sigh, went to tell Mac that he had to let the kid train, it's not the soldier's fault his face was all messed up.

That was Mac back then.

He did show a softer side though, behind closed doors, when Captain Armstrong showed up for their first field op. Damn officer. The guy hadn't been out to the field for a few years, so Mac helped un-fuck Armstrong's pack, make sure it was all cinched down and squared away.

But he never made Armstrong feel like a fool. Maybe it was because of the novelty, a company commander who took advice like that from his senior enlisted. Whatever the reason, Mac helped him out and didn't go blabbing about how messed-up the new CO was. No, he imparted that knowledge in an almost loving way to Armstrong. They were a team after all, and there's not too many people on your team when you start to move up in rank.

As a first sergeant, Mac didn't have any friends—at least, friends he could frankly talk to about his problems. Because he outranked about every enlisted guy around him and he had to put on a good show for all the officers, it got real lonely. But he could deal with it, because he had to be a hard-ass.

CHAPTER 4

NEW TIRES

Allen Thomas remained close to Patrick Exon, his friend from high school. Patrick saw changes in his friend after those two deployments, especially after the Purple Heart.

Allen talked about some of the things that he'd seen overseas and how he never wanted to see them again. No specifics, just that he'd seen stuff on his first two deployments that wasn't so great. Still, it wasn't so bad that he wanted out of the Army. Allen didn't want to quit soldiering.

Once when they were at the mall together, a loud noise—a dropped box or the boom of a slammed door—made Allen hit the deck. Then he wouldn't go to the mall at all, saying he wanted to avoid crowds. Sometimes when they were together Patrick would look over and see Allen just staring off.

It reminded him of the scene in *American Sniper* where the lead character sits entranced by a blank TV screen, wholly enthralled by it but at the same time totally oblivious.

"Looking back, I wish I would have tried to talk more," Patrick said. "In my younger years, ten years ago, I didn't have anything to compare it to."

But Allen was still Allen, just mellower, a little different. There was no wholesale change Patrick could put his finger on. He describes it as Allen "fading" a bit, even though his smile and laugh were still there.

That was just before Allen met Danica.

* * *

During the deployment workup in 2008, when most of the company went to Fort Polk, Louisiana, for training that they couldn't accomplish at Fort Bragg, Allen stayed behind to go to jumpmaster school so he'd be better qualified to train paratroopers.

Those few who hadn't gone to Louisiana were hanging out one night. Danica was there when talk turned to their pre-deployment Military Ball, the big fancy-dress dinner where troops in an airborne unit back then wore their Army Service Uniforms with all the medals and ribbons and the female guests wore dresses like it was prom night. The military ball might be the only time freshly minted privates get to wear their formal uniforms before they head out on their first deployment. Sometimes it's the last time they'll wear them before a funeral.

At the military ball the youngest soldiers get incredibly drunk and the oldest soldiers sometimes just get very drunk. For young and old, raw soldiers and those who are well-seasoned, all thoughts of future deployments are banished in order to focus on the moment and have a good time in the bosom of a base in the middle of the United States.

They were talking about the anticipated fun when Danica reached way up and put her hand on Allen's shoulder.

"Who are you taking to the ball?" she asked.

"Nobody," he said.

"Well, you're taking me," she replied.

And then she walked away, just like that. A few minutes later, out in the parking lot, Allen walked up to Danica and said he needed her number if he was taking her to the ball. Before the ball they needed to have a first date.

So he got her number.

For the date, she picked him up in her Chrysler Sebring convertible for a trip to the mall. He was appalled by the state of the car's tires—one was almost bald, for goodness' sake—so he drove the car because he didn't feel safe and had a premonition something might happen. And then, sure enough, on the way home, a blowout.

He changed the tire and drove her to work. Then he asked if he could borrow her car and went with it straightaway and bought her a full set of radials.

He bought her a set a tires on their first date.

That was Allen for you.

Danica was smitten. After all, once you accept tires from a guy it's a bona fide relationship, right? But Allen was unsure. The one thing he was absolutely rock solid about was his job as an Army sergeant. It was relationship stuff that brought uncertainty even as they saw more and more of each other.

Allen was worried about training, and he knew a deployment was around the corner. He wasn't quite ready to dive into something long-term, he said, as they spent more time together. She nodded her head and said it was OK, that they'd figure things out.

And they really seemed to be figuring things out in those wonderful few months between when they met and when Allen needed to deploy.

Danica's mom, a pretty traditional Serbian-American woman grounded in family and self-reliance, lived in Fayetteville, so Danica and Allen and her mom would spend Sundays together at Manna Church in town. It wasn't a stuffy Serbian Orthodox place, it was a church with guitars and preachers in Henley shirts singing lyrics projected onto a screen behind the stage.

Danica herself was still Serbian Orthodox, but her mom never expected her to be "by the book" about it. Allen had been raised Southern Baptist, so Manna Church was good enough for everybody. Allen was just happy to have met a twenty-year-old woman who wanted to go to church every Sunday.

"We both believed, and we had our faith, and that's all that mattered," she said.

So Allen tagged along with them on Sundays. Church. Family time. It was perfect. Faith was something that brought them together and something they never gave up on, one of the solid rocks they started building their burgeoning relationship on. Family. Friends. Church.

And beer. Pabst Blue Ribbon was always a source of mutual happiness, though Allen also liked to drink his weird version of a black and tan: Guinness and Fat Tire ale.

Soon enough they were inseparable. Well, as inseparable as they could be with the Army always, always, always cutting between them like a chaperone at a school dance. He was an infantryman, an 82nd Airborne Division paratrooper, and for him the career would always come before family life, he said. And she knew he meant it.

She'd grown up as the stepdaughter of an active-duty guy. Her sister married into the Army, too. "It sounds kind of silly, but I always knew that I would kind of always be on the back burner to his job," she said.

Allen was good at his job. He was a leader. He was a teacher. He was a soldier.

"I always knew that was his first priority, especially before we had children and married," she said.

Children. Marriage. A wish for the future—that's what she started having thoughts of.

While his old friend Patrick could see some changes in Allen—small changes—Danica didn't see anything concerning. Or maybe he wouldn't let her see. She didn't know what PTSD was back then—couldn't even tell you what the letters stood for.

Looking back, she's the first to say that she couldn't have really noticed any change, any deviation from the normal, because she hadn't known Allen before those other deployments. Danica met him when she met him, there's no way she could have known what he was like before the Army. There's no way she could have known what he was like ten minutes before they met, that's the ontological truth of the situation.

Looking back, she can't say whether the person she met in Fayetteville was the fundamental version of Allen, the true him. People change and adapt and get shaped. They are scarred and wounded and grow moment to moment. War changes people, but so does life. Every interaction they have has the chance to make a difference in their fundamental being. Was there something even then that Danica could have detected that would indicate a perilous road ahead? If there was something, some telltale sign, then what caused it? Was it his prior deployments or something that had been around even further back?

"When I met him he had already deployed twice, but, to me, I'm just meeting somebody. I don't know what he was like before. I don't know high school him," she said. "So I just met him and I thought that was him."

Was he a completely different person from when he was a teenager? The Allen she fell for might just have been a snapshot of a man who was ever changing in all ways. Perhaps there was no real Allen, some True Him that lay at the core of it all. Like Heraclitus's river, perhaps he was simply and always Allen, a human being in flux, depending on the moment.

Still, had Allen's very substance been altered by war? Or, God help us all, did war simply reveal the real Allen who had been there all along, in hibernation? Was he under there yet, waiting to be revealed?

CHAPTER 5

COIN

Bravo Company didn't know as they got ready for their deployment to Iraq in 2008 that they would soon be front and center in the minds of generals and statesmen. In retrospect, many of the men never found out at all.

Army units are like Russian nesting dolls. Bravo Company was part of Second Battalion, which was part of the 508th Parachute Infantry Regiment, which was part of Fourth Brigade, which was part of the 82nd Airborne Division, which was part of the Eighteenth Airborne Corps, which was part of the United States Army, which was part of the Department of Defense. And all of that nestled under the purview of the commander in chief, the president of the United States of America.

Any soldier knows "shit rolls downhill," so for Bravo to have understood their deployment and the orders that sent them abroad, they would have to have known what was going on at the White House.

For a soldier at the bottom of the food chain, though, there was little to understand. Nick "Armen" Armendariz was someone like that, a soldier at the bottom of the food chain, the tiniest nesting doll in the whole system.

Armen could be a jackass, as he would readily admit with a coy smile and a little laugh. He'd probably say it with a shrug of his shoulders to show that the truth of his jackassery is a fait accompli, and there's really nothing you or anyone else can do about it, so go fuck yourself. But Armen was also a fine machine gunner, a reliable soldier, and someone who could be depended upon in a firefight. When he was in tip-top shape at the height of his soldiering he had an angular nose and sharp chin, and he could turn that coy smile into a cruel rictus. He looked like he belonged among the guys from the Cobra Kai dojo who'd happily beat up Daniel LaRusso, that little goody two-shoes.

The upcoming deployment wasn't Armen's first. He had joined the Army right after high school, because going to college wasn't his thing. Being a soldier, hey, that was his thing, something he'd always wanted to do.

He went to basic training in 2006, then to Airborne school before being sent to Italy to join the 173rd Airborne Brigade. With them in 2007 he went for his first deployment to Afghanistan, up to Nuristan in the north. It's as mountainous up there as it can be flat in the south. Armen cut his teeth on combat in those mountains with seemingly endless firefights, guys getting shot and rolling down mountains. It was brutal, it was constant. And it was fucking fun.

The give and take of small-arms fire, mortars, and everything, that's what he trained for back in the States. It's what an infantryman is bred to do, and Armen found that he seemed custom-made to close with and destroy the enemy.

The best part of that deployment to Nuristan was that it seemed a fair fight, just him and his fellow soldiers shooting guns at the Taliban. It was Armen's team versus the bad guys' team. Sometimes they had a good day and killed the Taliban. Sometimes the Taliban had a good day and killed some Americans. But it was fair and square as far as he could tell. He came back from that northern Afghanistan deployment reveling in the glory of all those firefights.

Armen returned to his base in Italy and did the ridiculous things paratroopers do, like fist-fighting with an MP and then getting busted down to private. That sort of thing. So for the forthcoming deployment with Bravo Company, he didn't have the rank that would put him in a leadership position, but nobody could take away his experience. That left him with a pretty sweet gig, to be able to have a machine gun and fight without having to be in charge of anything or anyone.

Derek Hill had been on that first deployment with Armen. He came over to Bravo Company around the same time.

Hill was from Galax, Virginia, and had grown up close to his sister, Lisa Hill Lowe, even though they were twelve years apart in age, she remembers. He'd just turned seven years old when she got married, and he was always around her and her burgeoning family, in some ways more like a son to her than a brother.

He was a spur-of-the-moment type of guy, Lisa remembers. After high school he moved to Nashville and went to diesel mechanic school, then got a two-year degree. He worked at Lowe's, the home improvement store, for a while, but he just didn't like it. In 2006 he told his sister he was thinking about the Army, and then the next day he signed up.

Man, he was a happy guy. He was always smiling and asking after you, never focusing on himself. Lisa was worried that her twenty-three-year-old brother wouldn't like the Army, with drill instructors yelling at him and all in his face, but he said he'd be OK.

Boot camp and initial training in 2006 went just fine, and he'd been dating a girl. When he came home for a visit, he made what seemed like yet another spur-of-the-moment announcement: If they could find a preacher who wasn't busy, he and the girl he'd been dating were going to get married.

Hill got married after that short courtship, and that pulled him away from his sister. Then he moved to Italy with the 173rd Airborne and deployed.

He wrote home, saying he liked the Army and even had a best friend, Thomas Wilson. The two looked so much alike, they could switch nametapes on their uniforms and fool people. While Hill was on that first deployment to Afghanistan, months after boot camp, he had a medical issue come up when he was supposed to be out on patrol. He had to go to the hospital for some tests, so Wilson took his spot.

Wilson was shot on that patrol. Died. Hill came back to the States for the funeral and spoke at the ceremony. He blamed himself for that death ever after.

* * *

Soldiers like Armen looked forward to more of the fighting they'd experienced on previous deployments, and soldiers like Jared Lemon looked forward to finally getting into the kind of fights they'd been promised when they signed up. In late 2008, as Bravo Company prepared for Iraq, Lemon was a junior soldier with one deployment under his belt. He remembers clearly that he was bummed out knowing he'd probably just sit around a base doing nothing in Iraq, waiting for the end of that war.

Lemon had wanted to see real combat for about as long as he could remember. He had always wanted to be a soldier. Both his granddads had been in the Army, and when he was a kid up in Alaska, he'd always play Army—he'd never play Navy, no way.

Who plays Navy, anyway? Nobody has ever played Navy.

Lemon was an Eagle Scout, grew up near Anchorage, and climbed mountains all the time. Looking back on it, it was a hell of an accomplishment any time he went up a mountain. He'd hike up in Skagway, that pure land up in Alaska where the Klondike gold rush had loomed over everything a hundred years earlier.

He'd fish all summer long, catching enough for the entire year. He used to hate salmon, because his family always had it. Imagine having so much fresh salmon that you end up hating it. Halibut, well, now, that's a tasty fish. It became his favorite, and it still is.

He had his dark hair, his thick eyebrows, and a dense, rugged body forged by scrambling around in Alaska. While always ready to have an earnest conversation in low, subdued tones, Lemon also operated happily an octave higher, and at an allegro pace. Jokes and asides came quick, followed by a machine-gun staccato of laughs.

After high school Lemon got married and had a kid. He and the missus didn't have medical insurance, and when he got sick one time, the bills piled up.

Sometimes patriotic intentions drive you to join the Army. Other times it's hardship in the real world and you've got no other good options. For Lemon, it was a combination of both. He'd always wanted to join, sure, and the cherry on top was he could get insurance for the wife and kid. She didn't want him to go into the Army or the Marines or whatever it was he was about to do. She didn't support that stupid decision at all, he said.

Lemon did it anyway.

He went to see the Marine recruiter, but they didn't have a good offer, honestly. The Army, though, they could guarantee, with a contract in black-and-white, the job a fellow was going to get.

He chose infantry.

After weeks of boot camp and months of infantry training, Jared Lemon first arrived at Bravo Company's headquarters at Fort Bragg in 2007. When he arrived, nobody was there, because they were still in the middle of the fifteen-month deployment to Ghazni province, Afghanistan. Lemon learned he was going to be a combat replacement, which means he was going to be shipped over to Afghanistan and dropped into the company mid-tour to replenish the company's dwindling numbers, those who had been wounded in combat and sent back to the States to recover.

It sounded like the beginning of an exciting deployment, but for Lemon it turned out to be slow and boring. There were scant firefights, maybe a couple of potshots here and there from the bad guys. In 2007 there weren't very many IEDs to deal with.

It seemed like he was in a Humvee for hours at a time, driving from one base to another, from one Afghan outpost to another. The drive was always boring, locked in an armored vehicle, grumbling engines and whirring motors the only sounds to hear. Tiny, bulletproof windows, the only way to peek out onto the outside world. Once they finally got someplace, an Afghan *shura* meeting or something, the officers and senior enlisted disappeared into mud houses to talk to Afghan elders while guys like Lemon stood around outside in a security detail.

They had little more to do than fend off the local kids whose sole purpose in life seemed to be stealing the soldiers' ink pens and begging for candy. One time it snowed two feet and they were stuck on base and couldn't even take a boring drive to a boring *shura* somewhere. It seemed more like what he imagined was a police action than a war.

That first deployment wasn't satisfying at all: no action, not enough of what he'd signed up for. But no matter how slow it was, a war's a war. And when Lemon left that first tour in Afghanistan, he thought to himself, *Holy shit, I'm a war vet now.* He could count himself among those who had "Been There," same as the Vietnam guys he'd looked up to—he had that at least. But there was still something missing—there always seems to be something missing. The no-kidding bona fides are always out there someplace just over the horizon.

And now, after that first deployment, Lemon was getting ready to go on what seemed like another boring one. Oddly enough, he had always imagined going to Iraq. At least he imagined deploying to the Iraq he'd heard about in other people's stories when he was signing up for the Army and going through boot camp, and then all the training before getting to Bravo Company. He'd imagined himself in a place like Fallujah, where there was a fight—a real fight—the two sides slugging it out mano a mano. Young troops and old veterans alike talked about the Second Battle of Fallujah that happened in 2004 with the same reverence afforded to Khe Sanh or Iwo Jima.

Lemon knew there was always a chance of getting wounded or something. He knew his friends might get hurt, but that's the job, and it's all hypothetical anyway until an actual deployment.

"I don't even know if I should say this: You don't want your friends to get hurt," he said. "Imagine training for a job and you're really good at it. You want and desire to do that job."

But by late 2008, the Iraq War was winding down. It seemed like supremely crummy luck for Lemon that Bravo Company had drawn the Iraq card just when things were getting boring.

* * *

Jared Lemon's irritation with Iraq was then Commander in Chief George W. Bush's pleasure. The country was seemingly calm thanks in large part to a recent push by the Army and Marines to surge into the country and stamp out violence.

In 2006 the Republican Party lost control of the House of Representatives and the Senate in a midterm election that was in large part a referendum on the Iraq War, which hadn't been going well. Months later President Bush ordered some twenty thousand new troops into Iraq to turn things around with sheer force, but also leveraging a novel strategy that was all the rage in Washington and in Iraq. The strategy was known as counterinsurgency warfare, or COIN, and the public face of the strategy was Army General David Petraeus.

Petraeus had been leading the effort to create a new and comprehensive way of dealing with Iraq as it descended into chaos a few years back, in 2005. And it seemed to have worked swimmingly, which lent him an aura of military genius. (Never mind that the very building blocks of the doctrine would prove its downfall in the long term.) Petraeus used piles of money to build projects and win over local populations. He used ample American forces, diplomats, and their accompanying logistical largess to project American power and convince locals of the seeming inevitability of outcomes. A few years later, when the money, the troops, and the logistics dried up, so did many of the gains that seemed so impressive at the time. With a handful of military and civilian thinkers, Petraeus became the figurehead for a mindset codified in a new manual for COIN warfare, known as the Army's *Field Manual 3-24: Counterinsurgency.*

FM 3-24 laid out, in doctrinaire terms, how to handle a situation that seemed to precisely resemble the one the United States faced in Iraq at the time. It was, it seemed, tailor-made for a developed country with citizens who wanted infrastructure improvement and were ready to trust a duly appointed centralized government with the accoutrements of a trusted army and police. It told how to subdue an insurgency by gaining the trust of the population and emerging victorious. It told of how to use brainpower and diplomatic resources to win hearts and minds. It wasn't about sheer firepower, it was about a well-rounded approach to fighting an enemy that lived among the people.

Robert Gates, the defense secretary at the time, dumped troops and resources into Iraq for a surge. By 2008 it had gotten results, with violence decreasing across the country.

Even talking about it all just a few years afterward makes the effort, even the terminology, seem a bit crazy. The word "surge" itself seems like something that should be written with an exclamation mark behind it—Surge!—like the name of a bad water park or an ad for a high-caffeine soda pop. The word "surge" just seems downright hokey, like bad copy from a cut-rate ad agency.

But back then, it looked like the key. Was the relative success in Iraq because of COIN? It was hard to say, but everyone was talking about counterinsurgency and crediting it for victory. "We're all good Americans," said then Deputy National Security Advisor Doug Lute. "So we look in the mirror and say, it must have been something I did."

Like a business that focuses too much on its quarterly dividends at the expense of long-term solvency, the fruits of COIN warfare and the way the administration went about subduing Iraq would unravel a few years later. But that was yet to come. In 2008, while Bravo worked up for a deployment, Iraq seemed as if it was on the way to peace. Violence was dropping and local governance was pushing out insurgent influence. One of the primary reasons the COIN approach worked well was that tribes in places like Anbar were fed up with Al Qaeda in Iraq and decided to push back.

"He was born on third and thought he hit a triple," Barnett Rubin, a former State Department official and deputy to Ambassador Richard Holbrooke, said of Petraeus's seemingly perfect strategy in Iraq. "The surge had worked, but the main part was politics."

Rubin worked for Holbrooke, the top diplomat for Afghanistan at the time, so Barnett had a front-row seat to everything unfolding.

For his part, Petraeus always maintained that the strategy in Iraq wasn't ever meant to be duplicated and shipped to Afghanistan.

"FM [3-24] had, of course, been published in December 2006 and implemented successfully in Iraq during the Surge of 2007/8; however, we all knew that Afghanistan was very different from Iraq in a host of ways, not the least of which was the sanctuaries available to the enemy outside Afghanistan," he said in an email.

"In fact, the first slide in a briefing I gave to Secretary Rumsfeld back in September 2005, after doing an assessment of the situation in Afghanistan on the way home from my three-star tour in Iraq, was titled Afghanistan [Does Not Equal sign] Iraq. And I laid out all the differences."

Petraeus's slides notwithstanding, the conflation of Iraq and Afghanistan was unavoidable. A soldier who fights in any country for a year is going to transfer lessons learned to the next place he fights.

"When you're coming from Iraq to Afghanistan, you're seeing things with an Iraq lens," said General George Casey in an interview. He was the Army chief of staff at the time who said he worried about such myopia.

At the Pentagon, though, generals have to keep up with each other. They have to keep an eye on shifting political winds, not just the realities on the battlefield. Everyone saw Petraeus's star rising and they didn't want to get left behind, so, in turn, everyone clamored for a slice of the COIN action, pointing to Iraq to show it worked.

Thoughts turned to Afghanistan and whether the apparent panacea would work there. From the military's perspective, it was worth a try. At the top, careers were being made thanks to COIN. Petraeus was rocketing up into the Defense Department firmament due to his vocal embrace of this thinking man's style of war. This general, who could run a half marathon faster than you could jog around the block and then dig into strategy documents wearing granny-style reading glasses, was setting the pace all the other generals needed to follow.

Petraeus had burnished COIN doctrine to a high gloss thanks to the apparent success in Iraq. Nobody seemed to think about the governance and political aspects of all this, the things that had to happen to make these gains last.

Nobody seemed to care about history if it meant looking back more than a few years. Defense officials' memories didn't stretch back to Vietnam or other conflicts, they seemed to only think about the present, as if all problems and situations were novel things to be solved with tactics that seemed to be working at the time.

It's a recurring theme in American military operations, that we don't really care about history when we're looking at today's conflict. History never really has a seat at the table, it's too crowded with people who care about the immediate present and the not-too-distant future. Perhaps most significantly, it's crowded with people with sharp elbows thinking about military promotion boards.

Down among mid-ranking officers, FM 3-24, the COIN manual, was on everyone's reading list. The thing was so popular that the University of Chicago Press published it, complete with olive drab covers and with the page edges rounded off so it looked more rugged. It was a military manual published as a fifteen-dollar paperback, made to look like it could be thrown in a rucksack, and it sold more than 40,000 copies plus another few thousand e-books.

The flip side to all this COIN talk was that the military aspect of it depended heavily on building up societies in occupied lands. COIN relied on civilians in the occupied country to make it work. Thus it needed diplomats and aid workers from the occupying force. It needed troops who knew how to do more than blow stuff up. And it needed the State Department, which had institutional know-how, cultural expertise, and cadres of people who had been around the country before the shooting war began and would stick around afterward.

To work, to really work, COIN needed to have the coordination of a lot of moving parts that don't easily mesh.

"The essence behind 3-24 was civilians and military working together," said Elisabeth Kvitashvili, a retired officer from the United States Agency for International Development, known as USAID, and the State Department. She helped draft the manual. But nobody ever figured out if the military needed to lead the way and create a safe environment for diplomats and aid workers, or if those civilians needed to do humanitarian assistance as a prerequisite for the populace to trust the military. The chicken-or-egg question was never answered.

"State and USAID didn't have the bandwidth," Kvitashvili said. "We just didn't have the capacity."

While the military can call down to Fort Bragg and order up a few thousand troops to head into country on new orders, the State Department can't really do the same thing. They can incentivize deployments and maybe force folks to head over for a few months at most, but there aren't direct orders like in the military. Even if people did want to go, there weren't enough, not the sheer numbers found at the Defense Department.

The Defense Department could get that call, though, ordering up a few thousand troops to go someplace new, to do whatever they were ordered to do. Maybe there would be a new reason to call America's 9-1-1 force down at Fort Bragg?

* * *

When he took office in 2009, President Barack Obama didn't know exactly what he wanted to do in Afghanistan, only that he wanted to do something. During the campaign and transition, there had been conversations about Afghanistan, but nothing had been decided.

"Obama really didn't like having that decision put on him immediately, but he was ambushed by reality," said Barnett Rubin, whose official title was senior advisor to the special representative for Afghanistan and Pakistan in the US Department of State from 2009 to 2013. "They had not decided what their policy would be at all. When you're campaigning you set up all these focus groups to keep people busy."

One of the reasons Obama chose to keep Robert Gates as his secretary of defense was a belief in the notion that things had been going better recently in Iraq and Afghanistan. Continuity would show he trusted the Pentagon, which was important, since Obama had no military experience.

One guy with some experience in foreign affairs was Vice President Joe Biden. At meetings Biden asked guys like Defense Secretary Gates: What was the point of more troops? He asked the generals what was to be gained. But Biden was the vice president, not the president.

Richard Holbrooke was another man who had extensive experience in the region. In January 2009 Obama appointed him to a newly created position, the US special envoy to Afghanistan and Pakistan. The larger-than-life Holbrooke was a diplomatic wizard, but he could really make people angry—including the president who'd appointed him.

It didn't take long for Holbrooke to burn his bridges with Obama and lose influence, because the president simply didn't care for the man, according to multiple accounts. Holbrooke was perceived by many—including the president—as stuck-up and haughty, so Obama didn't want to listen to him. Holbrooke, for his part, knew he didn't have to be loved by the president, but he did need to have influence with the president to accomplish tasks he felt invested in.

Over a dinner with Rubin, Holbrooke confided that this COIN stuff seemed like some of the same failed programs the United States had tried in other conflicts, like Vietnam—they'd just changed the names for them. Holbrooke complained he would have been able to bring history to the table if Obama and others would have trusted him, but he wasn't really given a seat, despite being a high-ranking envoy.

Holbrooke realized that COIN was loved by all as the latest fashion and that the new president seemed to like it. Rubin remembers that Holbrooke said he'd decided to go all in on COIN if that's what it took to get the president to listen to him. If he had some influence with the president he could guide policy, he thought. So the giant of the diplomatic corps also gave COIN his thumbs-up.

CHAPTER 6

ENABLERS

The men of Bravo Company had spent months preparing for a deployment to Iraq.

In many ways a company gets ready for combat—not combat in any particular place, but combat generally. It's not the specifics of a locale or its people that an Army unit spends much of its training time on. An Army unit might do a couple of extra trips to a desert base in California or Texas if they're expecting to spend time in sandy environs as they might find in Iraq, and there's maybe a few perfunctory language sessions, learning the Arabic version of "Hello" and "How are you?" and "Stop or I'll shoot." The local word for "shit" or "fuck" must also be learned, though not through an Army textbook. There are a handful of culture lessons, too, but no eighteen-year-old is there to become an anthropologist, so all he remembers is: Don't shake hands with your left hand when you're over there.

The layout of a pre-deployment workup is, thus, pretty much the same for a unit going to Iraq or Afghanistan or anywhere else. Much of Bravo's training happened at Fort Bragg, where the company was based. It's among those lush and leafy miles upon miles of deciduous forest that Army units trained to deploy to the Middle East. That meant long hikes with full packs along paved roads, shooting rifles on ranges covered in grass, and jumping out of airplanes even though there was zero chance they'd be doing that on the next deployment.

They learned how to shoot weapons, blow things up, work together, and endure misery. That's the essence of training for the bulk of soldiers. An Army unit trains to kill whatever enemy it can whenever it can, and beginning in boot camp soldiers are told that their purpose in life is to get into combat, kill the enemy, and keep their buddies from getting killed by the enemy. Enemy, enemy, enemy. All cultural and language training takes a back seat to the bread and butter. Soldiers are taught to desire combat, to thirst for it, and that if they can just do what they learn in training, well, they will prevail against the enemy, because the US Army is, of course, the greatest fighting force on the planet, goddammit!

There's added juice to this message in the 82nd Airborne. The division is always up there in the pantheon of units that contribute piss, vinegar, and a storied history to the notion of the Army's greatness. First formed in 1917, the division long boasted having a representation of fighting-age men from across the country, which gave rise to its nickname, the "All American," from whence comes the distinctive shoulder patch with two *A*'s next to each other. The 82nd took part in World War I and World War II as well as wars and not-quite-wars ever since. By the time Bravo Company was part of it, the 82nd boasted that it always had units ready to deploy on eighteen hours' notice to forcibly take airfields or do whatever the US government needed parachute infantry to do.

In Iraq and Afghanistan there wasn't much paratrooping to be done—jumping behind enemy lines and all that—but there was plenty of war to be fought, and if the Department of Defense was calling up reserves and the National Guard, then you can bet regular units like the 82nd were going to get constant deployments.

Those soldiers grew up as kids playing Army in the woods, and then many of them labored through high school, waiting for the day they could enlist and head off to boot camp. They watched movies like *The Green Berets* and imbibed hagiographic tales of manly heroism, and it helped drive deep into their heads and into their very souls a desire to be like Grandpa, like Dad, like John Wayne, and to experience combat, to *know* in their bones what being a soldier is really like.

They thought they would be soldiers once they got through boot camp. But then they got a huge surprise after going through the miserable weeks of basic training—they were told they weren't really soldiers, not yet. Senior troops around them reminded them that they'd not yet been to war and didn't yet know anything about the real Army. And once they'd been told that, they looked all around them on base and saw soldiers who had earned the right to be called soldiers. Older troops were often brutal to these new additions to their units. The new guys got called "boots" for having just graduated boot camp, or "cherries" because they hadn't yet been deflowered by combat operations. Even though these young men had rank on their uniforms and got a paycheck, they didn't have the experience that meant they were veterans of conflict. It's a truism in the US Army the same as it has been for militaries throughout time: Seasoned troops shit on the new guys.

Then and now, they were told they can't really be soldiers until they've gone on that first deployment. That gets internalized, implanted somewhere deep within that boot-ass cherry. It makes the soldier want combat experience simply in order to fit in. And through all the months of training as they get ready to go on that first deployment, they're not thinking about how to say "hello" in Arabic or which hand to use when they shake, they're only thinking of one thing: the Combat Infantryman Badge, or CIB.

The badge itself is a tiny Springfield Arsenal musket, model 1795, on a blue background that they get to wear above their ribbons on a uniform jacket. They can wear a patch of it on their cammies, too. The badge shows a soldier's been there. But you don't get one just for being in a war zone. In order to earn that CIB a soldier has to be shot at by the enemy and then shoot back. It means he's done the minimum necessary to gain the respect of the rest of the Army and veterans across all ages and wars.

Soldiers can be perplexed when they talk to a civilian and try to explain that just because a person was in the military it doesn't mean they ever went to a combat zone. And a soldier is likely further astonished when they have to explain to a civilian that just because someone was deployed to a combat zone, it doesn't mean they actually saw combat of any kind. This is one of the basic dividing lines between soldier and civilian—the soldier has a genuine appreciation for what it means to be in combat. The Combat Infantryman Badge is the only way to prove a soldier actually did what people think they all do: go to war and shoot at the enemy.

During those months of preparing for deployment, the young guys of Bravo Company longed for war, in part so that they, too, could be part of the club. It's that way across much of the military, part of the zeitgeist of units that thrive on combat like Army paratroopers or Marines. In fact, the Marine Corps makes a big deal about praying for war, actually imploring the Almighty to allow for the worst shit imaginable to happen so they can take part in it. It's the same feeling for a soldier, especially a new soldier who doesn't have that CIB yet. Down deep it becomes an animal desire to kill another human being, shoot him right in the chest or, better yet, in the face. That gets to the heart of what's taught in those months of training for a deployment. Through all the training, field exercises, rifle ranges, and qualification badges, it ultimately boils down to one thing: Kill.

But in 2009, the young soldiers' longing for war wasn't likely going to be satisfied by a deployment to Iraq. It wasn't the same as it had been for years following the 2003 invasion of the country to oust Saddam Hussein. For about half a decade, Iraq had been the place where Marines and soldiers wanted to go because that's where they were likely to find themselves in combat.

When President George W. Bush turned his attention to Iraq, the war in Afghanistan became a seeming backwater, with little attention from the president or his closest advisors. Because of that focus, by early 2009, Iraq wasn't as violent as it had been. It even seemed that there might have been a fundamental shift toward stability. There had been a tactical, strategic, and political change throughout Iraq. The Marines out in the western stretches of the country took credit for the Awakening, a movement among local tribal leadership who decided they'd had enough of Al Qaeda in Iraq and would tentatively throw their lot in with the Americans. (Only the Marine Corps would have the audacity to take credit for calming down an entire country through operations in one province.) In a matter of months Marines had turned the cities of Ramadi and Fallujah from hellholes where they'd fought vicious battles into cities where they could walk down the middle of the street alongside local residents with little threat of a firefight.

By the end of 2008 it seemed the Iraq War was winding down, and what crummy luck for Bravo Company, having to go someplace boring.

The military had also been slowly solving the IED problem in Iraq. It had founded a group, the Joint IED Defeat Organization (JIEDDO), which was a research think tank to figure out what kinds of IEDs were commonly found on the battlefield and to come up with tactics and gadgets that could prevent them from blowing up Americans.

JIEDDO, pronounced ji-ay-doe, had been around for a few years at that point and had been focusing almost solely on Iraq. They didn't even pay attention to Afghanistan at the time.

Back in 2008, Iraq was a country where US troops operated primarily on flat ground. It was a place with well-developed roads where hulking Mine-Resistant Ambush Protected (MRAP) armored vehicles could drive just about anywhere with less worry than a Humvee and where IEDs were pretty much old artillery shells wired up with a timer or some kind of detonator to use as booby traps. The armored vehicles had been designed to stop exactly that.

Sure, there were occasionally explosively formed penetrators, slugs of copper on top of high explosives, that shot out as a liquid-hot piece of metal that could go right through armored vehicles, but those were not as routinely used as standard old IEDs.

And despite the relative calm in Iraq, a soldier could expect gunfights with insurgents, too. Some snipers taking potshots were de rigueur, but so, too, were the occasional shoot-outs with Al Qaeda dead-enders. A guy could expect to have mano a mano gun battles every so often.

* * *

That action was what Sergeant Alex "J" Jauregui had signed up for.

Jauregui, born in Guadalajara in 1985, first came across the US border when he was three. He came across illegally. He went back to Mexico for a while, then came back to the States with his mom when he was six, but this time they were caught at the border and detained.

Their punishment? They had to go through the immigration process the legal way, just like anyone else. No draconian deportations, just a stern talking-to and a reminder that everybody's got to do things the way they're supposed to be done. They had an interview with an immigration officer and got their visas just like that. America turned its benevolent countenance toward his family and deemed them good.

In a way, Jauregui's Army career started back then with the knowledge that the United States was, indeed, what it had claimed to be: a land of opportunity and welcoming arms.

Jauregui grew up in Williams, California, northwest of Sacramento, where his mom hoed in the fields and his dad drove a tractor. He played soccer and football and ran track in high school. He worked the fields with his parents in the summer. He worked the fields and worked the fields and worked the fields.

Sometimes J's old high school friends went off and joined the Army, then they came back home to Williams in their ACUs (Army Combat Uniforms) looking sharp as hell. If they were infantry and in their dress uniforms, they'd have that beautiful baby-blue fourragère around their right arm that showed everyone who knew anything that they were infantrymen. They got attention, sure, but it wasn't the hemming and hawing of everyone else that impressed J. No, what impressed him was the pride those soldiers showed in themselves. The uniform made them different. He decided the Army was the way to go.

J didn't come from a broken family or need to get away. He just wanted the best for himself, and that's what his folks wanted for him, too. He wanted to be a good American, to give back to the country that had given his family a new chance.

Alex Jauregui joined the Army in 2003 on a contract to be a mechanic. It seemed a smart, responsible way to guarantee his future. He'd learn a trade and be able to market it after the service.

He was stationed at Fort Bragg in North Carolina, home to the 82nd Airborne Division, and he was always among all those Airborne guys—all those paratroopers with their beautiful baby-blue fourragères around their right arms—but he didn't rate, because he was a mechanic. J deployed in 2004 to Iraq, doing route security for a bunch of KBR Inc. contractors who were doing God knows what. It wasn't glamorous for him—actually, it kinda sucked. It wasn't even worth talking about.

In 2006 he was back in Iraq for another deployment, this time as a wrecker operator, kind of like the AAA tow truck guy, but in a combat zone. On February 4, 2007—he will never forget the date—a truck in his convoy hit an IED and caught fire, and J scrambled back to pull his buddy from the flaming wreckage. The guy's name was Randy Matheny—how can he forget the guy's name when something like that happens?

Then the infantry, the "grunts," showed up as a quick reaction force, riding into battle like some kind of big-screen action heroes. They were ready to fight if they had to, to charge at the enemy and shoot 'em up. It was something mechanics like him weren't trained for. In fact, mechanics had been trained to run away if there was a fight.

It didn't take but a short conversation with one of those grunts for J to realize he was done being a POG, a Personnel Other than Grunt. There's no glory in being a butcher, baker, or candlestick maker in the Army. J decided to switch jobs and go infantry. He needed to get some.

Once he declared his intentions to change jobs in the Army, J, a guy with two combat tours—but not as an infantryman—had to go back through parts of boot camp. How about that, a guy choosing to go through boot camp again! He got reclassed to infantry, and in 2008 he was assigned to Bravo Company, so he had plenty of time to work up with them.

Bravo Company had just gotten back from the Afghanistan deployment that Lemon and other guys had dropped into the middle of, so he was surrounded by salty assholes.

J was already a sergeant, but since he didn't have any infantry experience he was in a weird spot that the machinery of Big Army couldn't really compute properly. Technically speaking, a sergeant is a sergeant is a sergeant as far as the Army's concerned. Technically speaking, you can't get to sergeant without doing all the things a soldier needs to do to be a sergeant and so you should be capable of doing any job that a sergeant's supposed to be able to do. It seems like it's not even worth saying, it's so obvious. Thus, a generic sergeant over here should have the same leadership qualifications as that sergeant over there.

But J had been a mechanic, dealing with wrenches and fucking oil changes, not infantry assaults. How could the Army expect a mechanic to find himself in an infantry unit and immediately be ready to lead salty grunts like Jared Lemon?

"Our job was to get out of an engagement, not to get into them," he said. "It's completely different, support versus infantry. They don't relate."

So Bravo Company started him out at as a basic rifleman, toting an M4. But he was a motivated guy, and strong—damn, those legs were like unstoppable pistons—and smart, and pretty soon he was a team leader waiting for the next deployment. He became a sergeant fully capable of doing any of the sergeant stuff the Army might throw at him.

* * *

Bravo Company was in the middle of their months-long preparation for deployment as headlines about Iraq heralded more and more the relative peace and calm. It left them with a feeling that their hunger for war wouldn't be sated. What good is it to be a paratrooper deployed to a combat zone where there's no combat?

The Army was doing its fair share to quell violence in the country. Thanks to the surge, or maybe the infinite wisdom of COIN—or both—levels of violence dropped across the country. In Baghdad and Mosul, under General Ray Odierno and General David Petraeus, using counterinsurgency doctrine and overwhelming numbers of troops solidified the gains in the waning days of the George W. Bush administration.

And in the 2008 presidential race Barack Obama had campaigned explicitly on the wrongness of the war in Iraq, on the need to end it and focus instead on the Afghanistan War. It looked like the new president would completely upend things, making Afghanistan the place where troops like Bravo Company wanted to go. Iraq was poised to become the relative backwater with little attention from the president or his closest advisors.

Bravo's slated deployment promised to be a huge bust for men longing to get that CIB. They figured they'd be going to a war that seemed to be all fought out. It might even be boring. They might get tasked to stand guard on bases or worse, help pack up shipping containers of surplus war matériel and supplies to be sent back to the United States because it wasn't needed in Iraq anymore. These possibilities were a far cry from what so many of the men in Bravo Company wanted, from what they'd been trained to do—from what they'd been *promised* ever since they shook hands with their recruiter and signed their contract with the United States Army.

In December 2008, the US had nearly 161,000 troops in Iraq. In the other undifferentiated blob of war, Afghanistan, the US had only about 38,000. A skeptic of the whole endeavor of the Global War on Terror might ask, "Why repeat it all in Afghanistan?" But a newly elected president looking to ensure he didn't look like a weak-willed stereotype of a liberal politician might ask, "Why not give Afghanistan a real go?"

Graeme Smith, an author and researcher with years of experience in Afghanistan, remembers that just before the American presidential election there was a flurry of engineering work at Kandahar Airfield, bulldozers and all that. He sidled up to an engineer and asked him what was with all the activity. The guy replied that if Obama won the election there'd be a surge and if the Republican candidate, John McCain, won the election there might be a push into Iran. Either way, the airfield needed to be bigger, the guy had said.

A few months later, President Obama was inaugurated, and he set about fulfilling his campaign promise of shifting focus from Iraq to Afghanistan. He was a novice when it came to foreign policy, particularly when it came to military matters. But he did know a few things immediately. He knew Defense Department officials had already requested nearly 20,000 troops to be added in Afghanistan, enough to just stabilize things and then they could make further decisions. Obama knew the prior administration and the Pentagon had set conditions so he could escalate the war in Afghanistan, had prepared the way for a surge in that country that could mirror, in many ways, the one that seemingly had been so successful in Iraq. He also knew that he didn't want to feel bullied into military decisions by top Pentagon officers, so he called for suggestions from top brass and from big brains at think tanks before he decided how many troops he wanted to send as a surge. He wanted studies that he could call his own, suggestions from his own administration rather than leftovers from the Bush era.

A few short weeks later, before the reviews were all finished, Obama announced in a speech on February 27, 2009, at Marine Corps Base Camp

Lejeune that he would wind down the war in Iraq. In late March he announced he'd be sending seventeen thousand troops to Afghanistan as part of the mission shift to that country. There'd also be four thousand troops sent specifically as trainers for Afghan forces. It was a number he felt confident in. He wanted no more and no less. But then, as he got ready to sign the order to send the troops into harm's way, the Pentagon said it had made a mistake in the calculations and they'd actually need a couple thousand more troops on top of those seventeen thousand. They'd forgotten to include the so-called enablers in the deployment numbers, the men and women who serve support roles in-country. It was as if Obama were getting ready to sign a contract for a new car and the salesman all of a sudden said, Hey, sorry, this doesn't include any tires.

Deputy National Security Advisor Doug Lute was the guy who had to go tell Obama that the numbers were all screwed up.

"Mr. President, this is awkward, but the Pentagon's request which you approved didn't include enablers," he remembered telling the new president.

Obama stared at him quizzically, Lute said, then he pushed his chair back from the *Resolute* desk in the Oval Office, a desk still relatively new to him. He was confused at the sloppy staff work at first. Then he was enraged. This president who always portrayed himself as stoic and steady was red-hot mad, but what could he do? He had committed in a public speech to sending those troops, and the Defense Department already had the machinery moving. Officials like Petraeus were already making public statements.

The president felt he had to add in the enablers, add more troops to the mix.

And the four thousand troops to be sent as trainers? Those four thousand were thrown in almost as an afterthought, a sap to the NATO folks and other allies who had been wringing their hands over the lack of troops in-country who could train up the Afghans and serve in support roles. It was a way for the US to show it would be a team player in the international community even as it started to take charge again of the shooting war in the south and east with more American troops in a surge.

Those four thousand troops were Colonel Brian Drinkwine's Fourth Brigade, which was in the middle of preparing for a deployment to Iraq.

Drinkwine was a US Military Academy graduate with a cleft in his chin and a round face whose thick body served him well when he played goalie for West Point's ice hockey team. As a brigade commander, Drinkwine had risen to a position crucial to testing a colonel's command mettle and whether he deserved to keep rising in the ranks and pin on a general's star. A brigade commander gets one chance at success and does his best to prepare carefully for combat to come.

Drinkwine's brigade was the next available for deployment, so they were called to do the job. It's as simple as that to shift the fate of four thousand soldiers and to derail even the best preparations and plans. Drinkwine had to get his brigade ready for Afghanistan.

CHAPTER 7

ADVISE AND ASSIST

An Army company is sort of like an immediate family, always in close contact and together. It's designed to be the largest unit that can operate in battle such that the top officer and the lowliest enlisted soldier might directly interact. It numbers a few hundred. The next step up, the battalion, around one thousand strong, is like an extended family where people know each other but aren't always around each other. The four or more companies in a battalion come together for major training operations, and the battalion commander can shape the companies under his command. The brigade, made up of a few battalions, so roughly four thousand soldiers, is a conglomeration where the parts don't routinely see each other but can come together for large operations.

A brigade is pretty large, but at the same time a brigade was essentially the smallest piece on the strategic chessboard that top generals at the Pentagon and planners at the White House could move around. They couldn't shuffle battalions or companies, because they're too small. President Obama, plotting his first move and needing four thousand troops, had simply reached for the next brigade about to deploy. That was the Army's Fourth Brigade. And nested in that brigade was the Second Battalion of the 503rd Parachute Infantry Regiment.

And in that battalion was Bravo Company.

They'd be heading to Afghanistan instead of Iraq because they were the next unit up and because President Obama wanted to signal that he was serious about Afghanistan, but he wasn't ready to make any big commitments until he'd undertaken his reviews. But he sent a brigade, those four thousand troops, to be trainers. And to this day nobody's really sure why, not even the guy who was in charge of the brigade.

Colonel Brian Drinkwine found out about his unit's change in deployment from Iraq to Afghanistan about four months before they were set to deploy. But he wasn't told what exactly his brigade would be doing, other than that they also had to shift the fundamental nature of their mission to focus on advise-and-assist rather than combat operations.

Down in Bravo Company soldiers like Jared Lemon didn't know about any of this. All Lemon knew was that he'd been around for the previous deployment and gotten his bona fides and now he was ready for another deployment somewhere. The reality of war hadn't affected him on that last deployment. There was only one guy from his unit who died, as far as Lemon remembered. But that soldier was a mechanic who didn't set a jack stand properly under a Humvee and it fell on him. That type of thing could happen down at the local quick-change oil place in town—or at least that's what a fellow has to tell himself. However, rationalizing a death of a guy getting squashed by bad jack-stand placement may indicate a rather casual approach to the whole thing, and if he had been looking more closely he would have noticed that rollover crashes, Humvees falling on guys, and stupid shit that actually would never, ever happen to your average American male in an average American city seemed to happen a little too often in a combat zone.

Ah, well, but who can care to think about that? A Humvee falling on a guy—that sure doesn't seem like war.

Since he didn't really experience the horrors of war on that deployment, Lemon wasn't able to observe, to scientifically document, how guys change when they get back home. One sergeant got all kinds of messed up on alcohol. Lemon knew him as a fantastic sergeant, but a few months after they got back, the Army threw him out because he became a drunk. As a low-ranking soldier, Lemon didn't see the maneuvering behind the scenes, didn't see whether that guy got counseling or a second chance, or whether his actions had been so irredeemable and unconscionable as to prohibit one. All he saw was a drunkard who was told his services were no longer needed.

Lemon got himself a smart mouth a few months after getting back from that deployment, said something stupid to some NCOs and got in trouble, busted down in rank and everything. Meanwhile, it looked like he was going to end up spending his deployment packing huge CONEX boxes full of surplus gear in Iraq as part of the drawdown. He'd miss combat and be turning out the lights in-country on the way out.

Then their orders changed. Afghanistan, he heard. A guy like Lemon doesn't know about strategic considerations, presidential aspirations, or generals' plans. All he knew was it looked like he was going to get a deployment with some action.

How could President Obama have such a seemingly well-planned, publicly announced decision on how to approach the war, yet, at the brigade level, troops could be scrambling to figure out what the hell was happening? It's downright implausible—or impossible, even—for that to be true, right? But for a man or woman who has served in the military, who has been to war, the fact that there was so much confusion and craziness from top to bottom makes perfect sense, indeed.

While Colonel Drinkwine was scrambling to figure out what his troops were supposed to do in-country, Jared Lemon let the speeding tickets pile up from reckless driving in town. Who cared about paying them? he thought.

He was going to a no-shit war.

* * *

So was Lyle Pressley.

Lyle, a gentle giant of a man from North Carolina, always wanted to join the Army, but it was hard to enlist when there was a family business that depended on him.

His dad and his granddad had served, so he wanted to do the same. He had been looking at the Army and the Marines, but the family excavating business was strapped for employees around the time he finished high school, so he joined his dad at work. Since Lyle was enduring, quiet, and dedicated—not to mention built like Paul Bunyan—he stayed to help the excavating business get along. He had a quiet drawl and a slight stoop to his shoulders that lent him the air of someone who could easily bear any yoke with neither complaint nor difficulty.

September 11, 2001, happened and made him want to join even more, but you know how it is: Once a guy starts working instead of doing the other things he's always wanted to do, months turn into years. And years turn into life.

Excavating, excavating, excavating. A marriage. Life. A divorce.

Then the business finally stabilized, and Dad didn't desperately need him. Lyle's personal life was unencumbered, and he could think about the Army again. At the ripe old age of twenty-six he enlisted. He went to boot camp, jump school, all the usual stuff that a soldier goes through at the beginning, then he was off to the Army proper—he was off to Bravo Company.

Lyle broke his ankle during one of his jumps, but by the time he got to Bravo Company for his first deployment he was ready. He was one of those paratroopers who went to the Cadillac Ranch. He wasn't a cowboy-hat-and-boots type; he was more of a greasy-ball-cap-and-work-boots type and he knew deep down that he'd be good at soldiering. Though his body was already hurting from the ankle on up through his back, it wasn't anything he couldn't handle.

Every military unit's time and effort is spent on a mission, on fulfilling a task and purpose. The biggest units have a mission that gets subdivided and divvied up among the members of a subordinate unit. That subordinate unit's mission gets subdivided and divvied up further on down to the lowest level. Thus, while the Department of Defense's mission might be, for example, to eliminate the Taliban's control of Afghanistan, by the time it gets subdivided and divvied up through brigades and battalions and companies, the task of some lowly soldier at the end of the food chain is simply to shoot his rifle at someone.

It is military dogma that the unit above gives tasks and missions to units below, cascading in a marvelous flume of seeming efficiency. It is sacrosanct. It's how goals are supposed to get accomplished, how large missions are supposed to get accomplished. A company, for instance, on a deployment will get four square miles of land—maybe even less—that they're required to patrol and subdue. All those companies fall under a brigade that might be ultimately responsible for controlling a city or, if in a rural area, a parcel the size of an American county.

But Colonel Brian Drinkwine had no idea what his brigade's new mission was to be, only that he was being sent to Afghanistan instead of Iraq. To this day he professes not to know what his ultimate task and purpose was. He doesn't know what the brigade was *really* supposed to accomplish.

True, he knew his soldiers were supposed to be advising and assisting the Afghans, but to what end? And why? He didn't know. And even after undertaking his mission for a year, he never knew. All he knew was in the spring of 2009 the brigade would head over to Afghanistan and aid NATO forces across the country in the effort to train and advise Afghan military and police forces.

Colonel Drinkwine would let the message of the change in deployment trickle down through his subordinates and down to Bravo Company, but he didn't have time to make the rounds among his men right then. He had to try and figure out what exactly his brigade was going to do and where it was going to do it.

First things first: He had to reckon with the fundamental nature of what he was being asked to do, as best as he could understand it. Fourth Brigade was to be the first "security assistance brigade" the Army had ever sent on deployment, according to recollections of multiple people in the brigade and close to it, and Colonel Drinkwine had to figure out what that meant.

The security assistance brigade concept was born of the idea that troops need to be able to advise and work with foreign forces, not just fight in combat themselves. The theory behind it was that American forces would eventually have to leave a country, and the United States had to make sure the local forces would be prepared to take over and do everything on their own. This was the role the Green Berets were originally designed for, but once the United States waded into a massive war effort in both Iraq and Afghanistan, there was no way to provide enough of those highly skilled trainers to work with indigenous forces. Instead, the Army reasoned, they could take just about any old unit and tell them they'd be advising and assisting. After all, the Global War on Terror was premised in large part on helping local forces learn how to do things themselves. The GWoT wasn't supposed to be just US troops blowing things up.

The Army, in its infinite self-esteem, figured an entire brigade of soldiers could be made to advise foreign forces. From well-educated and experienced officers and senior enlisted to guys who couldn't pick Afghanistan out on a map, the Department of Defense figured they could all be advisors to foreign troops. It seemed this was as good a time as any to see if you could make a security assistance brigade work in practice as well as it did on paper.

According to the security assistance doctrine, soldiers best worked in small teams of a dozen or slightly more, and Drinkwine realized that if he followed best practices and doctrine, he'd have to decide to break up his brigade into 350 or more teams under his command. But there was no way that was going to work: He couldn't imagine having 350 disparate groups acting independently. And it wasn't like there was any other colonel in the Army whom he could ask about this because he thought his brigade was going to be the very first one to do things this way. With just four months to figure something out before deploying to Afghanistan, Drinkwine flew over with some of his top officers and senior enlisted personnel from the brigade. They traveled across the vast country trying to figure out exactly where he'd have his troops spread and what they might do once they were there.

While many of those involved with Fourth Brigade remember they were the first security assistance brigade, it turns out that they weren't. That very confusion and institutional amnesia says a lot about US strategy writ large, says retired Army Lieutenant General Dan Bolger, who was in command of a division of his own in Iraq around the time Fourth Brigade was leaving for Afghanistan.

It turns out that some other units had given the security assistance brigade concept a go already, but because the Army didn't do a great job at passing on lessons learned from unit to unit, few people if any from Fourth Brigade knew about it. As far as they were concerned, they were the first.

On his research trip, Drinkwine went out to western Afghanistan, including Herat, where Italian and Spanish troops were training Afghan police and military. Or maybe it was more accurate to say they were stationed out there not really doing anything at all. Herat was one of the more peaceful areas of the country, and there were few active threats. Drinkwine recognized that if he put his soldiers out there, they'd be like beat cops in a sleepy suburb.

Then he headed to southern Afghanistan, the heartland of the Afghan Taliban, where violence and extremism persisted, a place that had been severely neglected by the United States for years. Because of a lack of American troops and funding, it mostly had been left up to coalition troops from places like Canada and Great Britain to duke it out with the Taliban. In the south, Drinkwine's soldiers might get more action.

The Canadians were already preparing to be eclipsed by the American juggernaut, Graeme Smith the author and researcher remembers. Inside one of the plywood-walled buildings at Kandahar Airfield where the Canadians had their headquarters someone had tacked up a cartoon of a sandcastle about to be inundated by a massive wave adorned by an American flag. Atop the sandcastle was a little Canadian flag.

Drinkwine was scrambling, he had no idea what had happened way up the food chain to cause this mission shift. He didn't know at the time that his brigade's mission seemed so undefined and slapdash because it *was* undefined and slapdash. Sending a bunch of paratroopers into a combat zone to advise foreign military forces isn't using them for what they're designed to do. It's like using a sledgehammer as a tack hammer, or trying to change an axe into a scalpel.

US Army paratroopers are a world-class organization, yes, if they're used for the purpose they were intended: combat with the enemy, thought Doug Lute, the deputy national security advisor. But if that world-class organization wasn't being used for its intended purpose, then is it still a world-class organization? The best axe in the world is going to make a horrible scalpel.

Bravo Company and all the rest of the companies in the brigade were told they'd help advise Afghan military and police forces after getting minimal training to do that. In some cases troops were told to advise Afghans to do things the US soldiers hadn't ever done themselves. Infantry soldiers would be advising Afghan supply officers, for instance.

At best this was hubristic, to think the US military is so good that it can do anything some general or president asks of it. At worst it was paternalistic, condescending, and racist to assume red-blooded American soldiers knew better and could teach Afghans to do anything!

When they became advisors, the whole paratroop organizational structure was smashed apart and upended. The mission didn't just cut against the grain of paratrooper culture, it conflicted with the entire training objective of paratroopers, Lute said.

To illustrate his point, Lute recalled a trip he made to Afghanistan during which he met a group of soldiers advising and assisting Afghan forces. He asked to speak with the intelligence-analyst advisor. Some junior supply clerk from the National Guard stepped up and introduced himself.

"No, no, I didn't say I wanted to know who the supply clerk is," he said, chastising the kid.

But the junior soldier replied sheepishly that he was, indeed, the intelligence-analyst advisor, because there wasn't anybody else to do it. It boggled Lute's mind.

* * *

By 2009, Americans, including the Pentagon itself, had all but forgotten who's really supposed to be doing the bulk of this training: the Army's Special Forces.

Over the course of the Global War on Terror, the Green Berets became better known for firefights than for training foreign forces. But the Green Berets were originally designed to be tactical and cultural experts. They were specially screened soldiers who'd been given extensive training so they could help indigenous fighting forces. The whole concept had been born in the mid-twentieth century, and the organizational setup drew on experienced troops from recent worldwide conflicts.

In other words, Green Berets were designed to do what resembled COIN stuff before COIN became all the rage. The idea was highly skilled, well-trained, specialized troops with experience and wisdom were what was needed to effectively train and mentor foreign militaries. Special Forces teams then and now are relatively small, highly trained, and experienced in dealing with foreign militaries and operating outside of the normal parameters of the Army structure.

By the time Iraq and Afghanistan kicked off, some special operations forces across the board were migrating away from missions helping local forces get ready to fight into just doing the jobs themselves or fighting alongside local forces. There weren't enough Special Forces to go around, there never will be, nor can there be, because they're so well trained and well screened and take years to hone.

If the Army needs to train up an entire country's military and police—or two countries' militaries and police—and if the Army's all out of Green Berets, what's the answer? The answer is to give perfunctory training to regular troops and drill into their senior leaders' minds that their mission is to train foreign militaries.

* * *

As the White House and Department of Defense prepared for a ramp up in Afghanistan, career diplomats at the State Department warned about a rush into an Afghanistan surge, cautioning there weren't enough civilian resources available for the effort, that Afghanistan and its people were fundamentally different from Iraq and its people, and shoveling more troops into the conflict could backfire.

They knew full well what General George Casey knew: that it was way too easy for people to transpose Iraq onto Afghanistan and think they had a universal solution. And they didn't want it to happen.

"Flooding the area with well-intentioned soldiers was not a good idea," said Elisabeth Kvitashvili, the former USAID official. "We argued we needed a small presence to have maximum impact with Afghan interlocutors."

Sending in thousands of American troops, the State Department argued, might look to Afghans a lot like the 1980s when the Russians had, at times, more than one hundred thousand troops in the country.

In Iraq, the local populace was used to a powerful central government and knew the difference between civil and military authorities. Rural Afghans had long chafed under any central government control and were skeptical of anything that looked like agents of a faraway capital, whether they were civilians or military. In United States military doctrine, especially the COIN doctrine ascendant at the beginning of the Obama administration, civilian workers and military troops could forge a synergistic partnership in-country and work together to gain the respect of locals. That's what the handbook said, by God. At the State Department and USAID, though, officials worried that Afghans might not have read *FM 3-24* and they might just see everyone as part of an occupying force.

"Afghans were confused about the difference," Kvitashvili said. "If we were truly civilians we would be part of a neutral party. But now we were seen the same as the soldiers."

And flooding the area with military, even if they were there to train or advise and assist, ran the risk that US troops would simply take on more of the combat mission itself. Likewise, if they flooded the area with civilian resources and funding, the US government was going to end up doing more itself rather than relying on the Afghans.

More troops were a potential problem. More civilians were a potential problem. But orders had already been signed by the president. If troops were to be pumped into Afghanistan, there needed to be a discussion of where they were supposed to be going, right?

* * *

Around the time Bravo found out it was being sent to Afghanistan, the Marines were sending a brigade into Helmand province.

As the Marines geared up for their push into Helmand it didn't matter that people wondered why some of the best conventional troops available, US Marines, were going into a mostly desert province where only a small fraction of Afghans lived. It didn't matter that people from State and NGOs who had been working in the country for years said Helmand wasn't a priority.

Many of those wise hands argued that the military should have instead been focusing on Kandahar, the province where the Afghan Taliban had their capital. It also was a border province, abutting a notoriously insecure region of Pakistan through which militants traveled to and from hideaways over the international border and into Afghanistan. There were places like the Arghandab Valley in Kandahar that were nasty redoubts that perhaps should have been the focus of attention.

* * *

Colonel Drinkwine's troops, including Bravo Company, would be advising and assisting, helping Afghan soldiers and police learn how to do their jobs in the midst of a war. And the brigade had about four months to complete all their standard paratrooper training and then tack on an abbreviated version of what Special Forces troops spend years learning.

"All the security force assistance stuff in Iraq and Afghanistan was terrible. Start from that fundamental premise," said Nora Bensahel, an analyst at RAND Corporation, before adding about the United States military, "We have no idea how to do security force assistance at scale."

And in this case the United States wasn't just assisting, it was trying to rebuild an entire country's military and then keep it together. Amid the Russian nesting dolls that make up the Army's structure, the brigade, also known as a brigade combat team, or BCT, had become the most useful.

"My joke at the time was that the Army's answer was a BCT. What's the question?" said Bensahel.

Instead of sending a few hundred highly skilled Special Forces soldiers for a tailored training mission, the Army sent thousands of guys they had available, a conventional unit filled with young men, some of whom were on their first deployments. That group included Bravo Company.

In May 2009, the Army released a new manual that didn't get the same attention as *FM 3-24* but in some ways encapsulated the Army's thinking about advising missions even better than the COIN manual. The COIN manual was more of a Defense Department philosophical treatise laying out a grand mindset, while the handbook *Field Manual 3-07.1: Security Force Assistance* defined the immediate task at hand.

"The two pillars of security force assistance are the modular brigade and Soldiers acting as advisors," said the foreword, written by General Martin Dempsey, who would later become the Army's chief of staff.

In other words, the manual served as a direct rebuttal to the Nora Bensahels and various diplomats of the world, who thought it was crazy to put a brand-new PFC or a lieutenant with no real-world experience in the role of trainer, advisor, and mentor. "Security force assistance is no longer an 'additional duty.' It is now a core competency of our Army," the foreword read.

This was news to Bravo Company, who now had to start preparing for that job. But the machinery, traditions, and mindset of the Army can't just change overnight. The biggest, most difficult thing to do wasn't getting a president to sign a new deployment order—that was easy compared with actually getting the guys ready and qualified for a training mission. The most difficult thing was getting the Army to do something the top brass seemed to think could be done just by laying it out in a manual.

"Five months is a long time to prepare for anything," said General George Casey of Drinkwine's brigade. "They certainly had sufficient time to make that shift."

So thought the Army. But just because the commander in chief gave them an order that they were going to be advising foreign troops, that didn't mean the Army knew how best to prepare them for it—or that the men even gave a shit about being trainers in the first place. A paratrooper knows how to paratroop and typically doesn't give a rat's ass about advising and assisting.

* * *

Lieutenant Colonel Frank Jenio, one of Drinkwine's battalion commanders, didn't think the brigade's mission seemed confused or slapdash. It made sense to him. It made sense because he thought the orders were a bait and switch of sorts, and he figured he was in on it.

Frank Jenio is a man who multiple Bravo Company veterans said they'd follow into hell itself if he ordered a charge to be made. Jenio looked the very part of an infantry officer in charge of a battalion. He wasn't tall, but his squared shoulders—thrown back when he walked—made him seem taller. So did his haircut, about as close as a soldier can get to what's known in the Marines as a "high-and-tight": a short patch of hair atop a head whose scalp has been clipped as close as possible on the sides. He was a Ranger Regiment veteran who saw soldiers as a force for projecting American power abroad, and with an unstoppable pressure he had worked to make sure his battalion was ready to project that power.

Jenio's battalion, the 2-508, was just one of the battalions that made up the Fourth Brigade, and thus he was just one of the lieutenant colonels under Drinkwine's command. But he had arguably the best lineage for the job because he'd worked on General Stanley McChrystal's staff in the past, and everyone around considered the two men to be friends on some level. And since McChrystal had become the top American commander in Afghanistan, there was no reason to think Jenio wouldn't have a fast track to getting the general's attention and maybe call in a favor to get a choice upgrade in mission.

Jenio figured the mission was just a way to get US paratroopers into the fight in Afghanistan and that all talk of advise-and-assist was just diplomatic doublespeak and subterfuge. He kept preparing his men to go to combat, thinking all along that advise-and-assist was never the intent for them. Bravo Company fell under Jenio's battalion. In the world of nesting dolls, the battalion is where soldiers really find their identity. A battalion commander imbues his vision and spirit on the approximately one thousand men under his command. It's as a battalion that major training events get planned, with each of the companies under that battalion working toward a similar training goal.

Jenio had spent a chunk of his career in the Ranger Regiment, a group even more elite than a paratrooper unit. Ranger Regiment soldiers are special operators—they get to wear their own tan berets and everything. He was a man accustomed to combat, accustomed to fighting.

Rangers, unlike Green Berets, aren't bred and trained to help mold indigenous forces. Rangers are bred and trained to fight. In the special operations world, Green Berets can be like stealthy stilettos, whereas Rangers are like cleavers.

While an officer is in charge of a unit, there's also a senior enlisted man right there next to him who's supposed to give him wise and sage advice, to make sure the officer is doing everything by the books and to keep him grounded. These senior enlisted—at the battalion level and above they have the rank of sergeant major—may not get saluted, but they're arguably the very lifeblood of a unit.

Sergeant Major Bert Puckett was Jenio's top enlisted advisor, an experienced paratrooper with tactical and operational bona fides. He'd also been in Ranger Regiment. Hell, Puckett actually jumped into combat in Grenada back in 1983 when he was a young soldier, a rarity these days, as most paratroopers don't ever actually get to jump in war. But Puckett also spent a good part of his time in Ranger Regiment and that colored the fiber of his soldierly being. It gave him much the same mindset as Jenio.

This lucky battalion, 2-508, had a Ranger Regiment commanding officer and a Ranger Regiment command sergeant major. Thus, the senior officer in the battalion as well as the top enlisted man didn't want some namby-pamby training mission. From the beginning they wanted to train their guys to kick in doors and kill bad guys. They saw their role as preparing paratroopers to fight wherever they might go.

"Our focus was theater agnostic," Jenio said, in Army officer-speak. So whether it be Iraq, Afghanistan, or the dark side of the moon, Jenio and Puckett were preparing for conventional, bare-knuckled combat with the enemy.

"If you have disciplined leaders, you can always turn it down," he said, like a man or an entire unit's fighting spirit had a stereo's volume knob. "But you can't suddenly turn it on if you're not trained."

They'd been training to turn it up all the way. It was the old-school hard-core paratrooper mentality. And during the workup to the deployment they'd fought to get their battalion extra time on the range and extra ammo and extra training, all to be as lethal as possible. When they found out they'd be headed to Afghanistan, they doubled down on their efforts. It was in their very DNA as Rangers, and they thought Afghanistan would call for full volume. Did the battalion just go through extensive rifle range training in the daytime? Well, get them more ammo and have them run it in the dark. In the rain. Once more! Run it again!

Jenio thought the whole advise-and-assist mission was likely just smoke and mirrors to cover up the fact that the United States was sending in four thousand men from the 82nd Airborne. "Marines are going in to kick ass and the other ones are just trainers?" he said. "At the political level it briefs very well: They're trainers."

Puckett said the battalion did some perfunctory lessons on advise-and-assist, but it was mostly what he called "check-the-block bullshit," something to tick off a checklist quickly so they could get back to training to fight.

But when the brigade finally deployed to Afghanistan in the spring of 2009, Jenio suddenly found out there was no clever ruse devised to sneak the brigade into combat. There was no tricky doublespeak to get Frank Jenio's paratroopers face-to-face with America's enemy. No, the brigade—his battalion included—had actually, truthfully, honest-to-God been sent to Afghanistan to advise and assist. No shit. Just as Drinkwine had learned the truth of things four months before deployment and then gone to Afghanistan to try and figure out what the deployment would actually mean, Jenio, too, realized that his battalion was going to be advising and assisting, split up into small teams and spread across hundreds of miles of Afghanistan.

Good God, they really had been sent to be trainers? *Trainers*? God did not create paratroopers to be namby-pamby, and yet somehow the divine—or more importantly President Obama—had forced Jenio's troopers into this deployment.

But Jenio was a Ranger, dammit. He was not one to give up. So Lieutenant Colonel Frank Jenio started scheming about how to get his men into a real fight.

PART II

DEPLOYMENT

CHAPTER 8

THE HALLOWEEN

ZOMBIE MASSACRE

In late August 2009, Colonel Brian Drinkwine's Fourth Brigade was sent to Afghanistan and spread across hundreds of miles of territory to support NATO forces who were, in turn, advising Afghan military and police units. At the brigade level, the mission always seemed to change for his troops. From the beginning of the deployment, in midsummer 2009, the unit had already been parted out like an old Chevrolet, with battalions and companies tasked from Herat to Helmand.

By the end of the deployment in 2010, Drinkwine said he had thirty to thirty-six different commands under his purview, he never really knew for sure. How could he even tally them all? Good luck deciphering who he reported to on the American and NATO side of things. Likewise, it was near impossible to determine exactly which American and NATO units reported to him. It wasn't a typical setup in any way. The lines of command were tangled together. On a chart it would have looked like a diagram of a plate of spaghetti.

The war had begun so auspiciously back in 2001. Osama bin Laden had holed up in Afghanistan under the benevolent disregard of the Taliban, which had run the country for years in the 1990s. From his hideaway, Bin Laden orchestrated the September 11 attacks on the United States, which caused then President George W. Bush to move swiftly to invade Afghanistan, topple the Taliban, and begin a hunt for Bin Laden.

Just a couple years into the war in Afghanistan, as the American forces and coalition partners shifted the mission into a nation-building effort that required more money, troops, diplomats, and attention, the Bush administration shifted resources to Iraq, invading in 2003 to topple Saddam Hussein. Much of the American military machine focused on Iraq while Afghanistan smoldered. By the time Drinkwine and his troops deployed in 2009 the goals of the war were as tangled up as Drinkwine's lines of command.

Colonel Drinkwine and his troops' fortunes were tied up with the priorities of various coalition commanders. Meanwhile, southern Afghanistan was in turmoil, remembers Ben Hodges, who was a lieutenant general at the time and one of the top-ranking Americans in-country.

Hodges became the director of operations for Regional Command–South in August 2009, around the same time as the men from Bravo settled into their deployment, and he was echelons above them, watching the movement of entire divisions. He was able to see the context of the whole southern Afghanistan operation. When Hodges first arrived, Dutch General Mart de Kruif was the International Security Assistance Force (ISAF) commander in southern Afghanistan. De Kruif commanded in Afghanistan before any big talk of a surge of American troops. He seemed to know the Europeans had signed up for a training mission and that the Afghans needed to lead the way in their own country. De Kruif seemed to have the long game in mind.

De Kruif led when a coalition of allies seemed still in charge of this plodding war, before Obama decided to make Afghanistan an American focus again. He seemed of the mindset that since each Afghan province had separate Afghan military corps, and those commands were typically paired up with one or another allied country, and since regional commands had their own way of doing things, he let each of those commands do their thing. It was a federal system, with control devolved—which, come to think of it, sounds a lot like the system of governance set up in Afghanistan where the central government doesn't have as much sway in the daily lives of its citizens as in a place like Iraq. The Afghans were doing their own thing in conjunction with, but not wholly dependent on, ISAF's decisions.

Americans operated as they wanted in the east. Down south the Brits did their thing in Helmand—the joke was it was known as "Helmandshire." Up in the north there were places where Swedes and Hungarians were in charge of things, for the love of God. Imagine that, a cocky American would think, some *Swedes* were in charge of the *Afghan* war? And yet nobody from the allies' hierarchy seemed to want a whole-sale change in strategy.

Then came British General Nick Carter, who replaced de Kruif in November of 2009. By that time, General Stanley McChrystal was fully in charge of American troops and seemed to be getting his confidence up. The stars were aligning for a major change in the conduct of the war, and it wouldn't hurt anyone to get those résumés fit as a fiddle for future promotions.

Bravo Company began its deployment by getting scattered out from Fourth Brigade and pushed under an ISAF command. It and a handful of other companies from the brigade were sent south to train Afghans in Regional Command–South, with a focus on Helmand province.

After all, that's how so many of the NATO and allied countries had sold this war to their constituents, as a peacekeeping endeavor. For many allies, the Afghanistan conflict wasn't supposed to be combat. But even so-called training missions meant close proximity to fighting in ways that Italians, Germans, and other Europeans didn't anticipate.

Most of the time the troops in a battalion can expect to be, at most, a few miles away from headquarters and each other. Jenio's battalion was spread out with units nearly two hundred miles from each other. They even had a scout and a mortar platoon attached to a Marine Corps unit.

Jenio was going to follow orders, but he wasn't going to let some allies run roughshod over his battalion. So while ISAF called on 2-508 to provide a training squad here and a training squad there—like they were ordering up an à la carte breakfast at a diner—Jenio and his top officers would have none of it. They wouldn't send anything smaller than a pla-toon out on training missions because they wanted to make sure their paratroopers could hold their own if they got into a firefight, remembered Scott Brannon, who was Jenio's operations officer and a decade later had risen to the rank of colonel himself.

Bravo Company originally was detailed out to a British commander in the field, Colonel Jasper de Quincey Adams, a wavy-haired dragoon commander with a posh accent who owned a horse farm back in Britain. Under Colonel de Quincey Adams, Bravo Company was given the task of helping to train and mentor two groups of Afghan troops: the Afghan National Civil Order Police (ANCOP) and the Provincial Reserves.

The ANCOP was first developed in 2006 as a gendarmerie, a premier police force in Afghanistan, typically patrolling borderlands and places outside population centers where the regular police can't easily operate. The ANCOP was known for less corruption and more professionalism than the Afghanistan National Police. The national police, in contrast, were best known for corruption and for practices like *bacha bazi* (using young boys as sex slaves). Provincial Reserves, on the other hand, were old pensioners who might still be able to fit into uniforms issued decades ago and, though they might be unfamiliar with newfangled weapons, were still able to shoot antique Lee-Enfield rifles and man checkpoints if they had to.

The British troops, under Colonel de Quincey Adams, fought regularly in Helmand province against the Taliban in places like Sangin and Marjah years before Americans learned those names. But the British troops had been sent to Helmand province to fight the Taliban, while Bravo Company and the rest of the brigade had been sent to Helmand province as trainers and *not* to fight the Taliban. The American paratroopers found themselves stationed on a base alongside the British troops who often went out on the kind of combat missions the Americans had trained for, the kind of missions they longed to do.

It wasn't uncommon for the gritty Brits to come swaggering back into camp, along with a few companies of stoic Gurkha fighters, and nonchalantly boast about some of the scraps they'd been in with the Taliban. That was almost painful for the Americans to experience.

Take then Sergeant Rob Musil, the frenetic war philosopher. Musil wanted a fight because he knew it was something he was plain good at. When he arrived in-country with a squad's worth of men under his charge and got ready to move to a smaller base, Musil was told by a supply sergeant that his squad would be issued ammo at that next base, just a short convoy ride down the road.

But his men still remember Musil upbraiding the sergeant in his wild and loud and unforgiving way, yelling "Fuck no!" right to the guy. He said they wouldn't go anywhere without a full load of ammo for their rifles right there, right now, because they were in Afghanistan and they had to be ready to fight no matter what. Ammo down the road? Fuck that. He and his men were issued their ammo, fully expecting to use it. But they didn't use it. Musil and the rest of the company were introduced to the reality of those incomprehensibly safe roads where they really didn't seem to need ammo.

The Brits went out and fought with the Taliban, and the men of Bravo Company, meanwhile, busied themselves traveling Afghanistan's Route 601 to inspect checkpoints and have brief sit-downs with the ANCOP or Provincial Reserves. Nothing ever seemed to happen. They weren't even able to do much advising or training of the Afghan forces because of the distances involved in getting to the units they were supposed to advise. They'd load up in armored Humvees and head out a few hours to a checkpoint, drink some tea and talk with the Afghan commanders there, then come back to the base. They'd maybe take some potshots here and there, return fire on occasion, but nobody was ever hurt, and they didn't kill anybody as far as they could tell. There were no real firefights. Those first months in Helmand province in the fall of 2009 were downright boring for Bravo Company.

It was a real drag for the guys who had never deployed before, stuck doing this advise-and-assist nonsense rather than getting out there and fighting. Sitting around and training some Afghan forces doesn't motivate the typical soldier. Many of the younger men in Bravo Company couldn't see the wisdom in training Afghan forces to do the real work of war. A paratrooper drinking tea? This is not what their training, their pre-deployment workups, had promised. They had been taught that American soldiers were just about the only soldiers who knew how to fight properly and that everyone else did things incorrectly in some way or another. An army maintains its esprit de corps in large part through chauvinism and bluster and thinking they are the best of the best.

It was an animal desire by this point to get into combat, a yearning of an almost sexual nature, to finish the promise of the months of training and indoctrination with an explosion of action. It's a simple truth that men who go to war want an orgasm of violence for the sake of violence itself. Don't let them tell you any different. Most don't really think the endeavor might kill them. They don't think about living with the fallout of killing other humans, something that will remain with them for years and years and years. They just want to be to be a part of that club who has been to war.

By contrast, some of the older guys, those who had been on prior deployments, weren't itching to see more action. They knew what was out there, what could happen in a firefight. They knew what the truth of the matter was, and they knew that firefights weren't the be-all and end-all. They knew the death and destruction and injuries and losses of friends that could come as a result of firefights.

But they were able to feel that way, to feel sated, because they already had their bona fides. They had their CIBs to pin to their ACUs. Sure, some of the older guys said they didn't want any more war stuff, but they could only say that because they'd already had it. They were members of the club. It's not every soldier who is wary of war, it's the *experienced* soldier who is wary of war. And the only way to get that experience is to go through war.

But then Bravo Company found themselves down in Helmand on this training mission thing. It was boring. They didn't really get shot at once. Not once!

Jared Lemon remembers that it wasn't like he really hoped for combat or to get wounded. But at the same time, you know, if it happened, he was ready for it.

Lemon was no warmonger or anything, but he had trained for it, and the last deployment was a bust, so he hoped this one might live up to the billing. Lemon had some decent bona fides because he'd deployed before, but he wanted the no-shit bona fides of real combat.

His platoon was initially assigned to mentor the ANCOP out near where the Marines were operating in Marjah in Helmand province and, according to all their intel reports, where all the bad guys went to give the Marines a run for their money. That first half of the deployment was so slow for Lemon that he decided to use his time studying for the NCO tests and get ready to try for promotion to sergeant, to finally put an end to his old life where he'd been busted down for being disrespectful.

William Yeske also longed for his own bona fides. He'd decided to join the Marines right out of high school in Connecticut, but his parents talked him out of it by promising to pay for him to go to the University of Connecticut to get a degree. He was a sophomore sitting in the dining hall at college when the planes hit the towers on 9/11, and though it resonated with him, it didn't prompt him to immediate action. He'd gone the college route and sealed his fate.

Tall, lean, handsome, and smooth-talking, Yeske seems like he was born to give an elevator pitch for a venture capital firm. While at college he met a girl, started getting involved in a motorsport racing team, and designed a digital storage platform back when most people were just getting familiarized with Google searches. The girl left, he sold the patent on his system for what seemed like buckets of cash, and then he started heading down the wrong path.

He'd often go down to the casino for a laugh and sometimes would turn fifty bucks into a few thousand. One weekend he woke up and realized he'd spent a few thousand dollars partying—nothing illicit, mind you, which makes it even more remarkable he could spend so much—and realized he needed a change, so he signed up for the Army on a Special Forces contract at the age of twenty-six. Another 18X sucker to help a recruiter make quota! In boot camp he has a distinct memory of their drill instructor, a Ranger who seemed a bit screwy from his time in combat, making the platoon do naked jumping jacks in the shower. The drill instructor justified the exercise by saying that in combat, when a guy steps on a booby trap and gets blown up, he might ask you to check to make sure his dick is still there. *Hmm, kinda weird. Don't think I really need this lesson,* Yeske thought to himself as he hopped up and down in the buff along with the rest of the platoon.

In the Special Forces training pipeline Yeske pulled the tendon in his left calf so bad he couldn't complete the training, and he was sent to the 82nd. He showed up to Bravo Company in December 2008, the night of the company Christmas party, and was assigned Allen Thomas as a squad leader.

As he checked into his barracks, Yeske saw a soldier swerving toward him, clearly tipsy, and Yeske—twenty-seven years old and gregarious but just a newbie soldier—greeted the drunken soldier: Rob Musil.

"Hello," said Yeske, the smiling new guy.

"What the fuck did you say?" Musil replied. "Shut your fucking mouth, I'm a sergeant."

It was a fitting introduction to the 82nd and to Rob Musil.

This was Yeske's first deployment, but as an older soldier he understood the idea behind COIN. He'd even gotten a copy of Petraeus's COIN manual to read. During workup he'd gone to EMT school and knew how to help save a man if things got real gnarly.

Yeske and his platoon sat down with Staff Sergeant Matt Hill, who was a combat veteran himself and had had enough of fighting to be sated, to have his bona fides.

Hill's accent was so Bostonian that it sounded like someone imitating a Boston accent. He started out at Fort Hood in Texas with the First Cavalry. Hill knew the realities of combat, having been with 2-508 for the previous deployment. He knew about firefights and IEDs and the importance of being prepared for them, but he also knew about stuff like "green-on-blue," which is when local Afghan forces opened fire on the Americans who were there as advisors. He knew there was never a moment to be relaxed in-country, even on your own base.

Hill gave the platoon a talk about how if things seem boring, then everyone might start getting complacent, and if everyone got complacent, then they'd be tempting the Taliban—even tempting fate, or the gods of war, or whatever—to take advantage of their lack of preparedness. They always had to remind themselves and each other not to forget what might happen, what could happen any day. They had to remain prepared for war in case war found them.

In Helmand, Bravo Company had gotten used to driving mile after boring mile on roads for what they thought were cockamamie training missions. Since they were in vehicles all the time, they didn't have the mystical union that an infantryman with boots on the ground has with a piece of territory. They weren't connected to the earth itself, where every footstep required a man to be aware of subtle changes in the landscape.

They watched from their vehicles for IEDs and sometimes found them, obvious ones found in obvious places. They kept an eye out for Taliban ambushes that never came on missions that seemed to be the same day after day.

Despite what Hill told them about not getting complacent and needing to remain sharp, there was nothing to make that lesson take hold. Simply put, they didn't have to pay a premium in life or injuries for complacency. If a turret gunner daydreamed, it didn't really matter because he never needed to shoot at anything anyway. It was a cushy deployment.

"New guys who'd never deployed were just bitching. It doesn't matter what you do, guys are going to bitch and complain," Mac said, recalling that time.

But Mac knew what it meant to get shot at, to see guys get hurt. To get hurt himself.

"When it comes, it's gonna come, and you're going to wish it didn't," Mac would tell them. "If you're over here and don't fire a single shot, it's going to be boring but we're all going to go home."

For those boring months in Helmand, Mac—like Hill—worked to fend off complacency, because if the shit came they had to be ready for it. Then on Halloween 2009, some of the company inadvertently rolled into a firefight that went so well that it's cited by some as a textbook example of how to maneuver on the enemy.

Third Platoon had been out visiting some of the ANCOP, the comparatively well-trained Afghan police. It had been a four-day-long mission of drinking tea at checkpoints and running boring basic training for police units. At the end of it all, the men from Bravo loaded up in their Humvees, accompanied by a contingent of Afghan National Army (ANA) troops in their hunter-green Ford Ranger pickups, to drive back to the British base together. The Ranger trucks were lightweight, more maneuverable and speedier than American Humvees. The American vehicles were loaded down with extra armor plates, and their suspensions squealed under the weight, their engines groaning with the effort of hauling around all that extra steel.

The contingent of men from Bravo Company in their straining Humvees had to halt at a culvert, a drainage ditch, under the road that was a veritable magnet for IEDs. It was mind-numbing, stopping at every single ditch to take a look and see if there might be an IED. Stop and check. Stop again for an IED check. And another IED check. The term "IED" itself started to hum in the background all the time, like deadly white noise. Every convoy became the same. Sometimes they found an IED, but none of those IEDs ever blew up on them, so it just became a routine tedium.

Yeske came to call these drives their "IED training mission," because it seemed that they did more stopping and checking for bombs than anything else during those first months in Helmand. They'd sometimes see a spot where there was an obvious IED, then call for the explosive ordnance disposal (EOD) guys. Since Bravo was working under a British unit, they had to wait for British EOD. It might take hours for them to show up, and when they did arrive, they'd examine the bomb and then figure out a way to drag it out and blow it up safely.

Sometimes the Afghan contingent—not bound by the Army strictures—grew impatient and zoomed off in their Rangers, taking their chances. October 31, 2009, was one of those days when the Afghans took their chances.

The Bravo Company convoy had been waiting for the EOD after running into a passel of IEDs on the road when a group of Ford Ranger trucks went flying past. Off they went, out ahead of the Americans, then around a bend in the road and out of sight.

EOD showed up soon after that, dealt quickly with the IEDs, and the guys from Bravo got on the move again, with Allen Thomas in the lead truck, Yeske in another, and Hill in the back of the formation. Once moving, they came around another bend a few miles ahead and saw one of the Afghan Ranger trucks smashed into the wall of a building near the road, the engine smoking. Yeske couldn't figure out what had happened to the poor truck and at first assumed a wreck. It wasn't uncommon for those zippy vehicles to be driven crazily off the road.

But in a few moments the Americans in the Humvees realized what had happened and what was still happening when they arrived. The Taliban had sprung an ambush on what they thought was just a convoy of Afghan soldiers, a soft, juicy, lovely target bumping down the road without American support. It made for a fight the Taliban were pretty sure they could win.

Unfortunately for the Taliban, the ill-prepared and hasty Afghan National Army pickup truck convoy was followed shortly by a bunch of American paratroopers from Bravo Company. What was worse for the Taliban was this was a bunch of paratroopers who had trained for more than a year to destroy the enemy in a situation just like this. All the ranges and training missions back home had been for this right here. And those American paratroopers were tired of their boring advise-and-assist mission and wanted nothing more than to unleash the full fury of the promises made to them since boot camp.

Sergeant Allen Thomas, in the first Humvee, was standing up in the turret that stuck out of the top of the truck and he opened up on the Taliban he could see with the mounted machine gun.

Yeske's Humvee had an M240G machine gun and an MK19 grenade launcher in its turret, with Tyler Koller behind the guns.

Before the Army, Koller was among the Priesthood of All Believers at a Pentecostal church in southern Illinois, where he had grown up.

Southern Illinois isn't Chicago, not by any stretch of the imagination. Once you get down an hour or two south of Lake Michigan, all bets are off—you might as well be in Indiana, or even Arkansas. Down there it's all farms and silos.

That's where Koller was raised, yelling at his mom to hurry up because she was a master of running behind all the time and making them late for church.

Church was the lodestar for the Kollers. Growing up, he was a Royal Ranger, man! If you don't know the Royal Rangers, it's a worldwide church youth group that makes the Boy Scouts seem like a wayward branch of Hells Angels. One of the principal tenets is for boys to "grow in Christlike manhood."

And then after high school Koller went into the Army, where he joined an Airborne unit and got one of those fantastic maroon berets that showed he was in a brotherhood, a grown-up Royal Rangers, with guns.

As Koller got ready to open fire, Yeske saw the gunner in the truck next to him turn his turret on two Taliban who were close enough that he could see one of the Talib's eyes open as wide as saucers before the Bravo machine gun cut them both down.

Oh shit, this is it, Yeske thought to himself in this, his first-ever firefight. "Taliban didn't have good effects on target," Hill says in an Army understatement. "They were scared. They thought they were attacking ANA and they attacked a bunch of paratroopers."

Up in the turret in Yeske's Humvee, Tyler Koller let loose on a tree line a few hundred yards away with the 40mm grenades from the MK19 machine gun. That gun sort of bloops out a succession of explosive rounds that resemble large golf balls, pretty much the same as what an M203 fires. The grenades come out slower than bullets from a machine gun and you can see them arc toward the enemy, watching their trajectory. Koller's first few rounds soared well over the target, but then he lowered the muzzle, used some Kentucky windage to adjust, and the grenades began hitting right where he wanted, a spot right by some trees where they'd seen some Talibs firing. He went to reload the gun and put the rounds in upside down, which jammed it up and put it out of commission. So Koller switched to his machine gun and let loose again on the tree line.

The Taliban aren't dumb and don't usually pick a fight unless they think they can gain something by it, but this time they miscalculated badly. The American vehicles bounded forward, one after the other, scattering the Taliban that they didn't quickly kill. Nobody from Bravo was even hurt.

One sergeant ended up with a bullet hole through the armpit of his uniform and a specialist swore up and down that a bullet ricocheted off his helmet, though nobody was too sure about that claim. The quick engagement was picture-perfect. It went exactly as they'd practiced it over and over and over again. They couldn't have done better on some range back at Fort Bragg. It was like a live-fire training exercise, except with Taliban serving as targets. Bravo Company reveled in the experience.

What a confidence boost it was. The whole thing was proof positive Bravo was well trained, knew what they were doing, and had talents that shouldn't be wasted on stupid advise-and-assist crap.

"It was weird," Hill, a veteran of multiple deployments, said. "Any firefight I ever went into, it never went that smooth."

After the fight they motored back to base and had burgers at the British Halloween party. It was surreal. Captain Adam Armstrong remembers the men from that patrol coming back to base and just glowing, beaming in ecstasy, knowing that all their training had actually worked. It seemed to them proof of a wartime calculation: All they had to do was apply the martial solution to a straightforward problem presented by the bad guys. If they just did what they'd been trained to do, there were no real surprises and nothing that could go wrong. If you just followed training, then you stayed safe, and the bad guys got killed. Simple.

Bravo Company called it the Halloween Zombie Massacre, a cute name for a firefight that was bad for the Taliban and great for them. No injuries. No casualties. It made them think they were ready to do anything that might be asked of them.

CHAPTER 9

JENIO'S WAR

He'd been in-country for more than three months, but Fourth Brigade commander Colonel Brian Drinkwine was still struggling to keep straight the locations and assignments of the thousands of men under his command. Bravo Company was just one small unit in that brigade, and they were stuck driving around the boring roads of Helmand province and contenting themselves with that Halloween shootout as the most action they were likely to face. Meanwhile, the 2-508 commander, Lieutenant Colonel Frank Jenio, was trying to get his battalion—which included Bravo Company—into what he saw as the real war.

Jenio and Puckett, the former Ranger Regiment stalwarts who wanted to get into the fight, had to follow orders, even distasteful orders like those that made their finely tuned war-fighting battalion into trainers more likely to drink tea all day than to pull triggers.

Part of Jenio's philosophy was that a well-trained paratrooper unit was certainly able to take on a training mission even though it wasn't sexy or what they wanted to do. These American troops could train a bunch of Afghans on anything from shooting a rifle to walking on a patrol, all in the American style, no problem.

"Take a good infantry company and they can do it," he said, adding ruefully, "Nobody wants to do that shit, they want to shoot people in the face. They don't want to go fuck around with a police unit."

And yet, they were fucking around with police units. At least for now.

Jenio embraced the training mission as best he could because Big Army said he must, and though he chafed at that mission from day one, they were still going to do it well, by God. And to make sure it was being done well, Jenio traveled around the region to talk with his troops spread among ISAF commanders to see how the boys were doing.

He found out his marvelously trained battalion wasn't even being used properly as trainers! Some of his men weren't allowed to travel freely off bases to work with the Afghan police units they'd been partnered up with. Others were restricted from leaving the combat outposts they'd been assigned to. The base commanders, often from a NATO nation, were too worried about risk.

Jenio's paratroopers were mostly just sitting around the base or their assigned outposts. The ISAF commanders in charge of his marvelous troopers weren't letting some of the men even leave the wire! When he found this out, that settled it, pushed him right over the edge. This was no way to use paratroopers! If they were going to be trainers, advising and assisting, they had to be able to go out and do it. His men needed to operate. Ah, shit, he figured he needed his own area of operations, his own battle space and his own slice of the war. No battalion commander is remembered for having his battalion farmed out all over hell and creation, drinking tea. There was ample fighting to be done in southern Afghanistan, Jenio knew. Sure, the Marines were down in Helmand, but Kandahar seemed like it was ready for some old-fashioned warfighting.

According to the martial catechism that was the COIN manual, a soldier learns that a crafty insurgent takes advantage of seeming weakness and turns it to his advantage. That's what Jenio did for himself, took advantage of the nooks and crannies of the Byzantine command structure he was part of. Nobody in Washington was paying attention—they couldn't pay attention all the way on the other side of the planet. The Obama administration wasn't sure what it was doing in Afghanistan and was trying to keep the domestic economy from cratering in the Great Recession back home. And Jenio's brigade commander, Colonel Drinkwine, had too many other problems to solve to keep tabs on Jenio, who began pulling every behind-the-scenes lever available to him.

There had to be some way out of this ill-conceived deployment, Jenio thought. And he just knew he could find that way out.

Jenio started dropping hints to any senior commanders he came across. "Training of police and army was Dick and Jane stuff," he told senior leaders. "I don't think this is the most effective way to use a brigade."

And so Jenio, whom everyone in the Army knew was a hard charger, was campaigning throughout ISAF to charge his guys right into a fight. His lobbying effort aligned almost magically with events in Kandahar province.

Scott Brannon, Jenio's operations officer, remembers that Jenio had previously served on General Stan McChrystal's staff, and every time McChrystal was close by, Jenio would visit with him and make the pitch to employ his troops as paratroopers in a hot combat zone. Brannon remembers that Jenio and McChrystal exchanged emails in a way you wouldn't expect a battalion commander to do with a general.

As the Marines swept into Helmand, there was pressure for ISAF and the US Army to do more in Kandahar, the province right next door. That pressure to do more came just as four thousand troops from America—Drinkwine's brigade, which included Jenio's battalion—showed up with little mission other than to serve as trainers. It was as if there were a few thousand fighters in southern Afghanistan available for freelance work.

At first Jenio thought he could finagle a way for his battalion to go fight alongside the British troops in Marjah, in Helmand province. "We were pining for Marjah," Jenio said. "I was practically kissing the Brits' ass to get to Marjah."

Voices across the US government and ISAF were asking why the Americans cared so much about Helmand. Kandahar is the Taliban capital, the place where Mullah Omar publicly donned the Prophet Muhammad's cloak, back in 1996 when the Taliban was ascendant, and presented himself to the world.

Kandahar has a major city, a no-kidding urban area from which the province gets its name. It's got transit lines to the capital, Kabul, and sits right next door to Pakistan. It serves as a conduit for the Taliban to slip across borders into the heart of Afghanistan. Kandahar province includes thousands of acres of legitimate farmland to grow the most famous pomegranates in the world. This mix of factors makes it a place that needs to be dominated in order to make a real difference in Afghanistan. Officials at the Pentagon and at State and even in the White House saw Kandahar's significance.

There were some Americans stationed in Kandahar, including one unit in the heartland of Kandahar's agricultural region, the Arghandab Valley. If Kandahar was the highway Taliban fighters used to get into Helmand, the Arghandab Valley was the fast lane. But this unit was a full-blown four-alarm disaster, in part due to its commander, in part due to bad luck. Men were being injured and killed left and right. The commander was out of control, according to those higher up in his chain of command, and several generals wouldn't have minded seeing him out.

The unit in Kandahar, the Fifth Stryker Brigade, was commanded by Colonel Harry Tunnell. He was a warfighter like Jenio, and he had earned the generals' ire. Tunnell was no longer able to run long distances because of a gunshot through the leg received years earlier near Kirkuk, Iraq, which got him a Purple Heart. After a long Army career, in early 2009 Tunnell found himself in command of the Stryker brigade sent to the Arghandab Valley.

Tunnell and his Strykers were a mismatch in just about every way for the terrain, for the battle, and for the local population. Even today, high-ranking Pentagon officials who have no reason to remember a brigade commander's name after all these years of war are able to remember Harry Tunnell, a rarity because brigade commanders came and went in Iraq and Afghanistan.

The Arghandab was essentially a gigantic orchard, a place nestled in a valley where in the summer pomegranates ripen and grapes grow abundantly along irrigated rows of canals dug out and built up over hundreds of years of cultivation. While Americans know Afghanistan for its poppy crops, in the Arghandab it would have been a waste to grow much other than the world-famous pomegranates. That plowed-up ground was difficult to walk on, and worse to drive across. And yet, Colonel Tunnell was sent there with his brigade to prove the utility of the newest high-tech fighting vehicle the Army had built at the time: the Stryker.

Strykers are eight-wheeled hulking beasts, essentially armored personnel carriers digitally connected to one another through a wireless, networked computer system. They were supposed to be the forefront of digital technology, able to act as an organic unified being on the battlefield and then fire their 105mm cannon much like a tank. But when a unit rolls into battle in a Stryker, it's dependent on that beast, wholly tied to it.

When the terrain is right for it, the Stryker does its job as smooth as butter. When the terrain is as it is in the Arghandab, with tiny ridges of land and ravines of tilled-up soil, sunbaked and hardened, Strykers fail. They move slowly across the bumpy land and make it easy for the bad guy to know exactly where they are, where they will be, where to put the pressure on, and where to avoid it. It didn't help that the Strykers looked a hell of a lot like the Russian armored personnel carriers they used to invade the country in the 1980s.

* * *

Todd Greentree cut his teeth as a State Department foreign service officer in El Salvador in the 1980s. By the time Afghanistan rolled around, he'd seen four other wars. Greentree doesn't talk like other diplomats, and he doesn't act like them, either. While most diplomats prefer to stay in the base air-conditioning or, better yet, avoid going into war-active countries altogether, Todd Greentree loved to get out in the dirt. Greentree was stationed in eastern Afghanistan when the Strykers were first being sent down to Kandahar, before Tunnell and his men ever got to the country. He was assigned to go along with the Stryker unit to provide a civilian presence.

Greentree was sitting with a senior Army officer when he got his assignment. The Army officer chuckled and said, "You want to take a bet on how long before one gets blown up?" Greentree said he didn't because it seemed bad form, but the officer wanted to get his bet on the record anyway, so the officer said loudly, wagering with no one in particular, that it would be, max, two weeks before one of those tin cans got blown up. Turns out he was spot-on.

Tunnell's Strykers went into Kandahar in the fall of 2009 to provide combat power before there was a plan on how to use that power. Tunnell's confidence didn't appear to be shaken by the lack of a plan. He went in seemingly ready to fire those 105mm cannons at anybody who messed with him. But there were a couple of problems with that. First, the American forces in Afghanistan had already begun the shift to COIN warfare. That meant anyone who went into an area with the mindset of wanting to kill everything had simply gone out of style, leaving aside the question if such an attitude was ever effective or ethical to begin with. Second, a kill-'em-all attitude in a commander trickles down to the troops. A brigade full of soldiers ready to kill anything is but a hop, skip, and a jump from a willingness to engage in war crimes.

Tunnell's focus, according to those who remember his efforts, was on combat, not COIN. He wouldn't—couldn't—change his mindset, superiors and others remember. Greentree said when he got to Arghandab to talk COIN it was like trying to help a football team learn how to play baseball. One day Tunnell's commanding officer was talking about the shift to COIN and how Kandahar was central to it all. Tunnell, though, seemed to ignore everything his boss had said and instead laid out vague plans to do a clearing operation in Arghandab. It sounded like Tunnell wanted to sweep through the area as though it were World War II. It blew Greentree's mind, Tunnel's apparent approach to the conflict, his approach to his commanders. Before long, Tunnell had made enemies at the Pentagon, and at NATO and ISAF. The Arghandab proved to be unwelcoming, too.

On the very first operation using Strykers, Tunnell's men were able to lay waste to the Taliban. They attacked through an open area that seemed custom-made for the eight-wheeled vehicles, bringing the fury of the fast armor to bear. They capitalized on the element of surprise. It was the first time they used these terrors of technology, and they leveled a Halloween Zombie Massacre–type of event against the Taliban.

It soon became clear that all Tunnell and his Strykers had on their side was the element of surprise. The Taliban doesn't take very long to learn their lesson, and once they did, it was all uphill for Tunnell and his Strykers. Pretty soon the Taliban were planting massive IEDs in the ground that the Stryker crews didn't know how to detect or deal with. Taliban bombs were flipping over the 38,000-pound behemoths. Entire American crews were getting killed or injured.

Tunnell's men seemed unwilling to operate without their Strykers and couldn't do much of anything in the Arghandab Valley besides opening fire from turrets whenever possible and using aircraft and drones for remote strikes on anyone and anything that looked like it might be planting an IED. Farmers were mad and Taliban and sympathizers were given free rein, people remember. Tunnell's men appeared to be left frustrated and began to take it out on the populace, which happened so much that a few men were eventually court-martialed for war crimes.

"Colonel Tunnell never, ever got it, he was never going to get it," said General Ben Hodges, a top ISAF commander at the time. "He showed up wanting to kill."

On the sides of vehicles was the motto "Search and Destroy." Tunnell stayed true to this motto. He didn't seem to see that the latest ISAF strategy wasn't just about killing as many Taliban as possible.

It wasn't about body counts, General Hodges remembered, and he said Tunnell appeared to not understand the shift to COIN and what that required.

Jenio had his eye on the Arghandab and was watching Tunnell's flagging effort from a distance, building a case that his battalion should take over for the Strykers. He remembers getting intelligence reports that there were times when the Taliban had enough freedom of movement to use a backhoe to dig holes and plant bombs. You can't watch everywhere at all times with drones, which were in short supply at that time in Afghanistan anyway. "You read about a thousand pounds of explosive being dug in with a backhoe," Jenio said. "How the fuck do they have the freedom of movement to do that?"

Arghandab was a mess, filled with pissed-off civilians and crafty Taliban. "The Taliban was in control of the Arghandab," said Todd Greentree.

ISAF and the United States needed an old-fashioned infantry unit— a ground combat unit that wasn't tied to Strykers or some other vehicle and was trained to fight in places like the Arghandab—to go in there and try to fix things, but there was no surge imminently forthcoming and no units available for it. They knew Obama would likely send more troops, more than the initial few thousand he'd already decided on, but if they came, they wouldn't get to Kandahar for a while, who knew how long? If only there were a spare infantry battalion sitting around somewhere in Afghanistan. And if only they'd want to go in there and replace Tunnell's Strykers. But surely there wasn't anyone available or crazed enough to volunteer for that, was there?

* * *

Just as Jenio knew he had this one shot at making his mark as a battalion commander, British General Nick Carter had a primo chance to make a big splash. An excellent performance here would boost a general's résumé, could bolster an argument to make him chief of the British Defence Staff—the top uniformed job in the UK military—a few years down the road. Because the fight in Afghanistan was a multinational effort, commanders like Nick Carter were in charge of troops from dozens of countries, including American troops. He could get more aggressive about the mission in southern Afghanistan with more troops under his command to take it to the Taliban.

Top uniformed officers talked about COIN, but they were also more than happy to just get things done rather than ensure the Afghans were the ones doing it. COIN doctrine was to teach a man to fish, yes. But the most important thing for officers with limited time in-country was to get some goddamn fish, even if that meant less reliance on the Afghans.

By this point in 2009, President Obama was signaling that Afghanistan was about to be the place where Americans were ready to send personnel and funding. Elation buzzed through the ranks of troops headed to Afghanistan. Suddenly with more troops and aggressive commanders, the Afghan war effort seemed like it might be able to move forward strategically—move forward in a way that hadn't been possible for nearly a decade.

"I remember saying, 'Finally we can mass somewhere and do a mission,'" Ben Hodges said.

As far as the big picture in Afghanistan, General Nick Carter made the fight in Marjah the main effort since there was an entire Marine Air-Ground Task Force (MAGTF) sweeping in for that purpose, and the Brits were champing at the bit to see the place they'd long fought over finally and decisively come under control of Western forces. Carter was the overall commander of the entire Western effort, McChrystal was just the guy in charge of American forces.

But Jenio knew as well as anybody that Kandahar was what the Taliban really cared about. He knew the intelligence reports, and since he'd served on McChrystal's staff, he knew the boss cared about it, too.

"In hindsight they didn't give a shit about Marjah," Jenio said of the Taliban. "They said, go ahead and take it."

Next door to it all, the Arghandab Valley had a strong Taliban, it had pissed off locals, it had plenty of IEDs. It was awful.

As heaps of resources readied to bear down on Helmand with the Marines in the lead, Arghandab practically begged, pleaded, for the same sort of attention. Jenio had angled for this very opportunity, and here the military stars aligned perfectly. Jenio's battalion, with Bravo Company front and center, seemed to be in a perfect spot all of a sudden, both geographically and tactically: Bravo Company sat ready and poised for action. The Army could rid itself of Tunnell and his ill-fated Strykers and fill the hole with a light infantry unit that prided itself on flexibility.

Jenio appeared to have the respect of McChrystal and a history of working with him. Just before the new year someone from a NATO country asked Jenio if he wanted to head into Kandahar. He said he sure would, but then, on second thought, Jenio said he didn't really have the final say. Despite his finagling and jousting for position, Jenio knew he was subject to the slow-moving cogs of the Army just like any other battalion commander. He'd have to wait for permission.

The brigade commander, Colonel Drinkwine, doesn't remember how it happened or who gave the final thumbs-up on Jenio's change in mission. But a decision was made somewhere and Jenio was told to get ready for the Arghandab. Jenio's battalion wasn't just going in to fill space, they were going to clean up after Tunnell. Moreover, they would undertake a crucial mission to cut off a main supply route the Taliban used to get from their de facto capital in Kandahar out into the rest of the country. The Marines were running all over Helmand making headlines while Kandahar was a gaping hole in the side of Afghanistan. Jenio's men and others in the

Arghandab would stitch up that wound, stopping the flow of anything and everybody able to traipse into the interior of the country, coming right in from Pakistan and then going back out again.

"We were happy as shit," Jenio said when his battalion learned they'd be heading into the Arghandab. Sure they'd still have Afghan military partners, still be advising and assisting on some level, but the Americans would take on the responsibility of pushing into combat areas. The Afghans would be like the parsley on the edge of the plate of a steakhouse dinner, somehow present but not necessary.

Colonel Drinkwine said years later he wasn't sure of the reason behind Tunnell's replacement, only that sometimes units wear out their welcome in an area of operations. "I hope there was not pressure to go in and kick the bee's nest in Arghandab," Drinkwine said a decade later.

General Ben Hodges remembered that he and General Carter didn't just put Jenio and his boys out there to fill space. No, they were happy to have a group of ready-to-patrol paratroopers led by a commander with the willingness and grit to follow orders—light infantry prepared to work with Afghans and get out among the people. They'd be at the forefront of flexing the coalition muscle in Kandahar in this renewed Afghanistan War.

And yet, the renewal of the war hadn't truly reached Kandahar, so the troops under Jenio's command would be a vanguard.

* * * *

"Johnny" knew about the Arghandab. He had been born in Helmand province and grew up close enough to it. Since he was working with Bravo Company as an interpreter, he had some idea of what they could expect. He was known as "Johnny" the interpreter to the American soldiers in part because he wanted to protect his identity and in part because Americans preferred Anglicized names. To this day, he worries about using his real name in any capacity because memories and grudges can last a long time in Afghanistan.

Johnny was born in Lashkar Gah, the capital of Helmand province, and remembers growing up under the Taliban regime, the one that played host to Osama bin Laden in the 1990s. As a child, he didn't have any sports he loved because the Taliban didn't allow him or his friends to play sports.

There were no girls in school because the Taliban didn't allow that, either. He had no real hobbies; he just went to school. He was a teenager when 9/11 happened and remembers the quick fall of the regime and years later he could still see in his mind's eye the military aircraft that flew overhead and presaged change for the country.

Once the Americans and their allies came to the country, new opportunities opened up for a young man with ambition like Johnny. He was still in high school at the time and started taking English classes, getting tutoring outside of school as well. People were excited then about a hope for a new government, a hope for a new life. Freedom. Peace. Stability.

No more Taliban.

Johnny decided he wanted to become an interpreter for the coalition forces. (It didn't matter much whether it was the Americans, the Brits, the Australians, or even the Germans—who spoke English, too. But let's be honest, he wanted to work with the Americans. They seemed the hottest ticket.) Everyone around him seemed to want that opportunity, even his English teacher. How could he not want to do his patriotic duty and help the troops who it seemed had come to his country, willing to invest so much in making sure Afghanistan escaped from the Taliban's grasp?

Oh, and there was the money. Compared with working at a grocery store or a gas station, becoming an interpreter for one of the coalition militaries meant a serious paycheck, and Johnny didn't come from a wealthy family. He was single, he was learning English, and he could already speak Pashto and Dari, the two predominant languages of Afghanistan.

It took Johnny a few years to learn English and to be old enough to apply for a job, but he finally made the trip to Kandahar Airfield, the massive military base in southern Afghanistan, and took the interpreter exam for a military contractor that had an acronym for a name, like so many. He passed the test and on October 6, 2009, became an interpreter for the US military, working for Bravo Company while they were still in Helmand.

Johnny was excited to finally join a military unit, to become a no-kidding interpreter. He was also scared. He'd never touched a gun in his life or even been around them. For the short time before Bravo was dispatched to the Arghandab, Johnny was placed with Third Platoon and partnered with a senior interpreter. Johnny stayed inside the base to get experience, translating whenever Americans had to speak with Afghan police or military units. The other interpreter left the wire and went out on missions. Johnny realized that he'd probably have to go out of the wire eventually, so he started lifting weights, running, and getting in better shape alongside the Americans. The broad-faced and quiet young man, who by his own account was neither skinny nor fat, got himself ready for something, anything, that might await him.

Then his platoon sergeant told him they'd be moving to the Arghandab. He said he was ready to help in any way he could, but he knew the Arghandab meant much more danger than sitting on a base. He and the nearly dozen interpreters who were also assigned to the company all knew that much better than any of the Americans.

* * * *

When a new unit takes over an area of operations, they usually get a few days or a few weeks to ride along with the outgoing leadership of the unit they're replacing in what's called "left seat/right seat" patrols. The men from the old and new units sit next to each other and talk about all sorts of things: what it's like in the area, things that don't get written down in briefs or memos, anything that will make the new guys' jobs easier.

With the Strykers, the left seat/right seat was like nothing the Bravo leadership team had ever experienced. Captain Adam Armstrong said he couldn't get any of the unit's officers to take him out on a patrol. The main reason was because they no longer really went out on patrols, as they were tired of getting blown up by Taliban bombs. The best they'd do was drive with the men from Bravo up to a hill overlooking the Arghandab, well out of harm's way, and give a few tips.

Nick Armendariz, who'd deployed to Afghanistan before, was out on that training meetup with the Strykers. Everybody rode up to a hill overlooking the Arghandab and the leaders from the Stryker unit pointed at places where they said Bravo simply shouldn't go. They didn't even go down into the valley but instead surveyed from a distance the stretch Bravo was getting ready to take over.

Up on that hill, the place looked amazing, nothing like the flatness and desert they had been seeing in Helmand. It was like a scene from another world, of undulating land and a river running through the middle of it, with some green underbrush even in the winter. From a distance, it was pristine. It was beautiful.

That view was all but ruined by the lower-ranking guys from the Strykers, the drivers and gunners, who wouldn't shut up about how crappy it was in the valley and how many casualties they'd taken and how they didn't even operate down there unless they absolutely, positively had to. Armendariz remembers looking at it all down below and listening to the soldiers they were about to replace in the valley and thinking, *Fuck, we're in the fight now. I got my wish.*

Armstrong remembers that it was damn near impossible from way up on that hill to try and pick out a place to build up a new base for foot patrols. Dave Huff remembers that as a junior soldier he didn't even get a brief or a lesson or anything about Arghandab, what to expect or what to know about the place. The Strykers were silent on anything tactically useful—all they gave voice to was the destruction they'd seen. It was as if Bravo was getting ready to go to an undiscovered land full of mythical dangers, a place that was spoken of as if nobody had set foot there before.

CHAPTER 10

A TENSE WALK INTO
A RADISH FIELD

Bravo Company had about a week after that turnover before they had to go into the Arghandab Valley. Captain Adam Armstrong remembers that they just sort of left Helmand behind and had few precious days to get ready for the new mission. Officers crammed like college kids getting ready for an exam, senior enlisted broke their backs and spent sleepless nights figuring out what was needed and what they might face. Many of the junior soldiers did what soldiers have done before big operations from time immemorial: They didn't do shit. The low-ranking soldiers of Bravo Company ate as many hot meals at the chow hall as they could. They worked out at the gym. And they waited.

A kind of stillness took over the company. Like the dawning of morning light, everyone began to see—began to really feel—that this mission change would be huge. They were going to be the first troops who'd walked into the Arghandab in years. They got ready for the firefights, the contact that they figured was inevitable. Soon enough the walk into the Arghandab was on them.

Armstrong knew the Taliban watched everything. They might not recognize faces, but a new uniform with new shoulder patches signaled there was a new unit in town. The Army's standard combat uniforms at the time were a gray, splotchy digital-pattern uniform designed to blend into everything, which had the effect of blending in with nothing.

In 2009 the Army decided to test a prototype uniform, known as UCP-D uniforms. It was the Army's ugly gray uniforms with some brown added into the camouflage pattern, made specifically to offer protection in Afghanistan. The Army didn't widely distribute the things, and Bravo was one of the few units to get them.

For the walk into the valley, Armstrong knew a new uniform would make the Taliban wonder about these new guys for a while and get them maybe a week's worth of surprise before the enemy figured out who they were.

When the actual day of mission shift came, Armstrong wanted to be on the move at the first hint of morning twilight. The company headed out of the main base around three or four A.M. on December 18, 2009. It was just before sunrise, when the sky just begins to glow, when they began their walk into the valley.

"It felt like something out of Vietnam," Armendariz said. "Walking in formation as a company-size element." They swooped into the cold valley on a cold morning expecting the full force of the Taliban, but they didn't see anybody. Every walled compound they came across they cleared with no resistance. There were no locals, no civilians, no anything. The tension kept rising as they walked because they'd expected so much and yet now there was nothing.

They had a mounted element, with Humvees and other vehicles who leapfrogged with them, holding space once taken. It was a major effort, a major operation.

"We were just waiting to get fucked up, just waiting for it," Armendariz said. All that pent-up frustration boiled inside them. They were finally done with the training mission they'd been stuck with and now they had the expectation of firefights, IEDs, combat. They ended up with a daylong walk into a silent valley.

And then they stopped in the middle of a farmer's field. Nothing but radishes all around. No infrastructure, no old fortifications. It was a radish field that had looked good on a map but which, of course, they hadn't been able to see because the closest they'd gotten to the valley was up on that hill. Now they were in the middle of a field in the middle of nowhere. They were home.

* * *

The radish field was immediately deemed a combat outpost (COP) and named after Albert Ware, an Army sergeant who died in the Arghandab the year before. But that doesn't mean COP Ware was worth a damn. They built the thing from scratch. When Bravo staked their claim, the place was nothing. There were only radishes that had been pulled up and left behind, scattered across the ground.

They didn't have access to big trucks to haul equipment. Mac remembers asking Jenio what additional equipment they could rely on for the big operation.

"What you see is what you get," Jenio responded to him.

Great, Mac thought. So he arranged to get every available Humvee with every available trailer to haul crap out to the radish field. Once they had gotten to the radish field, Mac and other senior NCOs ran convoys back and forth nearly nonstop for days to bring needed supplies out to the new COP. With dinky Humvees and trailers hooked to the backs of them they looked more like college kids with U-Hauls than the 82nd Airborne in the middle of a major combat operation.

Bravo made some basic entrenchments, and thanks to some Humvees with their trailers they quickly put up Hesco barriers all around the perimeter of the new outpost. Hescos are huge wire-mesh cages taller than a man. They store flat and are easily transported, but when unfolded they can be put together like Legos. The wire mesh is lined with heavy-duty felt so they can handle tons and tons of dirt dumped into them to quickly make walls a few feet thick, impervious to bullets and pretty good at absorbing explosions.

Hescos are little more than glorified chicken-wire cages until they get filled with dirt, but Bravo couldn't get their walls filled with dirt for weeks. The things hold so much earth that it takes a front-loader or a dump truck to fill them, and it would take time before the slow machinery of Big Army could push that kind of equipment out to this hinterland. A bunch of troops with shovels working day and night would barely put a dent in the job.

Bravo was busy pulling guard duty around the clock. They moved dirt when they could but the Hescos around the burgeoning base remained all but empty. They mostly just served as a screen for the outpost so nobody could see in, and maybe could bluff the Taliban.

"We had these Hesco barriers but no dirt in them!" said Dave Huff. "One day a strong wind came and just blew them over and I was like, 'Oh, shit!'" The Taliban could have shot right through the empty barriers with a .22 rifle if they'd wanted to. But they never did. It took weeks until Bravo finally contracted some Afghan workers to bring in dump trucks full of dirt to load into the barriers and make proper walls.

Mac remembers taking 550 cord, general-purpose thin nylon rope, and lashing that around the Hescos, then tying it to stakes in the ground to prevent the Potemkin village from blowing over. To this day he's mad that they couldn't get support out there, couldn't get some engineers to come fill up those crucial Hescos.

It was one of the problems with being a freelance infantry outfit—the Army was hard-pressed to spare logistics for them and couldn't help them out, so they had to get locals to come and do the job. It wasn't the only instance that hardscrabble Bravo Company had to make their own way out there.

As they waited for the dirt walls to get filled, Bravo dug in, making places to sleep, to eat, to take a dump. They dug out foxholes they could jump in if they came under attack or were mortared. They put up tents here and there. And they did the thing they had gone there to do: They went out on patrol.

When a bunch of grunts move into a new location, the first thing they typically do, after establishing a decent perimeter defense, is to start patrolling. No matter how much work needs to be done to build a base, the top priority for a small unit is to go out on patrol. Having an offense is the best way to ensure a defense. It's a cliché, but for an infantry unit it's absolute gospel. The enemy is less likely to get close to an outpost and will have a harder time attacking or digging in some IEDs if they're always worried about running into a foot patrol.

The patrols were quiet. There seemed to be hardly anyone in the valley, but there were some locals. Soon Bravo started finding massive IEDs while on foot patrols, bombs that had been buried for the Strykers to drive over. They'd been trained to look out for IEDs, scanning with their eyes for the signs of bombs: scruffed-up ground, wires, and whatnot. They'd also trained to sweep the ground with mine detectors, which really comes down to a soldier walking out ahead of everyone waving a metal detector in front of him, like an old man you might see at the beach looking for coins or lost jewelry. It's the same idea, only the military has olive drab metal detectors and troops wear body armor.

They didn't find any small IEDs, the kind meant to blow up infantry on foot patrols. The Taliban hadn't really needed to bury antipersonnel mines over the past year since Tunnell's Stryker troops hadn't been walking around, just driving the huge vehicles that require huge IEDs. The few locals who were around even started telling the Bravo patrols where the massive IEDs could be found. They pointed out locations of some of the deadly devices. The locals were just reporting bombs that were never going to kill an American and they might get a reward.

It was a pretty good deal for them.

* * *

Less than a week after Bravo Company walked into the valley, Christmas arrived.

They'd moved into the Arghandab on December 18 with that eerie walk into a valley they'd heard so much about and had prepared for. And then there was nothing, the place was all but empty. Where were all the awful things the Stryker guys had told them about? Where were all the Taliban fighters who supposedly depended on keeping the Arghandab open as the fabled supply line from Pakistan into the rest of the country? Why had they built up so much tension?

By December 25, Bravo Company was still keyed up and ready for something—anything. But they were also exhausted after a week of digging and building on that combat outpost where it was pretty much just Bravo Company laboring away in the middle of a radish field. The patrolling, the very reason they were there, was a day-in, day-out endeavor that left them bone weary and tired from walking through canals and dirt and always, always, always ready to get shot at.

This brand-new outpost might have seemed to have sprung up magically had Bravo not known they'd built every last bit of it by breaking their backs. When they weren't digging in the earth and building up defensive positions, they were standing guard and walking the perimeter. And when they weren't doing that, they were on patrol, climbing over walls and tromping through freezing canals. There didn't seem to be any time left for rest or adequate sleep, so that's what got bumped off the schedule first. Sleep is always a bonus, an extra.

No attacks, no firefights, and hardly even a sight of anyone in the Arghandab. So they were all coming off the massive rush, the high, of getting their own area of operations that promised to be action-packed and then wasn't giving them anything. William Yeske remembers the feeling that they were always being watched, yet nothing happened. He knew there had to be a reason that villagers weren't around, but the only reason he could come up with is they knew something was coming to hit Bravo. And still nothing seemed to come.

It was plodding for Allen Thomas, the sergeant with so much experience already. Out in Helmand and now in the Arghandab, Allen rarely called Danica. He let the other guys call home when the satellite phone was available. The other guys had wives, they had kids. And he was a sergeant with neither. It's not like you could just walk into a phone booth or an internet café out there. They had to wait their turn to use the satellite phone, a handheld thing that looked like a cell phone from the 1980s. It was a massive and hulking device. So Danica, who had moved back home with her parents in Indiana, didn't hear from Allen very often.

Allen and Danica had talked a bit about what they might do after the deployment, but that talk wasn't real. It wasn't concrete. The Army does a fantastic job of obliterating the past and eliminating the future for those on deployment. It makes the present the sine qua non. The present is the only thing that exists.

Once a soldier is on deployment it doesn't really matter where he went to school or when he went to boot camp. The only thing that matters is the sandbag being filled in the here and now, the rifle that needs to be cleaned as soon as possible, the patrol that's just about to happen. With a level of attentiveness to the task at hand typically known only to Zen monastics, the immediate task occupies the entirety of a soldier's being.

Cards and letters show up, and there's occasional phone calls to loved ones back home, but even those are also very much in the present. What's happening right now? How are you right now? Few people plan out their future with a girlfriend or spouse while they're deployed in a real combat zone. Conversations are about the present.

If a soldier starts to let the future into his mind, it's a bad sign. It means he isn't concentrating his entirety on the present. He's losing focus, and he's tempting fate. Allen was a squad leader in Afghanistan. He didn't need to talk on the phone or think about the future.

* * *

Bravo Company set up shop in the Arghandab Valley just days before Christmas, and their holiday season was defined not by cheerful anticipation but instead by patrolling the terrain, tuning in to its buried IEDs, and fending off the feeling of constant worry about when the Taliban would strike. But even with the focus on the fight, Bravo Company would know it was Christmas from the decorations. No matter what unit, no matter where they were stationed, no matter how long, American service members had decorations, come hell or high water.

The average Army company didn't really want for the most basic of the basics: ammunition and essential food like MREs (meals ready-to-eat). But they never had enough of anything. They always needed more replacement uniforms and more ammo and more food. Moving supplies from point A to point B in a combat zone has never been easy. Things got manufactured in America. Then that American-made bullet or MRE or uniform had to make its way by sea or airlift to someplace between America and Afghanistan. It sat in limbo for a while in the middle, wherever that was. It might be in Germany, it might be in Kyrgyzstan. Then it had to be convoyed in by trucks or flown in, because landlocked Afghanistan doesn't have any ports.

Whatever that thing is then got flown in on a huge plane like a C-17 cargo plane, likely to Bagram Airfield near Kabul or to Kandahar Airfield.

From there the supplies might get driven by another smaller convoy or flown by helicopter out to some smaller base. Another convoy or helicopter got it even farther out to some PFC in some company sitting in the middle of a radish field in the middle of the Arghandab.

It took a massive, logistically complex, taxpayer-burdensome—not to mention dangerous—effort to get any little widget out to the guys on the front lines. In most cases, the effort feels justified. Soldiers need equipment to help them do their jobs or to make the day-to-day slog a little more manageable: metal detectors, body armor, new boots and socks. It is amazing that any soldier receives any extras at all, beyond the essentials already provided by the unit.

More amazing still is the sheer volume of shit—in the form of care packages—that made its way to the front during the years of war in Iraq and Afghanistan.

Even the most remote combat operating post, including a chicken-wire encampment in a radish field deep in the Arghandab Valley, could be flooded with shoebox-size white USPS boxes precisely on time for the holidays.

An infantryman could be stationed by himself in the middle of nowhere, surrounded by Taliban and about to be overrun. All he would want, more than anything, is more ammo and more food, but what he would doubtless get is a care package filled with things he doesn't want or need. It's God's honest truth that an American soldier at war might find himself awash in garbage he neither needs nor has asked for. It's all sent over to him by thoughtful mothers, fathers, sisters, schoolteachers, Cub Scouts, and little old ladies from across the heartland.

Because lawmakers and the Army brass saw these care packages as morale builders—and because they had to respond to public criticism from little old ladies if care packages got delayed—the care packages were dispatched with haste to the four corners of the globe.

These care packages were filled with all manner of unnecessary and annoying garbage. It's an unspoken truth among grunts: Ninety-nine percent of the time care packages are unwelcome. In Iraq and Afghanistan they were often just pounds and pounds and pounds of junk shipped from Dubuque, Iowa, to the middle of Nowheresville, Afghanistan. Bags of stale coffee. Boxes of old candy that nobody wanted to eat. Pair upon pair of white athletic socks as thin as tissue paper that were on sale at a dollar store back in the States and would tear in two if worn on a combat patrol. There were American flags from Girl Scout troops and homemade cards from a first-grade class. Among the cards and the crappy socks, the stale Dubble Bubble gum and waxy, off-brand Tootsie Rolls, there was also the ubiquitous well-intentioned holiday decorations.

The Christmas care packages that Bravo Company received were filled with decorations that were shipped to a base in Afghanistan at great subsidy by the taxpayers of America and great danger to a number of convoys, much like the rest of the thousands upon thousands of care packages sent during the Global War on Terror. Sometimes those decorations got hung up because they were there and something needed to be done with them. Sometimes they just got thrown into the burn pit as quickly as possible so some young soldier might mercifully avoid wasting a half hour of his free time hanging them up, time he could use for sleep. It's a bad set of options any way you slice it. Sure, the Hesco barriers didn't have any dirt in them and some Taliban asshole could've shot clean through them with a.22 rifle if he wanted to, but they were strung with some from holiday tinsel from back home.

On Christmas, soldiers somehow find a way to squeeze some good cheer out of the misery of deployment. At COP Ware, on Christmas they set up a projector and watched the movie *Elf*. Some of the guys weren't but a few months out of high school. They made a show of being Grinch-like, wizened against Christmas cheer, but they also did want the holiday to be special somehow. So they found a place to settle into the dirt of the Arghandab and enjoy watching Will Ferrell walk through Manhattan wearing yellow tights. It was special in its own way. It was a good night, Christmas night.

Then the day after Christmas happened.

* * *

What never comes across in all the literature of war, the movies, the TV shows, and even the history books is how small of an area a unit is responsible for. A company that's foot patrolling has an area of operations, an AO, that's about nothing if you look at it on a map. An AO might be just over a square mile. If a soldier were back home in Ohio or Oklahoma, they could easily jog across the whole place in a half hour, maybe fifteen minutes.

Back in Ohio or Oklahoma, though, the soldier isn't wearing body armor. There are no canals to cross and walls to jump over. There isn't potential danger behind every tree, every footstep a possible problem. But on deployment, the space of the AO seems huge, because in that context it *is* huge. When every step a soldier takes could hit an IED or set off an ambush, it makes even the shortest walk an eternity. In suburban America, it's easy to just walk down the sidewalk to get to the end of a block. But imagine that same trip made by crossing through backyards instead. Every fence has to be hopped. Every shrub pushed through. Every swimming pool or hot tub waded through. And imagine if while hopping those fences you had to worry about every neighbor shooting you.

Well-trod paths cannot be taken, because those are obviously going to be booby-trapped. So the path of patrol involves wading through canals, hurdling walls, and breaking through brush and bramble. When patrolling the AO, the path of least resistance must likely be exchanged for the path of most resistance.

Bravo Company was responsible for a measly twelve square kilometers. That's three kilometers by four kilometers, or very roughly two miles by two and a half miles. A wee little rectangle of terrain. But on deployment that seems as big as all the great outdoors. On a given day a soldier might patrol only a kilometer or two, less than a mile, the equivalent of a few city blocks. And that patrol takes hours, sometimes an entire day. Sometimes more than a day, because every step is deliberate, slow, cautious.

When Bravo Company first arrived in the Arghandab and took their first foot patrols, an explosive ordnance disposal (EOD) team attached to them from the brigade joined them, to show them the ropes of walking through that dangerous land.

Some Bravo Company guys remembered the experience of going out with the EOD experts who walked in canals, using them like some kind of path, and moving at a snail's pace though the middle of the water. They seemed like they were either idiots or pussies, walking through the centers of canals.

The day after Christmas, Third Squad from First Platoon went out on patrol. About a dozen men, including squad leader Allen Thomas, William Yeske, and Jason Johnston.

Steve Towery was out on that patrol. It was his first deployment. He was from Fayetteville but grew up in a non-military family. Being around Fort Bragg made him to want to join the Army, so he did. He'd gone in for a Ranger contract but washed out from an injury and ended up in the 82nd, arriving at Bravo Company just a few months before the deployment was set to begin.

He never truly settled into the company and was always just a bit on the outside of things because he'd arrived so late, never really bonding with the group. He was one of the first men to go home for mid-deployment leave and had been out of Afghanistan when the Halloween Zombie Massacre happened. Just one more thing he missed out on. To be honest, he didn't necessarily consider what he'd done thus far to even count as a deployment in his mind.

Rudy "Doc" Ponce was the medic on that patrol. Doc, a born-and-bred Texan, graduated from high school in 2007 but had signed up with a buddy for the Army a year earlier in what's known as a delayed entry program. He was in the Junior Reserve Officers' Training Corps in high school but one year had shit grades so he wasn't able to travel with his high school's drill team to the national championships. He learned his lesson and boosted his grades after that.

He had planned from the beginning to go Airborne and then to Ranger school and join the elite Ranger Regiment. At basic training he realized he didn't have it in writing anywhere that he had been promised Ranger school when he signed up. He asked his drill instructor about it and the guy told him, Yeah, sure, it's guaranteed, trust me, now go away. When he graduated boot camp he was sent to Airborne and assigned to Fort Bragg. No Ranger school for Doc. If it ain't in writing, it ain't true in the Army.

Doc showed up to 2-508 while they were on deployment and waited for them to get back. He thus joined Bravo Company at the very beginning of the workup for the Arghandab deployment.

Jordan Flake, too, was part of that patrol. Flake was a tall, handsome kid, the oldest of four brothers who were all athletic and played sports in high school. Although he was skinny in high school. Flake bulked up and at times might easily have passed as a bodybuilder with a trim waist and more than 230 pounds on his frame. It was part of his genetic stock. One of his brothers at the time boasted a thirty-two-inch waist even as he tipped the scales at 275 pounds. Flake said one time he just gave up during a training session after seeing his brother squat a bar full of weights at the gym as if it were nothing.

Flake had a rough go of it as a young man. He remembers his parents had a rocky relationship and then a separation, and he lived his life insisting he would be loyal, loving, and someone you can depend on in any situation. He would be true to others.

In the Arghandab, they were moving cautiously and according to the cues they learned from the EOD team. Sergeant Allen Thomas was the squad leader. William Yeske was the radio-telephone operator (RTO), so he was responsible for wearing a heavy radio in his backpack. He was great at using the device, and the radio is often the lifeblood of a patrol—it's the way air strikes and mortars are called in, and the way you call a helicopter to evacuate casualties on a bad day. One of the crummy things about being good with a radio is that you're needed on every patrol. Not only was Yeske the RTO, he was also EMT-certified—not a full-blown medic, but still useful. So Yeske seemed to be constantly out of the wire and walking around.

Third Squad of First Platoon was out on what some of them thought was a so-called presence patrol, the kind to let the Taliban know that they were in town. In a COIN environment that kind of patrol is like cops on the beat, letting the locals know they were going to be ever-present. Those patrols are also about giving the local residents some peace of mind, developing relationships and building up some trust so the Afghans might point out where the bombs were rather than going out and planting them.

Captain Adam Armstrong was the company commander, the one who ultimately had the say in much of what Bravo Company did in that small area they were responsible for. The company commander had at his disposal multiple platoons, and each of those platoons had within it multiple squads. In some military operations, platoons operate with semi autonomy, but because of the nature of Bravo's deployment, Armstrong had a closer hold on the units under his command. He was the type of man who was happy to have a hand in everything, with his indomitable work ethic and compulsion to do the utmost in any situation.

Armstrong wouldn't have sent any unit out on such an unspecified mission as a presence patrol, though. He had an unspoken contract with the men that if he was sending them out it was going to be for more of a reason than just to walk around waiting to get blown up. He believed that if his men thought they were out on just a presence patrol they might get relaxed, allow themselves to get lackadaisical. Armstrong did his best to make sure they knew the reason they were out there, but a difficult reality of war, and one that sits heavily on the consciences of leaders in combat, is that there isn't always alignment between what unit leaders command and what the rank and file hear. Sometimes it can seem impossible to get the reasons for a patrol across to each and every man in their orders.

"If they get killed because they misinterpreted it, that's even worse," Armstrong said.

The real reason Armstrong had sent them out there, in part, was to scope out a mud-walled compound a few hundred meters away from COP Ware. Armstrong believed it was the place from which the Taliban could most easily attack the Americans' base. It was—or had the potential to be—a tactical jewel for the Taliban.

The squad was about eight hundred meters out from the COP, maybe less. It was the distance you might walk to get a cup of coffee in the civilian world. They were making their way toward the mud-walled compound to assess it, but the tactics they employed were running on some inertia from common tactics for patrolling in Iraq, for Iraqi architecture. When patrolling through Iraq, every so often units would find a house or a building, scale the wall, and take a pause on the rooftop to overlook the terrain. A small unit can keep hunkered down behind the low parapet found on top of many Iraqi buildings. That wall acts as a screen so a unit can't be easily watched and, what's more, the wall is usually constructed so it might stop at least a few incoming rounds. Maybe that's what they'd do here.

They decided to go into a walled compound, but it wasn't Iraq, it was Afghanistan. It was about four in the afternoon, and because it was late December, the sun was dropping in the sky.

The Taliban lured them right into position. There wasn't anything overt and it went unnoticed at the time, but in retrospect, it became clear as day how the Taliban moved Third Squad to just the right spot, step-by-step. They capitalized on the soldiers' relative unfamiliarity with the specifics of the environment.

A persistent nightmare of combat, an ever-present specter of a veteran's life, is the clairvoyance of hindsight. Things are crystal clear when it's over. Afterward, the evidence seems obvious, but at the time, not at all. In the then and there, the guys couldn't see that they were being pushed, steered, led down a path toward an IED. A broken branch of a tree here, some bent grass there, gentle ways that the Taliban nudged the patrol down a path like water in a creek bed. The Taliban caressed Bravo right into place.

The squad wasn't taking the easy route as they walked—that's one of the first lessons they'd learned in infantry patrolling. That would be dumb. That would be doing just what the Taliban wanted them to do. No, they were taking the hard route, hopping over walls and wading through canals. But the Taliban knows infantry tactics, too, and knew what it meant for infantrymen to look for the hard route. They knew smart, well-trained infantrymen will not take the easy route.

At the same time, the route can't be too hard, it can't be impossible to navigate. So the Taliban laid out a Goldilocks path for Bravo to follow. It wasn't easy, and it wasn't impossibly hard, it was just right. The pièce de résistance was where the Taliban's custom-made path took the Americans to the wall and into the compound. The squad didn't go to the lowest gap in the wall, the place where it looked like somebody might have jumped over before. And the squad didn't go to the highest spot on the wall, which would have been too much of a pain in the ass, nearly impossible. They picked the one that was just hard enough. Always choose the Goldilocks spot, where it seems just right.

Of course Third Squad proceeded with a metal detector out in front, with a low-ranking soldier working that thing, waving it back and forth like a beachcomber. By this time the Taliban knew the Americans' proficiency with metal detectors, so they wired their IEDs so the only piece of metal in it was about the size of a safety pin. One of Third Squad's main precautionary measures was rendered meaningless.

The squad had a team of Air Force EOD guys along with them, Jordan Flake remembers, but they weren't out in front clearing a path. They were around in case an IED was found, but what the hell, what if that IED was found by stepping on it? What good would those EOD experts be then?

Bravo hopped over that perfect spot in the outer wall, all of them walking in the wake of the metal detector's path. They didn't go inside any of the buildings on the compound—that would have been foolish.

They prepared to hunker down for a little while in that compound, Iraq-style, and send a team up on a rooftop to go into overwatch. Yeske, the radio operator, was struggling to get his radio to work. The mud in those Afghan walls was so full of iron that the radio could hardly receive a signal once he was inside the compound wall. So he busied himself with taking a tiny three-foot antenna off the radio and attaching the one that was ten feet long. Pain in the ass is what that was, and it took a lot of concentration.

Jordan Flake remembers just before they entered the compound Jason Johnston asked him for a dip of tobacco. Flake had an extra tin, so he threw the entire thing to his buddy and told him to keep it. Johnston seemed to always be broke and didn't have his own dip that day. Flake had also recently given him a pair of Oakley combat boots, an extra pair he'd brought along and could afford to give to his friend.

Flake had a special spot in his heart for Jason Johnston. He first met him when Flake checked into Bravo Company months earlier, back at Fort Bragg. Johnston always seemed to be broke back then, too. But he had a vehicle, and one day Flake needed to run an errand of some sort. Though he didn't even ask, Johnston just threw Flake his keys with no stipulations. He was generous with whatever he had and willing to help the new guy even as other people treated him like a new guy.

Johnston had only just recently joined Bravo Company in-country. That funky face condition, the one that let him grow a beard and got Mac all pissed off, had prevented him from deploying with them at first. The doctors wouldn't let him go. He could have easily just ridden out that excuse and skipped the whole deployment, but he fought and fought and fought and was eventually given the all clear from the doc and allowed to join Bravo in-country sometime after Halloween. Mac always had the utmost respect for Johnston after that. After knowing his friends were deployed, Johnston had begged to go into combat and fought like hell to get there. He was finally doing what he wanted to be doing: patrolling with his brothers in Afghanistan.

Back at the compound in the Arghandab, Flake and Johnston and Towery started walking up along a wall. One of them had grabbed a branch of a tree for balance and they were passing it from person to person so everyone could keep their footing.

Flake remembered that he was close to Johnston, could have given him a hug. Then he turned and took maybe two steps.

Yeske, who was tinkering with the radio, heard a *pop-POW!* No. It was more like a *crack-BOOM!*

The first thing, the smaller sound—the *crack*—was a detonator going off, a small explosion that sets off an even bigger one. And that first little explosion made a sharp sound just a fraction of a second before the huge jug of homemade explosive went off. It was a snare drum followed by a kick drum.

Yeske'd been messing with his radio antenna, but in that moment of the explosion he turned his head and looked right at it, saw a dust cloud go up. He remembers thinking in an instant it was kind of funny that he could see a shock wave sweeping over the scrub brush, rippling across the dirt. The shock wave was coming right at him. As the wave sprinted at him, he thought, *Holy shit, it just happened, this is it.*

Flake remembered that all of a sudden his ears went completely numb. The SAW gun he had been carrying was thrown from his hands and he was knocked out. When he came to—who knows how long that was?—he was on the ground and he opened his eyes and he saw Towery's foot sitting right in front of him, but no other sign of Towery, just that foot there by itself. Flake was missing a sleeve off his combat uniform, but his arm seemed OK.

Towery remembered flying through the air, face-planting on the ground, looking down at his mangled foot, and telling himself nothing had happened. He could just deny reality, no big deal. Then, on second thought, that wasn't too smart a notion, so he started fumbling around his individual first aid kit for a tourniquet.

And Flake heard Sergeant Allen Thomas screaming out, "Urgent surgical!"

Staff Sergeant Hill had stayed behind in the COP just eight hundred meters away to handle the myriad pains in the ass a platoon sergeant has to deal with on a deployment, everything from making sure the guys have enough ammo to making sure the satellite phone has batteries. He heard the blast, looked at the compound, saw a cloud rise up, and before the explosion stopped echoing through the valley, he dropped whatever BS he was doing and went into a full sprint to the tactical operations center (TOC). The TOC is the nerve center of operations. It is also where the company's radios and communications tools are housed. Hill had to get to the radio to learn what had happened. Sergeant Rob Musil had sprinted there, too. He and Hill gathered around the radio.

Eight hundred meters away at the blast site, it wasn't that Yeske's brain was moving slowly. No, it seemed to be moving at just the right pace. The shock wave had rolled over him, through him, having dissipated enough that it didn't knock him to the ground. That shock wave was maybe the way a dog feels as its shaking water off its coat, a buzzing shimmying that moves from one end of the body to the other, the way the dog shakes its head, its back, then its tail. That kind of shock wave is fast, but it's not instantaneous. It gives a soldier time to linger for a moment with the electric sensation of it traveling up his body.

Yeske's first thought after the wave and the accompanying cloud of dirt kicked up was a sense of wonder that he was the only person around who was still standing. It seemed that everyone else had fallen to the ground or hit the deck.

That's an odd thing, how was that possible? he thought, slowly. Well, it was no time to wonder. It was time to stay calm, to do his job and get on the radio and speak clearly.

Even in non-stressful times a radio operator can sound like he's screaming into the microphone if he doesn't take his time with the field radio. A good RTO trains himself to take a breath and exhale before talking. That way he doesn't force too much air through his windpipe. That little technique prevents a guy from sounding frantic. And a good RTO has mastered that by force of habit. So Yeske exhaled. He pushed the talk button on his handset and told the TOC that they'd hit an IED at the last position he'd radioed in a few minutes ago.

Yeske did some quick calculations in his head and made an estimate of what he thought the results of that blast might be. He reported one urgent surgical, maybe more. Getting that urgent surgical call over the radio was the start of the process to get a medevac chopper in the air and en route. That was the most important thing. Who cared if Yeske knew the details. The most important thing was to get that chopper on the way.

Back in the TOC they weren't sure for a second if they should take Yeske seriously. That was a big fucking boom and a big fucking cloud and now Yeske was calling in an urgent surgical, but he sounded as cool as the DJ from a drive-time radio show.

Armendariz was listening to the radio, had heard the boom. He was a team leader and geared up for the Quick Reaction Force (QRF), the immediate backup that gets there first after something bad happens. He listened as Yeske's voice on the radio told the QRF to watch out where they walked, giving them as detailed information as possible on where the patrol had stepped.

Every inch to the left or right of that path could have another bomb. *Fuck, this is the type of fight we're in?* Armendariz thought to himself.

They hadn't had any extensive training or experience with these bombs, the kind that would become so familiar in the coming year to troops deployed in Afghanistan, things laid into the ground and waiting for them to step on. Yet here it was. The full weight of their new area of operations was on top of them.

Armstrong was in the TOC and he turned toward his hooch, the place where his cot and all his gear was waiting. On second thought, that would take too long, so he told others in the TOC to just go. Mac was already in his kit. Hill and Musil threw on their gear and in a matter of moments were out the door of the TOC. They collected the QRF squad and the group of them were sprinting, sprinting, sprinting toward the explosion. (From then on Armstrong made sure to have his kit sitting right next to his desk in the TOC. There's never any time to lose. Lesson learned. It's still one of his regrets to this day.)

In hindsight, from that perfect vantage, maybe it wasn't the best idea in the world to make an all-out sprint to some guys who had just been blown up by bombs hidden in the ground. Odds were that, as Yeske had said, there were more IEDs somewhere between here and there. But at the time, it seemed like the right thing to do, the only thing to do. Men were hurt. Men needed help. And it was only eight hundred meters out.

While things roiled less than a kilometer away, Armstrong was stuck in the TOC working the radios, but that didn't take up 100 percent of his time. The moments between listening to radio chatter and helping to coordinate the response was filled with thinking. Those moments were steeped in the burdens of *what if*. They let Armstrong gather his thoughts and reconsider tactics, his men, his mission. He began to consider what had just happened, he stewed, retreated into his mind to think about what he'd done wrong, what he could have done differently. Those moments let him figure out all the ways that he had caused this, or at least figure out all the ways that he could put the blame on himself. Armstrong went deep into his head. *Was that a new IED or an old one?*

Is this unknown casualty hurt so bad he can't pull through?

Thus the company commander wondered about some unknown casualty with unknown wounds. His thoughts raced from the past, what had gone wrong, to the present. What was happening out there to his men that he wasn't there to see? Then thoughts went into the future. *That unknown casualty might not make it.* And as Armstrong thought about his soldier, he also started thinking about the rest of the unit.

Armstrong worried that his company had suffered its first death, months into the deployment. It had been so long since they'd arrived in Afghanistan that a casualty at this point could make the unit unravel. His mind raced as he thought about it all, with plenty of time to think, which isn't so good.

Doc Ponce, the medic, was at the rear of the patrol, back with Allen Thomas, the squad leader. They both went down with the blast, knocked on their asses. Doc remembers the blast as a brown thing that came at him, a blob of drab color.

Next thing Doc knew he was seeing stars. Instead of facing forward, the way he'd been when the bomb went off, he'd been spun around and was staring at a dirt wall. But he didn't know he'd been spun around. He just felt like he'd been hit in the head with a sledgehammer and that somebody seemed to have quickly built a wall in his way.

That's peculiar, he remembered thinking. *Where'd that wall come from?*

How peculiar that he would use the word "peculiar" in his mind at such a moment. But such is the way the human mind copes with a completely incomprehensible and new experience.

Doc just gazed at the wall, looked from the ground to the top of the brown mass looming in front of him, with painful slowness. Things were all mushy and logy in his head. He couldn't hear anything. His ears hadn't even started ringing yet, there was nothing. He could just see that brown, packed-dirt wall in front of him and it seemed to rise up forever. Doc's brain had been rebooted like a computer, and he was still waiting for all the applications to start back up again.

Then all of a sudden his brain started working. Doc got to his feet, trying to figure out why he was facing a wall. He'd been peppered with shrapnel, no, maybe it was bits of rock and dust—you could never tell with IEDs. But he knew he wasn't hurt, wasn't really hurt. That much he knew.

Doc's ears then started ringing, but not so much that he couldn't hear. That's when he heard the screaming. Everyone was screaming for him.

When a soldier's hurt, the first thing he yells for is the medic. It's one of the few things that's just like in the movies. In training they yell for the doc first thing, and that's what happened here. As if conjuring a wizard, they summoned the one guy around who has mystical powers when it comes to combat trauma, knows how to do something worthwhile in the aftermath of an explosion.

Doc Ponce was up on his feet and he could hear the screams, but he still couldn't figure out why there was that mud wall in front of him. As he tried to resolve that mystery he just directed his legs to run toward the screaming.

The first man he reached was Towery, whose foot had been taken off. Yeske had given the radio to someone else, picked up the EMT bag, and was already digging through it for bandages. Towery was still fumbling away, trying to put on his own tourniquet, when Yeske and Doc told him to let them handle it. What with the foot problem, Towery hadn't taken note of the various shrapnel wounds on his arms and hands. He realized his foot looked like hamburger and smelled like barbecue. Oh Lord, everything below the knee felt like it was on fire, too. It was all singed and smoldering. With practiced fingers, Doc put a tourniquet on Towery's leg and cinched it down to stop the blood pumping out of that suddenly worthless end of his leg.

Allen Thomas had been knocked back even harder than Doc. He had been thrown into a wall and inside that ballistic helmet his soft brain tissue bounced all around in a split second. The delicate pudding of the brain, protected by a thick layer of shock-absorbing liquid, bounced against the front and the back and the sides of the skull, the ballistic helmet barely providing any protection, and all that bouncing around of his brain likely broke apart some of the things that made Allen himself, synapses and dendrites and the very essence of him being shaken apart. Those kinds of injuries can be slow to show themselves, though. They can take months or years. In the moment, despite his foggy head, Allen tried to organize the squad.

Where was Johnston?

Johnston. All those nights of drinking and singing country songs together. Johnston, the one who introduced Allen to Danica. He was his best friend. Where was he? Allen was yelling for him and seemed to have lost control, his brain so banged up that the sheer force of his willpower couldn't overcome it. So much confusion. Allen was almost frantic in his effort to get control and to find Johnston.

Yeske recognized that the problem wasn't so much the devastation inside the compound, guys thrown all over the place like rag dolls, Towery with his bad foot, Allen struggling to gain control. The bulk of the yelling was coming from the other side of the compound's wall. But Yeske couldn't see what had happened over there.

The maybe fifteen-foot compound wall had its top five feet blown off by the IED, and somehow the blast sent Johnston and a soldier named Will Ross over the top. The screaming was Ross pleading for help on the other side.

Doc finally shook off the waviness and wonkiness and attempted to charge out to the guys on the other side of the wall, to reach the screams of "Doc!" But when he tried to run out of the compound he was stopped by Allen Thomas. The 250-pound squad leader was working to impose control on the chaos of the situation and of his own self. Thomas grabbed Doc.

"Where are you going?" Allen asked, according to Doc.

"You got this here, I'm going outside this wall."

"Fuck no, there could be another charge," Thomas said, even as they heard Ross screaming.

Doc wanted to get out there, to do the one thing he was put on God's green earth to do, to fix soldiers broken in combat. But Allen Thomas had Doc in his grip and told him he had to wait for the team to clear a path so nobody else would get blown up.

Damn, Doc remembers thinking, *those guys had cleared a path into the fucking compound and didn't find the bomb that just blew up, so what's the use in waiting for them again?*

Doc knew Johnston was over there but couldn't hear him hollering at all—and had to get to him. That wasn't just some soldier but one of his friends. Man, Johnston was *everybody's* friend.

Back before the deployment, when Doc was still new to the unit, he and Johnston were drinking together one night at the barracks and one of the other Bravo Company medics started giving Doc shit because he wasn't really one of the boys. He didn't have a deployment under his belt and blah blah blah. But Johnston, the same Johnston who was on the other side of that wall maybe bleeding out, that same Johnston had quietly told Doc Ponce that night at the barracks that he was definitely a no-shit member of Bravo Company. It was the first time anyone had told Ponce he officially had been accepted, was part of the team.

Johnston had even cheerfully offered retribution.

"Let's go fuck that guy up," Johnston had said mischievously.

"Nah," Ponce said, and had just kept on drinking.

He'd had the best retribution he could get. He had Johnston's approval while drinking beer at the barracks. And now here in Afghanistan, Doc was sitting on his ass waiting while Johnston was likely suffering on the other side of that dirt wall and Ross was screaming for help?

Doc called up the soldier with the mine detector and told Allen he would, sure as shit, stay in the cleared path, he'd step in the guy's god-damn bootprints for ensured safety if that's what was needed, but he had to get out there.

"Follow the footsteps, for the love of God, don't go outside the foot-steps," Thomas told him, and turned him loose.

By this time the other men in the compound were coming around, figuring out their injuries. Thomas stumbled from man to man doing his best to survey the situation, but not really acting like himself. The 240 gunner had been peppered by the blast, his eyes filled with dirt and debris, and he kept saying he couldn't see anything, he couldn't see anything, he couldn't see anything.

There was little thought of worry about a follow-on attack. The explosion—the first of that kind they'd experienced—had so rattled them that they didn't even think the bomb could be the kickoff of a complex assault. The unit instead devolved into figuring out who was hurt.

Looking back on it years later, anybody from Bravo will say this was the first big event of the deployment, maybe the defining moment for them. It was the first time they realized they weren't invincible. It was the first time they realized their tactics weren't perfect. It was the first time they realized they might not be able to shoot back at the enemy. It was brand-new for them, getting blown up like that. Whenever an unexpected variable is introduced into an equation, along with it comes massive confusion. A unit trains over and over and over again to do things a certain way when it hits the fan. With enough repetition, tactics become second nature. That's what made the Halloween Zombie Massacre so great. Everyone's training kicked in and they were able to execute a real-life variation on a training theme. They'd trained to deal with IEDs, yes, but they'd trained for the types of IEDs prevalent in Iraq.

From 2004 to early 2009 the military's focus was on two kinds of IEDs, the types of IEDs likely found in Iraq, according to Lieutenant General Mike Oates, who headed the Joint IED Defeat Organization at the time of Bravo's deployment. There were the IEDs made from connecting together old artillery shells so they'd all blow up at the same time, and there were explosively formed penetrators (EFPs) that could blast through inches-thick armor.

JIEDDO had first been established in 2006 to research IEDs, find ways to prevent them from harming US troops, and teach troops about best practices and how to use new technology—equipment like mine detectors—as it was developed. But once again, Iraq and Afghanistan were not the same. In Iraq the bombs seemed to be manufactured, and in Afghanistan they seemed more homemade, Oates said.

Iraq's artillery shells and EFPs had to be engineered. Buried artillery shells gave off a fantastic metallic signature, which a metal detector could pick up. Or the bombs would be detonated by radio signals or remote controls, which could be blocked with fancy electronic devices.

Afghanistan on the other hand was a land where the IEDs were made up of homemade explosive material, nitrogen-based fertilizers and the like. Since there was no way to detect the explosive itself, troops had to learn to look more closely for bombs. Metal detectors had to be used almost like divining rods, with utmost care and delicacy. And those Afghan bombs were often triggered by a trip wire or a plate buried in the ground that would touch off a detonation when the slightest pressure was applied.

General Oates remembered the Arghandab around 2009 and said the place presented a unique challenge because the landscape lent itself to planting IEDs. Thanks to all the cover from the orchards and vegetation as well as the canals, hedgerows, and ubiquitous walls, the nameless, faceless enemy could just watch and wait and learn and then, when the chance presented itself, plant bombs to blow up the Americans.

"Civilians think we're supermen and should be beating these guys into submission," Oates said, but the enemy was crafty and wise and knew how to fight and how to place booby traps. "A lot of these lessons were passed along from the Russian occupation," he said.

In 2009 JIEDDO was still focused in large part on Iraq, where on some occasions there had been one thousand IEDs reported in a month, Oates said. "There were damn few IEDs in Afghanistan compared with Iraq," he said, adding that Iraq still had the focus of the institution and much of the staffing and funding as well.

In mid-2009 and into 2010, Defense Secretary Robert Gates shifted JIEDDO's focus from Iraq to Afghanistan, Oates said. He remembers commanders in Afghanistan asking for ever more drones to provide surveillance. But as with manpower and other types of equipment, the shift to Afghanistan would take time.

"It's stating the obvious, DoD is a big ship and if you're going to turn it 90 degrees you're not going to do it quickly," he said. "They moved the institution about as fast as it could go."

Bravo Company, though, had no time to wait for the ship to turn around, because they were in the middle of it all. They didn't get the drones that could always surveil the ground, and they didn't get the benefit of JIEDDO because all that would come a little later to the Arghandab and to the rest of the country.

The IED Bravo hit that day in the compound had likely been a home-made explosive.

"One regret I have, still have to this day," Oates said a decade after the explosion, "we have not figured out how to detect homemade explosive."

This was where Bravo Company found themselves the day after Christmas, 2009.

These Afghan bombs, IEDs blowing up like this, was essentially uncharted territory, so there was confusion. Training for responding to an enemy attack involves positive action, a response to a stimulus. But responding to a bomb blowing up—what's the right answer? Stay in place and not step on other bombs? Get out of the area as fast as possible to get away from a possible follow-on attack?

Allen Thomas started wresting control and dealing with the tactical realities at hand. He pushed guys out to security positions as best as he could arrange, with men facing outward in all directions to reckon with the possibility of an attack. Yeske remembers Thomas's big voice as unimaginably hoarse from taking a mouthful of dirt in the blast. Nobody thinks about getting a swig of water at a time like this, and Thomas set to work, growling sandpapery orders as best he could.

While Hill and Musil and the team were sprinting their way from the COP, the men at the compound were just beginning to set in security and Doc was finally figuring out how to get to Jason Johnston with his unknown injuries on the other side of that godforsaken wall.

Doc followed the guy with a metal detector out of the compound. Inside the compound, Towery wasn't looking so bad even though he was missing a foot and some fingers. He had his tourniquet on and the helos were on the way, so he was good, Yeske figured. With that taken care of,

Yeske decided to follow Doc out of the compound, but as he did with Doc, Thomas grabbed him and said no way Yeske was going outside the wall.

After promises of following in footprints were made and reluctant agreement was given, Yeske was finally allowed out. It had only been seconds since everything happened, though it already seemed like an eternity. Outside the compound Doc and Yeske saw that Ross had taken up a security position, pointing his rifle out away from everything, out into the unknown, in case the Taliban did have something more in store.

When it's just one man by himself out there alongside a fellow wounded man, he's got no good choices to make. He can't just focus on his buddy, no matter how bad the injury. He can't do that because his number one priority is to defend the position against any enemy who might be approaching. If Ross didn't provide security, then they both could be overrun and shot down easily.

But at the same time, when a buddy's been injured, he could die in a matter of minutes or even seconds if there's arterial bleeding, the heart pumping fresh blood straight out of the body like a geyser. The soldier has no good choice. In the seconds between the blast and the arrival of Doc, Ross had chosen to repel any attackers. It was a sound tactical choice, despite the lack of any evident Taliban fighters taking advantage of the chaos.

As soon as Doc saw Johnston he knew it was bad. There's no worse feeling for a medic than to see a comrade, a friend, and to know—as a professional and an expert—that he's not going to be able to save the guy.

Fuck it, Doc thought. He was going to try. So he got to work.

Yeske looked at Johnston and had thoughts similar to Doc's: *Holy shit, there's no way this guy is surviving.* Yeske asked Doc what he could do, and Doc said—frankly—he wasn't sure. How about working on that leg there?

Now that they were on the other side of the wall, they heard Johnston's voice—it hadn't been loud enough to hear in the compound. He was telling them how much it hurt. He'd been ripped apart by the blast, a leg taken off and the other one a mass of smashed and pulverized bone, barely hanging on. His abdomen had been opened up, the force of the blast directed up and into his body.

Doc now knelt on the ground by his head and Yeske was down by his feet. Johnston's intestines kept coming out onto the ground. Yeske couldn't do much with them, though. There wasn't any place to put them if he scooped them up, no place to set them or tuck them to keep them clean and organized. They seemed to be everywhere.

As Yeske looked at the shattered body, he had a thought: *This guy looks like he took the whole blast, and if that's the case he protected the other men in the squad. He saved their lives.*

Yeske then had a momentary theological, philosophical, meta-physical meditation about the human body and the human spirit, about man's untold and mysterious capabilities to endure. Johnston had saved their lives. Perhaps there was something that could save him. And Yeske hung his hopes on the capacity still there in this sentient and yet-living being. Johnston was still there, despite the unimaginably shattered body.

"I don't see how he can survive, but I have no idea what the capacity of a human being is to hold on," Yeske said later.

Besides all that, Yeske reminded himself he wasn't a goddamn doctor or even a full-fledged medic and he took temporary comfort in his relative ignorance, hoping that what had seemed so obvious to him at first—that Johnston had no chance—was simply an ill-informed observation.

Yeske decided he needed to listen to Doc and do whatever was humanly possible, whatever he could muster to help Johnston.

Doc told him to check the tourniquets he had somehow applied to Johnston's stumps. Then Doc told him to talk to Johnston. And when Yeske focused on Johnston, the wounded man asked the question so many guys who have been blown up ask: "Is my dick still there?"

Yeske was amazed Johnston had the wherewithal to ask a question, any question at all. He was happy to give the guy hope and would have said "yeah" no matter what.

But he looked down just to see, and to his amazement, amid the mangled and missing legs and shattered pelvis, was Johnston's stuff. Fully intact. Yeske looked at him and, amazed and with honesty, said, "It's there. We're going to be laughing about this one day."

That seemed a major comfort to Johnston, a man otherwise torn apart.

Then, with little else to do, Yeske decided to pile up the intestines as best he could on Johnston's remaining midsection and wait. Doc gave

Johnston a shot of morphine and the shattered man went white, that ashen god-awful white that means the wounded is on the way out of this world. And he faded away.

Doc, lacking any other recourse, started giving him CPR, the last thing he could try.

Hill and Musil arrived with Second Squad about fifteen minutes after they sprinted out of the compound. It was a full-out eight-hundred-meter sprint that took fifteen minutes. On a running track, it would have taken them less than two. But in the Arghandab, with all the walls and canals and things to be bounded across, jumped over, or climbed, it took a painful eternity. When they arrived, they saw so many men in the compound sitting there reeling, shell-shocked, with helmets off.

Mac was one of the first to arrive. He saw Allen Thomas sitting off to the side now after having set up basic security positions. He was so shaken he was crying. Mac was the first sergeant, so he went over to him to tell him to get it together, especially right there in the middle of it all, right there where it all happened. They were "on the X" in military-speak, and it was time for Thomas to pull it together and lead.

"This is a roller coaster and you can't get off until it's finished," he told Thomas. "You can't do this on the X."

One of them pulled the ring on a violet-colored smoke grenade and threw it so the rescue helicopters could know where to come. Hill went out to check on Johnston and saw his pupils were dilated all the way, a signal he was dead. Towery was loopy by that point, having lost a foot and gotten all hopped up on morphine. He was also self-consciously in bullshit mode, he later said, trying to be peppy and witty in the face of it all. He looked at Hill and said, "I think you're an asshole. But you're a damn good platoon sergeant."

It was good for a laugh, a joke only a guy hopped up on morphine and adrenaline would dare say to his sergeant.

Mac looked at Towery's foot with a sort of approval and congratulated him on his war wound, which Towery remembers thinking at the time was pretty damn nifty.

"Welcome to the club," the grizzled first sergeant told him.

Then out of the sky, from a helicopter that showed up like an apparition, came an Air Force pararescue jumper (PJ), one of that branch's special operators who are trained to rescue downed pilots.

Yeske first took notice of the helicopter when a scorching-hot spent casing from the helicopter's machine gun fell on him. The helo had been laying down suppressive fire on anything that looked like it might cause trouble, and one of those smoking empty casings fell right into Yeske's gear, burning his skin. Then came the Air Force PJ, who roped down from out of the sky because there was no place they felt safe setting down the helo.

Somebody pulled Doc off Johnston, he doesn't remember for sure who, and told him CPR wasn't of any use. Johnston was gone.

The PJ descended onto the scene and made his way over to Johnston, who looked to be in most-immediate need. Musil waved the guy off with a signal that there was nothing to be done, then they made their way over to Towery, who'd been tourniqueted and morphined, and they helped load him into a hoist to get lifted up into the helo by a winch. The men cleared a hasty landing zone for another helicopter, and they loaded Johnston up in that one. Word got back to the COP somehow that Johnston was still cogent, still alive, still had a chance, Armstrong remembered. Who knows where that came from. Hope springs eternal, but Johnston was already dead.

After the wounded and dead were loaded up in the helos, the Air Force team flew away, and the remainder of the squad and Hill and Musil's guys fell back on the compound until it started turning dark. They hadn't moved. Johnston was gone.

Hill and Musil's guys stayed behind and sent Allen Thomas's squad back to the COP to recover from the day's events.

A squad had to stay behind because Bravo Company needed to do an after-action investigation of the scene to figure out the Taliban's tactics. They also had to find Johnston's night vision goggles, which had been lost in the melee. One of the unfailing rules of the Army is: Don't lose any gear.

And they had to find part of Johnston's leg that was still missing. So they settled into a defensive position to wait for daylight.

The next morning, the sun came up and right there in front of one of the men was a large portion of Johnston's severed leg. It had been lying there all night, close enough to be seen in plain sight if they'd just had some light. That freaked the soldier out, not just to have his dead friend's leg right there, but to know it'd been there all night, almost close enough to touch.

They cleaned that leg up, and whatever else they could find. That's when Hill had a few minutes to look around and see how the Taliban had steered them into the bomb, led them right along. The bent grass and almost invisible pathway, the perfect path to lure them in. It was a hell of a way to learn a lesson.

"You walk tall until you're humbled," said Nick Armendariz, who remembers thinking that he wanted the Arghandab to show them what it could offer.

It had.

CHAPTER 11

AFGHANISTAN WINTER

Jason Johnston died on December 26, 2009. He was Allen Thomas's friend, and it got into Allen's head in a metaphysical sense. The blast also affected him in a physical sense. It concussed him enough to get noted in his medical record. After Mac's talk with him at the compound, Allen was squarely on the roller coaster and determined to ride it to the end. He refused to take time away from his squad there in-country, he refused to sit out a single patrol.

That post-Christmas explosion was the first action from the Taliban in the Arghandab. This was the first contact Bravo Company had with the enemy there and it had been nothing like the Halloween Zombie Massacre. They hadn't even seen the Taliban, just the devastation that the Taliban could conjure.

Allen selflessly made space for other people's grief and tamped down his own. He still knew the other men in his squad had wives and kids and families back home, so he didn't use the satellite phone very often. When he did, or over messages on the computer with its creepingly slow internet connection, he connected with Danica. He made space for her grief. She had lost a good friend, and Allen allowed her that. Back then, she was still young and hadn't experienced loss on a grand scale, and Johnston was the first person she'd known to leave the earth with no natural reason to go.

Allen was her comfort even though they still didn't have any kind of official relationship and it seemed their future was still in question. Danica's grief was real, she felt it in her bones. And yet she knew nothing about what it sounded like or looked like to lose a friend to an explosion. She knew nothing of what it smells like when a friend's body is opened up and charred. She didn't know the details of Johnston's death. Allen hadn't shared much with her, so she didn't know what she didn't know.

"Whatever you need, I'm here," she remembers Allen telling her. So, like so many others in his life, she let him be there. She depended on him. She had no idea of the ways death eats away at a soldier, even a rock like Allen. His wasn't just a personal loss but also a professional failure. He had been the squad leader and Johnston had died. He was responsible for his friend and now Johnston was gone. Allen seemed to feel he had no one he could share that with, and Danica didn't know to ask him about it. She didn't know what she didn't know.

Years later, she doesn't remember which year, on December 26, they sat in a grocery store parking lot as she cried about the anniversary of their lost friend. In that parking lot she suddenly realized Jason Johnston was Allen's soldier, not hers. He was Allen's friend. She had taken all that space for grief and left Allen with so little of his own. She realized he'd taken all that emotion—hers and his and the squad's—and put it into a little box somewhere inside himself and closed the top.

For Danica, back home seemingly by herself, Johnston's demise made real what before was only theory: Death accompanies war. When an infantryman deploys there's always the possibility he won't come back, but that feels remote and vague, especially to people who haven't ever lost anyone they love to combat. In twenty years of war in Afghanistan where more than 750,000 troops deployed, just about 2,000 troops died.

Yet each of those few thousand who died had families, loved ones, and friends. They were all killed in ways their squad remembers, in ways their squadmates can still see, hear, and smell if they concentrate hard enough. Sometimes they remember it if they don't concentrate at all.

Danica hadn't ever lost anyone like that. She hadn't even known of someone who'd come back from combat wounded. She'd only ever seen combat on TV or in movies, distant fiction, not reality. Even in life her experience with war to this point was unreal. Danica's sister had married a soldier and a few years back they'd welcomed him home after some uneventful few months deployed overseas. It was happy, picturesque, a Hallmark-card sort of thing. It was pleasant, yes, that's probably the best word for it. It was an unharmed soldier coming home from a deployment with no obvious loss, no grief, no pain. It was happy. War had remained a distant fiction, not reality.

* * *

In the Arghandab, Bravo Company now faced reality, too.

Most of the company was ready to get back into it, to start patrolling as usual. But it seemed to the senior leaders like Armstrong and Mac that about one in three men thought they needed to take a beat, recover a bit. That percentage was way too high, too many who wanted time to recover. The first death in a unit can cause it to fall apart, especially if it comes after a few uneventful months so there's no expectation of combat trauma. It can make a unit shy away from battle. Armstrong and Mac wouldn't have any of that. They demanded everyone get back out there on patrol immediately.

Lieutenant Colonel Jenio came down to the COP from the battalion base, came to that COP there in the middle of the radishes. He told Bravo Company they were on the hunt, reminded them of why they were there, to fight the enemy. They were now in the fight they had trained for. The fight they had wanted. The fight they had gotten. It was imperative not only from a mental health perspective but—more importantly—for the mission itself that they get back out there quickly, Armstrong remembered.

They'd been bloodied, but they had to show they hadn't been beaten and hadn't lost a step. The Taliban certainly was watching to see how they'd react. Bravo needed to be a machine, an ever-grinding device capable of taking whatever came at them without stopping. They were all on the roller coaster that Mac had told Allen Thomas about. There was no way to get off until the ride was over.

It's quite a feeling in combat, to know that if your unit slows its pace it won't make the deployment any slower nor any easier. In fact it does the opposite, it emboldens the enemy to do more, to press their advantage. Any respite on your part is merely ignoring reality. It's just hiding. At best you can pass the pain on to the next unit by not patrolling, letting the area of operations fester and rot. But Bravo had been on the receiving end of that already when they took over from the Strykers.

Combat was now real for Adam Armstrong in a way it hadn't been before. Johnston was the first death under his command. The first death of one of *His Soldiers*. Sure, he'd been in places like Ramadi before and seen combat. He'd been a company XO there and driven bodies to the casualty collection point in his trunk. But those weren't men under his command. Those weren't *His Men*.

As the commanding officer of Bravo Company, he'd given the order that put Johnston at that compound, at the spot where that IED was placed. While he couldn't bear the responsibility for where each man on each patrol stepped and couldn't control their luck, he damn sure was responsible for a patrol's objective.

That first death can ruin a unit. Likewise, in a commander's mind a seed gets planted that can grow, can lead to creeping second thoughts, what-ifs. Thoughts of failure. It's always there after that first death, even if it's a still, small voice that can hardly be heard.

Armstrong was raised from those first days at West Point to be an officer focused on accomplishing the mission above all else. What they don't tell you at West Point is that you lose even if you are successful in your mission. You lose when the men under your command are hurt, maimed, killed, or broken psychologically. There's no way to really win once everything is tallied up—there's always loss. That's war. Even if the history books say you've accomplished the mission, even if there's no combat deaths, there's still loss. And it takes its toll on a person. If there's a combat death, then . . . well, then it's immediately tangible.

"Nobody tells you it's lose-lose," Armstrong said.

Back in the States, under clear blue skies with no threat of enemy contact, other commanders mention years later with pride that they brought everyone home. Armstrong resents it.

"I didn't bring everyone home, but fuck you," Armstrong wants so badly to say to these guys even as he nods his head in affirmation.

Bringing everyone home isn't the goal, goddammit. It's what you'd like to do, of course. It's not as if you want your soldiers to die, but war isn't a task where bringing everyone home is the top priority. That's the blunt, God's honest truth of it. If the goal was to bring everyone home, then you wouldn't go on patrol in the first place. You wouldn't join the infantry. You wouldn't sign up for the goddamn Army.

Johnston's death, for Armstrong—the company commander and West Point graduate—changed something. He felt he had planned and trained and prepared to this point more than anybody could believe, more than seemed possible. But Johnston's death meant he'd have to do more. That young soldier's death had to mean something.

Armstrong became even more obsessed with planning and training and preparing from then on, like a man possessed. He had to be out there on patrol not just as much as everyone else, but even more than everyone else, obsessed with taking on that risk because of the responsibility he bore personally.

The changes that swept over Armstrong after Johnston's death weren't limited to the immediate. He felt a new weight added to his body, his being. It was something else they don't tell you about at West Point. It was the weight of these troops as people, as flesh-and-blood creatures with moms and dads and sisters and wives and brothers and friends and kids and hopes and dreams. At West Point they don't tell you these men under your command aren't just yours for a few months while you're deployed to Afghanistan. Armstrong was coming to realize that having taken over Bravo Company he had also taken on an obligation for life, a responsibility for the well-being of these men. He had taken on a sacred and unbreakable bond he didn't fully understand at the time.

Bringing everyone home wasn't his goal. But he was coming to realize that on the other side of all this was an obligation—an obligation that would become an obsession once they returned home. The important thing, at the time, was that he was their commanding officer and he was in the middle of it all with them.

First Sergeant Mac barreled on because he had to. He drove the company forward, holding tight, white-knuckled, on the roller-coaster ride. But some cracks began to appear in his iron grip from the strain and stress, tiny fissures nobody else saw and that he didn't notice himself at the time. But they were there.

He and Armstrong had studied that valley as best they could with the limited time they'd had to prepare. They knew nobody had ever really taken it, even the Russians, who had done their level best. When Bravo walked into the Arghandab they weren't schooled up on these types of IEDs, the kind that target dismounted troops specifically with homemade explosives. Nobody was, not even the Defense Department's big IED research group JIEDDO. They were still paying attention to the bombs over in Iraq and had yet to refocus attention on Afghanistan and the tactics the Taliban used.

Mac had heard all the war stories from the guys who had been there before them but it didn't set in until he saw the big-bastard IED that got Johnston. Mac had seen plenty in combat before, been blown up himself, but had never seen anything like that. And when he saw it he knew, even told Armstrong, that sort of thing was the shit they were going to see every day from here on out. Mac was right.

CHAPTER 12

POWERPOINT

Down in the Arghandab after Johnston's death, down in Bravo Company's small slice of the valley, January and February were a cold and quiet time. Nothing grew in the orchards, and few locals walked the fallow fields. The temperature was cold and the landscape was cold and the people were cold. The whole place seemed the very definition of winter.

Yet Bravo Company patrolled and patrolled and patrolled though the ghostly land with the ever-present threat of death. Potentiality had become reality the day after Christmas with the loss of Johnston. Aristotle compares the relationship between activity and potentiality to the relation between wakefulness and sleep. Bravo had been awakened.

"After Johnston I was scared, oh my God," remembers Johnny, the interpreter, even though he wasn't out there for that incident. "That was the start."

Johnny had his fellow interpreters around him for support and says he was always treated like a member of the team when he was with the men from Bravo Company. But he was not a soldier, he hadn't gone through all the training they had: weapons, first aid, a combat mindset. Sure, he was a member of the team, but he was dependent on other men for his safety and security.

Interpreters slowly started to leave Bravo, recognizing the reality of the situation. They'd typically take a polite leave, graciously departing to go back to the relative safety of some other place in Afghanistan. They might quietly say "Thank you" to Bravo on their way out, but what they were thinking was, *I'm fucking outta here*. Over time, Bravo lost about half their interpreters, Johnny said. That meant more patrols for those who remained, for those like Johnny.

After that Christmas wake-up, Bravo recognized what was possible in the valley. The veterans who had been in Afghanistan before knew the fighting season had yet to arrive. Springtime was when the valley and its orchards come into bloom, turning stands of trees into dense copses thick with leaves, flowers, and fruit. Spring would spur grasses and shrubs into their full growth. Those now-bleak areas would soon be even more full of danger. But in those cold winter days no one else stepped on a bomb. No one got into a firefight. There were no casualties. In winter it's hard to plant IEDs. Rock-hard dirt and no vegetation. The Taliban knew that. So they waited. They weren't stupid.

The US Army lets its troops rest in between their deployments. A modern-day American soldier would be stupefied if told their deployment would go on indefinitely, they wouldn't stand for it. The same thing goes for the Taliban. They get it, too. But they were savvier about when they chose to take time off. While the US Army relied on massive amounts of manpower to provide units to rotate through Afghanistan, keeping a constant presence in the country, the Taliban—with fewer troops and logistical oomph—just decided to all but call it quits in the off-season. They waited for fighting season, the spring and summer, to get all their men deployed. While the US soldiers were walking around in canals freezing, the Taliban went on their own R&R. Places like Pakistan's border areas and Balochistan have long been known as spots where the Taliban, especially the more accomplished fighters, could pop over the border to rest and refit under the Pakistan government's policy to at the least ignore the whole situation in Afghanistan and at the most provide support to the Taliban.

And so in the Arghandab, for a couple months, the men of Bravo patrolled in the cold and busied themselves with finding and digging up ponderous IEDs designed to blow a Stryker vehicle sky high but not foot-mounted patrols. They found those big-mother IEDs, but the dreadful patrolling through frozen fields was misery. Even if they found those IEDs and disabled them, Bravo Company had seen what could happen when they didn't find the smaller ones. They had come to know that the Taliban didn't have to be perfect. All the Taliban had to do was get an IED in the right place at the right time. Meanwhile, if Bravo was off their game for a moment, not paying attention for one second, or just had a minute's worth of bad luck . . .

Bravo was on full alert on every patrol, with every man watching and inspecting and surveying every inch of ground so he might not become the next Johnston. It's typical of war for men to be always vigilant, but in this case, in this valley, there was an added stress of not knowing what each footstep might bring. If even in late December—a time of nothingness and rest—Johnston had been blown up, that meant they could be hit in the least likely places at the least likely times. The Taliban didn't need to attack the men physically, they were doing it psychologically. Every step on every patrol became a nightmare of anticipation, the kind of thing that drives a man crazy. With IEDs, a soldier has to try to think about it from the other guy's perspective. It makes every walk a game of chess. A soldier has to be thinking about where the Taliban might have put something. Here? There? Where? And yet they'd missed the signs of the IED that killed Johnston, signs that had been clear as day in retrospect. So what might they be missing on every patrol?

As they patrolled, the point men would sweep and sweep and sweep with handheld metal detectors, every single step of the way. Traditional patrol formations were thrown out the window, echelons and wedges and squads spread out in all sorts of ways to deal with possible enemy contact that had been developed over decades to deal with gun battles and firefights. All out the window.

Now they walked single file, just as Yeske had done when he went to recover Johnston's body. One after another, with the metal detector sweeping up front. If there was enemy contact, a firefight, they'd just have to drop to the deck, right where they stood. They couldn't go diving off into some cover, because if the ground hadn't been swept by the metal detector, then they knew better than to step on it. They would have to lie down in the open, which was contrary to all the training they'd gotten as far back as boot camp and in their DNA as humans. It was a far better proposition to face gunfire or mortars or whatever right there in the spot they knew didn't have any bombs than to go leaping into a what seemed a safe ditch only to trigger a bomb that would blow a guy's balls off.

It was better to walk through canals when possible, up to their chests in nasty water with animal piss and shit, dark as mud, water that caused their asses to chafe and get raw and infected, that made their toes all wrinkly and shriveled and then rotten with the wet, that disintegrated American-made uniforms, blowing out the crotches of trousers. Better to walk through water and piss and shit that made their suede combat boots fall apart, with their rifles up over their heads in one hand and their pack of smokes in the other—keeping the two things they most cherished from getting wet—than live in doubt. Bravo Company could be 100 percent sure they wouldn't step on a bomb in a canal because nobody, not even the Taliban, could plant a bomb in a canal.

They came to see the all-encompassing wisdom of the EOD team that had taken them out on some of their first patrols. They now knew the team was wise to walk through the centers of canals, to take things slowly. They had thought they were pussies just a few weeks earlier. Bravo learned the EOD troops were veritable sages.

But it all wore them down, even in the calmest, most nothing's-going-to-happen part of winter, all the way on the other side of the calendar from fighting season. The best Army in the world was walking through canals and having their nuts chafe away in hopes that they wouldn't step on a bomb buried sometime the year before.

It didn't take much of that strain, like the awful moments in a horror film waiting for the ghoul to jump out of a dark corner, to make men crack. Something was out there.

It was enough to make men downright terrified to leave the wire. The Taliban were smart enough to let the Americans wear themselves out walking around the valley for a few months. No need to get into a Halloween Zombie Massacre, there was no way they could win that sort of thing. The Taliban had been off their game for a moment and wouldn't let that happen again in the Arghandab.

And yet.

Bravo Company was out there, patrolling and doing what Tunnell's unit before them hadn't been able to do. They were starting to impose some control over the Arghandab Valley. So what if the Taliban was probably waiting for fighting season and that's why things were so calm. They weren't obviously in the valley, and Bravo was.

* * *

Just days after Johnston died, Allen Thomas went home the first week in January for his mid-deployment Rest and Recuperation Leave.

It's an odd thing, mid-deployment R&R. Soldiers on a deployment of a year or more got about two weeks in the middle of a combat deployment to relax back home in the States. They left the summer heat or winter freeze of Afghanistan and got on a plane, usually without anyone else from their unit, and flew by themselves to spend a few days at home where nearly everyone around them had been all but untouched by war. For two weeks, men found themselves in civilian clothes, seeing Mom and Dad, the wife and kids, or just some old buddies.

On R&R the relationships of civilian life were unthawed as the soldier tried to squeeze every drop of normalcy out of the time. They drank beers. They went to the mall. They slept in their own bedrooms rather than in some tent or plywood shack with dozens of other men snoring and farting and jerking off and waiting to go back out on patrol and maybe step on an IED. And while men were on R&R, they spent a good amount of time just counting down the days until they had to get on a plane all by themselves, without anyone else from the unit, and go right back to war. R&R was nothing like the months-long gap between deployments where units retool and refit and have time to settle in back home. In between deployments, a soldier could really reset along with the rest of his company or battalion. But R&R was just a pause. It was a time-out with a ticking clock.

Nick Armendariz remembered when he went home for mid-deployment R&R to Newport Beach, California, and friends asked him whether anything was actually happening in Afghanistan. They assumed he must be bored over there because the only thing they ever heard about on the news was Iraq. The news in the papers and on TV hadn't yet shifted its focus, and if it had it was on the Marines operating in Helmand. Bravo Company felt as if they were on the edge of a war, a new war, but it only meant something to them because they were there on the front lines.

Allen Thomas had just gone through what had been an objectively horrifying experience, losing a friend to an IED and dealing with the immediate chaos and confusion of all that. Armstrong and Jenio's theory on forcing men back into routine wasn't just some cockamamie effort to be tough. It was a way to wedge men into a routine that could prevent them from spinning out of control. Allen left that routine, left the immediate support network of men who understood what had happened and had been there. He went back to a place where no one really knew and no one really understood, where he was by himself to think through it all.

For a few weeks, Allen escaped a place that had just revealed itself to be a hidden land of bombs and booby traps with no enemy to shoot at. It was a land where his friend had been blown up just like that.

Allen arrived home for R&R and Danica had no idea that he'd be coming back. Her best friend had come to visit her in North Carolina for the New Year. At the time, Danica was living in the house shared by Dave Abt and Allen in Fayetteville because those guys were deployed and the place was empty. Allen decided he'd surprise her by just showing up unannounced.

Danica took her best friend to the airport one day in early January to fly home, and when she got back to the house, Allen was inside taking a shower. Surprise!

The future of their relationship was still undefined, but they were certainly a couple. He came home to visit her before going to visit his mom and dad, which meant something. Danica remembers that they were certainly a couple at the time but that the future wasn't definite. Even though Allen was a combat veteran, at the end of the day these two were the same age as college kids, with the same effervescent and gauzy thoughts about the future.

Kids weren't on their minds. Danica didn't have any thoughts of a career or anything. She was twenty years old and knew Allen wanted to be a career soldier. She had spent years fermenting in the culture of the Army, so she knew that if a soldier wanted to pursue a career, the partner took a back seat.

Danica looks back and wonders if she was an afterthought to Allen, but then recognizes that he came back to see her on R&R. His decision to come back to her seemed intentional and meaningful, even though there was no codified future plan. When he used his precious satellite phone minutes, she was who he used them on.

She knew something was different, though—he wasn't quite his old self. She had awoken to the possibility of death with the loss of Johnston. But when she reunited with Allen, she realized there was more than the binary black-and-white, live or die, come home or don't. Danica saw for the first time a gray area where a man could come back changed. Alive but broken. She knew people had always said that when a soldier returns from war he's never the same as when he left, but there was no way for her to know what that meant. She started to realize it. Allen was back and he was changed. Perhaps she was just able to see something she hadn't before because their relationship was deeper. Maybe Johnston's death had opened her eyes to something.

"When he came back on R&R things were different," Danica remembers. She saw this time as him unwinding from war and preparing to go back, caught in a two-week-long whipsaw of emotions. Allen had also just days before been subject to the physical effects of being near an explosion—perhaps he was still recuperating at the most fundamental level. There was likely a lot going on in the head of Allen Thomas, and she was not able to fully grasp it at the time. It's only looking back a decade later that she sees clearly the TBI, or traumatic brain injury, the PTSD.

"Now I have knowledge of it, but then I didn't," she said.

They were in Fayetteville, and Allen's parents lived in College Park, Maryland. He had friends in Baltimore, too. So they drove up to Baltimore to visit one of his best friends. They decided to go to a karaoke bar.

Allen had some beers, and some more beers, and everything was fun. Then he and Danica went outside for a smoke away from everyone.

He broke into tears, out there losing control over himself in a way she'd never seen before. She had seen him cry before because he could be an emotional fellow, but never in a situation like this. She had never, ever seen him show such bald feelings when it came to the Army and himself as a soldier.

She saw the awesome and impossible sight of Sergeant Allen Thomas breaking down. Then, as quickly as he'd started crying, he stopped. It was all over and under control. He was back to the happy old Allen and said he was OK and ready to go back into the bar. She had figured he'd either come back from war or he wouldn't. But here was something else, a gradation along an infinite scale of gray.

"The rest of the time he was fine," she said. Yet he was different. Sometimes he might just stare off. "I could see him chipping away."

A few days after that, Allen packed his bags and he was off again, back to Afghanistan, back to Bravo in the Arghandab.

Allen and Danica fell back into their pattern. He called her sporadically, like before. His soldiers still had wives and kids and he didn't. That went on for a few weeks until in late February, right after Valentine's Day, when she sent him a note on Facebook Messenger: "You need to call me as soon as possible."

Allen stoically replied that he didn't know if he could, what with other soldiers needing the phone more than him and all.

"I don't think you want to find out over Facebook what I have to tell you," she wrote him.

So he called, worried. And though she hadn't a clue how he'd take it, Danica told Allen she was pregnant.

She waited for his response.

"Oh my God, I'm going to be a dad?" he said, stunned. And then excitement, sheer joy, set in.

"Oh my God! Oh my God!" he repeated, unbelieving.

Danica, thousands of miles away on the other end of a satellite phone, had rarely been happier, knowing she and Allen Thomas were finally officially together and that he was happy about the prospects of having a family. She was excited to hear his excitement. Then she realized she was about to go through almost all of the pregnancy—her first—alone. The deployment was only half over. Allen wasn't scheduled to come back home until just weeks before the baby's arrival.

* * *

Allen, with two combat deployments under his belt and a Purple Heart from a previous Iraq deployment, had always thought a life of soldiering lay ahead of him. Suddenly a different future presented itself, and it included Danica and a child who was already on the way. He didn't have to—maybe didn't want to, he said—do this infantry thing forever.

The phone calls changed. He talked to her now, actually talked. Now Allen was one of the men who needed those satellite phone minutes. He told her he'd come to a determination: He'd maybe had enough of being an infantryman. He still wanted a career in the Army, yes, but a quieter one. He just needed to get through the few remaining months of this deployment and then he could come home and change his job in the Army. There'd be no more frontline stuff. Three combat deployments felt like plenty.

They talked all the time now. His voice had a new tone, his thoughts speeding ahead almost faster than he could talk. Marriage. A complete change in the idea of an Army career. Renewal. He even used some of that precious satellite phone time and called his mom, unbeknownst to Danica. Shortly after, Danica got a letter in the mail from Allen's mother.

"I guess you're my son's fiancée now," Danica remembered it read.

Yeah, I guess so, she thought. Allen hadn't asked her to get married.

Sure, she was pregnant in the United States while her now-fiancé patrolled daily through bomb-laden fields in Afghanistan. But the deployment would end. He would come home. No problem. She could do this.

"I just felt so safe and protected," she says, even though he was on the other side of the planet. "I loved everything about him. And so I had known that I wanted to be with him."

In her head she thought about the future, too, of going back to school, of marriage and more children. She and Allen were already thinking beyond this deployment. He just had to finish it up and come home.

* * *

Lieutenant Colonel Frank Jenio had gotten the Second Battalion of the 508th Parachute Infantry Regiment into the fight all right, hadn't he? That's what they all wanted, wasn't it?

His battalion, 2-508, was fighting in the Arghandab in large part or, depending how you look at it, because Frank Jenio had done everything he could to get them there. You might say the battalion, including Bravo Company, was now in Jenio's War, if you wanted to be philosophical about it. The United States Army, a massive organization that is part of the even larger American war effort, rarely gives a single man a chance to have an outsize effect on an entire battalion's fate in the way that Jenio had been able to do with his men. But what was happening might well have been called Jenio's War.

Don't let that be misconstrued as necessarily a bad thing. Jenio was just giving so many of the men in his battalion what they wanted: a slice of honest-to-goodness war. It's only after a man gets blown up that he might regret going to war. Before that, he's just as likely to be pleased as punch to be there.

And they were there.

"Jenio saw an opening, a gap, and he took it," remembers Lieutenant General Dan Bolger, an Army commander who was paying attention to events in Afghanistan even as he commanded in Iraq at the time. "Frank understood what these paratroopers were trained for."

Bravo Company was just one part of that battalion. Other companies in his battalion were likewise reaping the fruits of their new assignments. Take Charlie Company. They were in the fight now, too, down in the Arghandab, just on the other side of the river from Bravo Company.

Bravo could hear them, the Charlie Company guys, just a few miles away. There were firefights, there were explosions. Bravo could hear it all happening, could even see the flashes and streaks of rifle fire, tracers. But as far as Bravo's deployment went, those few kilometers between them and Charlie Company were about as far as the other side of the moon.

Charlie Company's story is a story all its own, of course, worthy of retelling and remembrance insofar as every unit's story is worthy of remembrance. But this is a story about Bravo. Inside a battalion there's overlap among friends in the companies, personnel get shuffled between companies between deployments and even during deployments every so often. Charlie's story bled into Bravo's and vice versa. And Bravo, Charlie, and a few others were in the Second Battalion of the 508th, all under Jenio's command. He'd trained them. He'd instilled in them his fighting spirit, his ethos. He orchestrated their move into the maw of the Arghandab after their bogus training mission in Helmand. He was in many ways their linchpin and the embodiment of 2-508.

And then all of a sudden he was gone.

Lieutenant Colonel Frank Jenio wasn't killed by a sniper or blown up by an IED. No, it wasn't a battlefield tragedy that caused him to disappear. It was something far, far worse for a career officer than being mowed down in battle. It was a bad PowerPoint presentation.

After Johnston died in late December, after Bravo realized they were in real combat, after Jenio and everyone else in the battalion knew they'd finally gotten what they'd been hoping for, that's when the PowerPoints leaked out.

Battalion headquarters, a few kilometers away from COP Ware, had daily briefings like just about every headquarters on the planet. After the battalion moved into the Arghandab, reports of injuries and deaths across the battalion became a regular feature of the daily briefing, and the practice of reporting every casualty made those daily briefings real downers. Jenio and Sergeant Major Bert Puckett decided to let the team add in a joke slide at the end of the briefing, dark humor to lighten things up. They called it a "demotivation" slide. Just something to make the guys laugh.

But they didn't really supervise the soldier, some lieutenant or something, who was picking out those slides. And when a young man in a combat zone isn't being supervised, he can quickly slide down a slippery slope. The PowerPoint slides became increasingly raunchy, more tasteless and questionable by the day. Each day's offering was a little worse than the day before.

When things devolve by increments, it's difficult to say when they should stop.

People from the battalion remember one in particular that should have been a red flag, a sign that things had slid far enough. It was a picture of a close-up of a guy's armpit that looked, at first glance, like a woman's naked crotch. *Oh jeez, that was a little much*, the staff thought as they groaned and laughed nervously. But nobody said anything, so the slides kept sliding. Raunchy jokes and inappropriate gags never get milder.

One morning the demotivation slide that popped up showed a white basketball coach beside a Black player with a caption that was a joke. It was a joke about slavery.

About slavery.

Someone leaked the slide, sent it up the chain of command. Drinkwine saw it and took it to General Ben Hodges, and from there it landed on the desk of Major General Curtis Scaparrotti, who was commanding the 82nd Airborne at the time.

To this day nobody knows for sure if Jenio's bosses were looking for a reason to get rid of him. Maybe his peers coveted command of a combat unit and wanted to swoop in, much the same way he'd swooped in himself? Or the reason might have been as simple as the Army's explanation at the time: Something had to be done to uphold Army values. Everyone's got a take on what happened. But the objective truth of the thing is that Jenio and Puckett—two white men—were responsible for a briefing session that included a joke about slavery.

They weren't even there the day that slide was briefed. They'd been out touring the combat zone and visiting troops. But they were still in charge of the unit, and—even if by looking the other way—had condoned those other PowerPoints, creating the climate that resulted in that inappropriate joke. The Army was changing, maybe, becoming kinder and gentler? Or it was just finally doing the right thing to address pervasive and systemic issues like racism. Either way, Jenio and Puckett were quickly relieved of command. This was a promotion-ending fate worse than death.

It happened so suddenly in early January 2010 that Puckett remembers he was out on a battlefield circulation tour, at a COP somewhere, and he was told he couldn't go back to his base even to pack his bags. General Scaparrotti, the one who made the ultimate decision, was a man who eventually rose to become a four-star general. That means that over the course of a multidecade career he made thousands of consequential decisions. Yet to this day he says making the decision to relieve Jenio was the hardest decision he's ever had to make.

It wasn't that Scaparrotti thought the PowerPoint was remotely close to being acceptable. Rather, Scaparrotti had been around for decades and knew the gravity of cutting a commander loose in the middle of combat. Decapitating a battalion in the middle of the fight could derail the unit. Plus, Jenio and Puckett were superb soldiers, had long been good men. Likewise, though, keeping a command team that somehow allowed jokes about slavery—how can an organization abide that happening?

Hodges remembers talking with Scapparotti about it and the two wondering what kind of impact it would have on this battalion in the middle of a combat operation. Then Hodges gave his plain opinion.

"I said this is one of the best battalions in RC-South," Hodges remembers before adding about Frank Jenio: "But he can be replaced."

Scaparotti agreed completely.

Jenio and Puckett were told to put on civilian clothes for a flight back to the States, and 2-508 had lost its commander and its command sergeant major. Those two arrived back in the United States on a commercial flight like a couple of tourists, put their feet on US soil just as their battalion was beginning to fight and die in the Arghandab. The action in Arghandab represented Jenio's wish to turn up the volume on combat, and there he was, back in the United States and out of command, only a few days after his trip to visit Bravo Company's COP Ware to bolster them following Johnston's death.

Puckett got back to Fort Bragg and was informed he ought to just wait to be told what to do next. He talked to another sergeant major at the base who told him not to bother with even showing up for work, just to hang out at home while the Army figured out what would happen next. Would there be an investigation? Charges? A court-martial? Would he get bad paperwork and slowly fade into retirement, disappearing like a ghost after a career that had shone so brightly? Being relieved was the worst thing that had ever happened in his life. The disgrace. The snatching away of a career just like that. It was bullshit, he said, that he could be dismissed for some PowerPoint that he wasn't even there to see himself.

Once he was back home Puckett started drinking heavily, he recalls. When a senior soldier has been relieved there's a window of time where he thinks, maybe, just maybe, this won't kill his career. Maybe, just maybe, it will be different for him.

While Puckett was at home for weeks, then months, just stewing, the wounded and dead of 2-508 came back. They came back after being hurt and killed in places he and Jenio had sent them. Puckett felt he had to go pay his respects.

Puckett attended some funerals because that's what the senior enlisted man does in a situation like that. After he'd done it a few times, he remembers, someone from the Army got in touch with him and said he wasn't allowed to do that anymore. Puckett wasn't their senior enlisted man. The Army took even that away from him. He couldn't pay his respects to the boys he'd trained and sent into harm's way. And with that, Puckett came to accept that his career was dead.

Jenio, too, was all through. The Ranger Regiment pedigree, time at special operations command, and having honed 2-508 to perfection, all for naught. And just after he'd engineered getting his own area of operations pregnant with combat opportunities, a sure shot at some colonel's wings and a maybe general's star. Gone like that.

And Bravo Company was stuck deep in the shit with their trusted commander back home in the States. But the Army's the Army, and in the blink of an eye, another officer took over for Jenio. Another sergeant major stepped in for Puckett. The deployment continued as all deployments do, and always will.

So concerned were some that a loss of leadership would cause 2-508 to founder, they forgot that, since Jenio's soldiers would follow him into hell if he ordered them to do so, they were also prepared to do their jobs no matter what may come.

Because Jenio seemed irreplaceable as a commander, he had, paradoxically, made himself imminently replaceable. He'd trained his battalion so well that they could operate without him. And they did.

CHAPTER 13

HANDS UP

January was a cold, miserable month of patrolling with nothing substantial as far as firefights or IEDs. So was February.

Those two months seemed as nothing to most of the men from Bravo, a time they've nearly forgotten because nothing happened. Grab a beer at the bar and ask most of them about January and February and you'll get a shrug. Nobody tells war stories about those nothing months.

Yet that was the time Captain Adam Armstrong remembers Bravo was able to accomplish what the Department of Defense, President Obama, and the blessed *FM 3-24* COIN manual had sent them there to do: They partnered with Afghan forces, went out among the people, and did the daily grind of counterinsurgency operations.

It's because they weren't getting in firefights and weren't stepping on IEDs that they were able to concentrate on COIN. There's no way to prove a counterfactual, but hell, maybe it was *because* they were doing COIN that they didn't get into firefights or step on IEDs. No way to know.

Armstrong launched patrol after patrol to learn about their area of operations. They walked over, through, and across as much of that land as they could, mapping the terrain into their brains.

They did their best to meet every farmer—every male inhabitant—they could. And they took photos of those men, building a database of the people in the area, little dossiers so they could know who was supposed to be in the area and who wasn't, so they could cross-reference identities if they got intelligence about someone who was a suspected insurgent.

They started projects in their area, rebuilding small bridges over canals. They delivered some speakers to a mosque in the area. Armstrong started developing a relationship with the local bigwig that seemed to be legitimate and heartfelt. They did it alongside Afghan forces, working shoulder to shoulder with them, or *shona ba shona* as the Afghans said it.

Man, it seemed as if the COIN doctrine, the partnering operations, might actually be working. It had been worth the endless toil to build COP Ware out of the radish field. It had been worth enduring patrol after patrol and the early casualties. It seemed as if Jason Johnston's death might even be redeemed in some way because they were accomplishing a bigger mission.

Under Armstrong, Bravo's quotidian nut-chafing patrols were doing exactly what was needed. It's sometimes the everyday efforts, nothing blockbuster, that can turn the tide of conflict. History remembers the blowout battles, not the endless days of nothing happening.

But nothing happening in the Arghandab was something, indeed.

Nothing happening was in large part the point of it all.

The Arghandab served as a ratline, military parlance for an illicit pathway for the enemy to sneak along. A ratline isn't a ratline if nobody scurries along it, and there was less scurrying. The effort was noticed by commanders up the chain.

"I am pretty sure I visited with the 508th in Arghandab and was impressed by what they were doing," said David Petraeus in an email, of the time when he was the commanding general of Central Command.

"Of course, the contrast with the Stryker Brigade actions was marked, as the Strykers had generally not been a clear and hold force to the extent that was needed—in part because we didn't have sufficient forces to hold in the way that we needed to do," Petraeus said. "The additional forces, over time, enabled us to do that."

* * *

Then, on February 23, the nothing days ended and the casualties began.

It started with a lieutenant and a PFC, both of them on the same day, injured by stepping on IEDs. The lieutenant headed back to Walter Reed, injured but missing no limbs.

Two weeks later came another PFC, injured by an IED.

"We were fighting in all directions and there wasn't an actual front," Mac said. "Just because you take a piece of ground, it doesn't mean you're winning."

Since Mac had rank, he wasn't the one patrolling two or three times a day. Instead, he was the one telling the men to go patrol two or three times a day. The Taliban bombs weren't always meant to kill, they were meant to maim, and they did.

Every time Bravo changed the way they did things, the Taliban changed the way they set in bombs. Every day, it seemed like the two sides were adapting and changing, nothing ever the same. That was some of the awfulness of it. There was no consistency. It was an ever-evolving chess game. The Taliban would figure out new tripwires, so Bravo would come up with something new, like the time one of the guys had his wife send him their kid's Spider-Man toy fishing pole with a heavy sinker on the end of the line. They'd whip out that toy rod and reel and cast out into the unknown, reeling it in slowly to see if it hit anything. Sergeant Hill tied a length of 550 cord to a baseball and threw the thing out there. It worked when it didn't work, which is to say when nothing happened. If that baseball came back to them without blowing up it meant there weren't any tripwires or cords out there. They were doing anything they could to try and outwit the Taliban.

"If a soldier finds something he thinks will save his life, he's going to do it," said Lieutenant General Mike Oates, the commander of JIEDDO, who studied IEDs for the military.

Even when new equipment and techniques came to Afghanistan, the men operating on the ground sometimes didn't have access to it, remembers Scott Brannon, who served as Frank Jenio's operations officer on that deployment.

New equipment would sometimes just arrive and there'd be no training on it and no experts to show the troops how to best use it. So the men would rely on what they knew rather than to try something that was unproven that they didn't know how to work. It led to the paradoxical environment where a Spider-Man fishing pole was used in combat while the newest DoD gadgetry sat in a box someplace.

* * *

Mac, the stalwart, found himself thinking too much. Like when one of the men from Bravo stepped on an IED and Mac showed up in the QRF to hold his hand and tell him everything was going to be OK, but the guy was missing a leg.

He had to tell the guys, tell himself, that the next day was going to be OK. But would it? He wasn't even sure the next day would be OK.

And there was that one day when he yelled at a soldier who was unsure of his ability to do his job. Mac chewed his ass and told him not to be such a pussy and to get into the fight. Well, that guy got blown up a few missions later because he was out there not being a pussy. He was following Mac's orders, and he was blown up.

Mac thought to himself, *Was that because of me?*

* * *

For the month after Valentine's Day, Danica was planning out her life with Allen, and he was planning out his life with her. He was so excited about the pregnancy, about the future, and even about his next phase of life in the Army. The deployment had become a series of tense patrols through god-awful fields that might be laced with IEDs. And those patrols had the occasional stop to visit with the villagers and locals who were in the valley. Bravo knew the importance of being able to talk with the local population, of moving among them, even if that was a potential hazard.

One day in March, Bravo Company was out on patrol when they set up a snap checkpoint in the road, a common practice. An American patrol would just decide to stop vehicles and people, give them a look-see, like cops on the beat. Jordan Flake was out there on that patrol, and they set up a checkpoint at the intersection of a road—a screwy way to do it, he says in retrospect. Too many variables at an intersection. Flake was put in a position where he could best bring the firepower of his SAW to bear if needed. They were out there with some Afghan police, doing a partnered mission. Those Afghans were useful to talk to the locals, but anytime they were involved it was hard to make sure things went smoothly, maybe like doing carpentry without a tape measure or something. With the Afghan forces there was always a feeling they were winging it to some extent. They could never be sure things would be just right. In this case there was an Afghan policeman who was sort of in Flake's way, not too much, but enough that he might edge into Flake's line of sight if he needed to fire the SAW.

Soon after they set in the checkpoint, Flake remembers a man and his son came through riding a tractor. They were just farmers doing their farmer thing, they seemed nice enough.

Five minutes later, as far as Flake reckons, a different young man came walking their way real slow and real weird. The soldiers told each other to keep an eye on the guy. The man kept walking toward them, mumbling to himself. When Flake thinks back on it now, he remembers the guy had a spiffy new set of black clothes on, spotless, as if he was dressed for a special occasion.

Flake thought something wasn't right with this guy, but that realization didn't come with ample time to decide and react. In retrospect, there's always ample time to look at everything that happened and make sense of it. At the time, things moved so fast, it was hard to make a decision. It's always hard to make a decision. It was hard even to process that there was a decision to make.

This guy was an odd fellow, and he came on as fast as time itself, unstopping.

It seemed he was about ten feet away now, and the Afghan cop and the guy started yelling at each other, or were they just talking loudly? Damn, the cop was in the way now, hollering at the guy. Flake couldn't shoot even if he wanted to, or at least that's what he tells himself in retrospect.

But he could have shot. His job was to be the first one to decide to shoot if there was trouble.

Yet Flake had let that man keep coming, step after step, time flying by in every moment. After all, deciding to kill someone isn't easy.

It's easy enough to talk about killing when you're a spectator. Watching war films, it seems downright simple to know who the bad guy is and when to shoot at him. It's easy for someone from the outside to say what they would have done. For people who have been there, they know it's not so easy in the moment. Sure, in war there's sometimes a bad guy with a uniform and a gun who's shooting at you, and that makes the decision straightforward and even easy, but a soldier rarely knows for sure what the hell is happening even when he's in the middle of it.

Still, for people who have been there, they can often look back on things and make a declaration about it. In retrospect even a soldier who *knows* how hard it is in the moment can look back and think there was a clear-cut, obvious course of action. In the moment it's not easy at all. When it's a guy coming at you wearing civilian clothes, it's not easy at all. It's not easy when it's a guy taking a step closer. And another.

Deciding to kill someone is not a decision that can be undone. The act is final. Definite. After an event is done and over with, there's a teleological certainty to it. It almost seems that it had to happen the way it did. But at the time, each moment is pregnant with possibility, with a different direction that can be taken. There is no inevitable. That moment when Flake could have acted took forever and yet at the same time was gone immediately. Afterward, there is only one way for the event to have happened, and that can't be changed. But there is no telos in the midst of war, no predestined outcomes in the here and now.

Everyone's had a moment, a few seconds of their life, where the fabric of time stretches, expands. Maybe it's a motorcycle wreck, with the skid and then going over the handlebars—waiting for your body to hit the road in a suspended-moment's eternity. Perhaps it's a more pleasant reverie, a high school basketball game with a high arcing three pointer finding nothing but net, that traced arc lasting an eternity as it's happening, yet gone in a moment. Gone, yes, but it can come back again and again, recalled from memory to be replayed. Perhaps that moment is something more important in the grand scheme of things: the moment a partner sees their child's head crown as a woman gives birth, that wonderful forever that lasts but a moment.

And in those moments, a thinking person knows for certain that time is not set fast in stone. It can bend and warp and shrink and lengthen. It's only a fool who thinks that a second lasts a second, or a minute lasts a minute.

No, a second can last a minute. A second gives enough time to think and reason and wonder and reflect. And to act, even. Or not act. Time to feel a sinking dread in the stomach, a visceral dread. A moment like that can last forever even as time races forward. A moment like that, a moment filled with meaning, also rips the fabric of time itself. It creates a place, a time, that a person can return to at will, or where they're sometimes transported to against their will.

Those moments create places where, like Billy Pilgrim of Kurt Vonnegut's *Slaughterhouse-Five*, a man can just come unstuck in time. Vonnegut reveals the truth of time to us, that Pilgrim goes through the horrors of World War II and finds himself unwittingly jumping from past to present to future, hopping through the moments with no control over how it happens. He goes from combat to civilian life and back again.

For Billy Pilgrim, for Flake, for Allen Thomas and other combat veterans, those rips in time where a man comes unstuck are very real. Go ahead, ask any of them about it. Those rips in time can be nightmares. And just as Billy Pilgrim learns that free will is a passing fancy, gone in a moment, so, too, does a man like Flake or Allen Thomas. Free will's a funny thing because while we have control over what we do, at the same time it might as well be an illusion, because the possibility of action lasts a flash of a moment and then is gone, turned into the hard fact of history, of the past. Something unchangeable. Free will becomes a prison of regret.

Visiting a moment is more than remembering it. Remembering is what you do when you talk about multiplication tables or who led the majors in dingers the year you turned twelve. *Visiting* a moment like that actually transports a person from the present into that past. He relives it in the most literal sense. It makes a man seem like a crazy person, staring off into the distance, living a past moment as if it's happening right now.

Once a man has been to war, Billy Pilgrim doesn't seem crazy, and *Slaughterhouse-Five* doesn't seem like science fiction. Billy is the normal one. He's normal to a man who has experienced one of those eternal moments, those rips in time. He's normal to a man like Flake who knows that moment as a suicide bomber took a step closer. Another. When he started yelling at the policeman, when the policeman raised his gun and pointed it at the man. When the man mumbled something new as he raised his hands and took another step.

When he mumbled, "Allahu Akbar."

* * *

"Suicide vest" doesn't really explain what bombers use. That's a sterile term that makes it sound like part of a three-piece suit. It's easier to understand it if you list the parts, if you open it up and look into its guts.

Start with inch-thick slabs of explosive that often look and feel like modeling clay, cold and gray. That's typically shaped into a rectangle the size of a coffee-table book, nothing more detailed or defined than an elementary-school art project. Then likely come the industrial ball bearings, dense steel the size of marbles. They're laid out in a mosaic. The quarter-inch shiny metal balls are arranged next to each other in a geometric pattern like tiny grout tiles on a floor. Or on the walls of a church. Or the floor of a mosque.

The whole thing's then wrapped up in clear packing tape to keep it all together. Somewhere in all that is woven a detonation cord and a blasting cap, a tiny bit of explosive attached to a trigger that makes it all go off. This is its anatomy. Simple and lethal.

Such a vest might even be wired up so that a cord runs down a bomber's leg, connecting to a button on his kneecap. That way he doesn't have to use his hands to hit a trigger—he can just fall to his knees. That is smart stuff because then he can put his hands up and take a step closer to his target.

* * *

In that moment where the young man mumbled "Allahu Akbar," nothing was determined. Flake was a young American in an uncertain place watching another young man who had walked toward him. And now the man had his hands up. A fellow human being.

In that moment, Flake could have made a choice, in theory he could have changed the progress of history, exerted his free will on the situation.

Shoot or don't shoot. But as that moment, unstoppable, slid by, there was so much to calculate!

There's something deep within a soldier's breast, fundamental to a person like Flake's very nature. There are those who have dark souls, bad men moving among us, but we must believe in a fundamental goodness in ourselves and those we interact with. If we lose hope in that, we might as well give up on the project of life itself. We must believe in the good. For a soldier like Jordan Flake that goodness was as much a part of him as his soul, unchanging and pure. It was the unflinching human love that lies within us all, that thing that was deep within Flake in that moment where he was trying to make a decision to end another human's life.

It was the divine.

The infinite held in a passing moment. The very breath of God swirled around Jordan Flake, reminding him that the young Afghan in front of him, too, was a man.

Or perhaps Flake just didn't act, simple as that. Who's to say?

* * *

As is the case with any suicide bomber, every step closer they can get increases the odds that the explosion, the ball bearings, will find their mark. Those ball bearings are indiscriminate in their destruction, their goal simply to do as much damage as possible to whatever human is in their path. Their mark is anyone, and there's no rhyme or reason in their path of flight. Just like with a shotgun, the chance of hitting the target diminishes the farther you get from it. The suicide bomber's bet is that there are so many ball bearings, the odds are pretty good at least one of them will find a target. Especially if he can take a step closer.

And another step closer.

And another.

* * *

Suicide bombers prey on the better angels of our nature. Suicide bombers know the Flakes of the world, know they will see the eyes of another human being, a brother made in God's image. Perhaps they have that goodness buried deep within them, too, and thus know how to exploit it.

Hmmm, is that too presumptuous, to try and get into the mind of a suicide bomber? If so, then despite any intent they have in their minds, the reality is they *can* and *do* play upon those tender mercies. And Flake, seeing that image of God coming toward him, thought nothing could be lost by taking his time. Everything could be lost by rushing to fire his rifle.

The strange Afghan man, Flake later found out, was yelling at the policeman because he said he desperately needed something. He needed to get through the checkpoint, please, his wife and child were sick. Please, he begged. His pleas came tumbling out as he stepped closer and closer.

Suicide bombers look into a young soldier's eyes and take full advantage of those mystic chords of memory. "I am loath to close. We are not enemies but friends." The young soldier waits a moment.

A precious child of God himself, Flake did not, could not, level his rifle and shoot the Afghan.

* * *

That delay, that moment of humanity, comes back to Flake again and again even now. Or rather he goes back to it, unstuck in time. He waited, the Holy Spirit itself staying his trigger finger and the tremblingly awful life-ending act he was contemplating. In memory, in hindsight, he knows his delay let the bomber get closer. The delay to consider this Afghan's life put himself in deadly danger. It put his friends in deadly danger. Flake risked death in order to not risk sullying his humanity.

The calculations are not easy. And they have to be done quickly before that fleeting free-will moment passes. Why couldn't Flake have done it differently? In that moment of sympathy, empathy, and trust, in that moment of delay, that precious Afghan child of God, the one wearing a suicide vest, went to his knees.

***

***

***

Boom

***

***

***

In less than a moment the trigger set off those slabs of plastic explosive studded with ball bearings, those mosaics reminiscent of holy places, which the young man had hidden beneath his new black clothes. It instantly pulverized the torso of the young man wearing it, sending bits of him in all directions. It also sent those hundreds of ball bearings shooting out in all directions like a massive shotgun.

That blast and the bearings went toward Jordan Flake and toward Allen Thomas.

Flake remembers the bomber's rib cage exposed by the blast and coming toward him. A slow-motion horror.

The explosion was enough to knock people over, throw them in the air. That shock wave could lead to horrific injuries like a collapsed lung. The bomber was already in pieces: legs, arms, head, scattered all over.

It's all about odds, like so much else during deployment. The odds are good that a ball bearing will find its mark. But at the same time, the odds are really good they'll miss. It all depends on how you look at it. Glass half full or half empty.

Flake was hit just by the force of the explosion, which laid him flat. He was close to the bomber but wasn't hit by a single ball bearing, he was just felled like a huge tree. And he got back up, essentially unharmed. For a moment he looked as if he'd been grievously wounded—a fellow soldier told him to call for the medic because his face looked like it had been split open.

Flake knew better. His face felt just fine. But there was *something* on his cheek, right by his mouth. He was going to stick his tongue out to see what it was, a force of habit. But he stopped himself from doing that. He reached up with his hand instead and pulled off a chunk of the bomber's face that had been blown off and affixed itself to Flake's cheek. Other than that, nothing from the bomber hit him.

The odds were on Flake's side. They weren't on Allen's.

One of those hundreds of tiny ball bearings hit Allen. That roughly quarter-inch ball of steel that had been carefully laid out in that suicide vest and heated to a scorching temperature in the moment of the explosion tore through Allen's flak jacket and into his chest, punched through one of his lungs, and came out his back. It didn't have enough energy left to blast through the last layer of his body armor, so it just skimmed down along Allen's back, like a hot marble in a pachinko game, leaving a scalding burn mark on his skin in its wake.

His left lung was all but ruined when the ball bearing ripped through it. The other lung collapsed from the pressure of the blast. Allen was knocked unconscious, his lungs not functioning, and was nearly dead. Flake, on the other hand, the one who waited a moment too long, was a bit dazed but otherwise fine.

It's all about odds.

Flake prided himself on being able to decipher body language, to be able to read a situation better than those around him. He kept his head on a swivel, he noticed stuff before others did. He wasn't trigger shy. He wasn't scared. It's what messes with his head years later, that he saw all the things that should have alerted him to the danger, that should have prompted him to shoot. But he didn't. In that moment, even all the evidence sitting right there in front of a man isn't enough to make him kill another human who might just be trying to get his sick wife and kid through a checkpoint.

"Anyone on the outside would say what they would do," Flake says angrily. "You don't know what the fuck you would do."

And now his squad leader, Allen Thomas, couldn't breathe. They'd listened to Texas country together. They'd both dipped Copenhagen. Allen had trusted him with his life.

Flake remembers Allen, when he was conscious, saying in clipped words he couldn't breathe, he couldn't breathe. When Doc got to him, Allen said, "You gotta save me, I have to get home to see my kid."

Allen turned grayish-white as he lay there with neither lung working correctly. Yeske, who was on that patrol, remembered Allen taking on the ashen color of a person who's died. Doc did four needle chest decompressions on Allen, inserting into the wounded man's chest a huge needle that looks almost like the one you use to inflate a basketball, which released the air gathering around Allen's lungs rather than in the lungs. Yeske with his EMT training helped Allen as they waited for the medevac helicopter to show up.

Allen wasn't dead yet. Somehow Doc and Yeske—and Allen's own incredible strength—had gotten that one lung to start working

enough in the time before the medevac helicopter touched down. Doc
remembers two Black Hawks arrived to evacuate Allen and the couple of other soldiers who had been hit by shrapnel and needed to be
checked, though they weren't horribly hurt. When the helos touched
down a big, fat flight medic trundled out of the helo. Doc remembers
thinking to himself the dude probably had the nickname "Lunchbox" or
something. Everybody loaded Allen—a big man—onto a stretcher and
started carrying him to the helo. Well, that fat medic dropped his side
of the litter, so they dropped Allen.

"Fuck off!" Doc remembers telling the fat medic, and he grabbed two
handles on the litter and mustered the adrenaline to safely get Allen the
rest of the way. Doc remembers somebody had recently told him to expect
that one in three men from Bravo would be wounded. Jesus, the toll was
starting to grow.

Once in the air, medics on the helo had to insert four chest tubes into
Allen before they arrived at the field hospital at Bagram Air Base just
outside of Kabul.

A chest tube, a flexible bit of plastic pipe, is typically installed by a
surgeon when a patient has a buildup of fluid or air around the lungs. It's
commonly done as part of any major thoracic surgery in a hospital under
sterile and controlled conditions. In Allen's case, as in other battlefield
emergencies, it's done with haste by a medic because a patient's chest is
filling with blood from an internal wound, or with air. Any little hole in
the chest means every time the wounded takes a breath a little bit of air
gets pulled into the space between the lung and chest wall. Slowly, that air
goes in and doesn't come out, pumping up that empty space like a bike
tire, all that pressure or tension squeezing on the lungs.

A chest tube is a rarity out there on the battlefield and only resorted
to in the most extreme circumstances. Allen needed four.

From Bagram he was stabilized and soon sent to Germany for emergency surgery. They saved him, kept that one lung working. And from
there, just a month after Valentine's Day and learning the news that he was
to be a father, Allen headed back again to the United States.

* * *

The next time Armstrong pushed out a patrol to where the bombing happened, to show the Taliban that they couldn't keep Bravo Company down,
they saw pieces of Allen's uniform up in a nearby tree.

That was one of the Taliban's dirtiest tricks, festoon some branches
with a guy's uniform scraps, like trimming a Christmas tree. The Taliban
would do that, then sow the ground all around with IEDs.

It was terrible to see Allen's uniform up in the tree. It felt like the
Taliban was laughing at them. But it wasn't worth it to go get the stuff
down. There simply had to be so many IEDs around the tree. What if
someone else was blown up just to remove the provocation?

No, Armstrong left the scraps up in that tree, and he helped the men
of Bravo Company to see it as their own rebuke to the Taliban and that
suicide bomber.

You may have gotten one of us, but we're still here.

CHAPTER 14

WALTER REED

Back home, Danica, in her first trimester, got a phone call. Allen had been wounded.

It was a phone call all military partners or spouses know might be out there, a ubiquitous possibility. A spouse hopes for and plans on the deployed soldier coming home just fine and carrying on, certainly. They also unwittingly plan for the soldier's death as well, even though they might never admit it or even know it's what they're doing.

Actively wrestling with the possibility of death is hard. But once a soldier is deployed, imagining the *possibility* of death just sort of happens. The soldier's over there in Afghanistan and the spouse, the loved one, well, they're still back home. And life continues. For many spouses, groceries and bills and kids and school and dinners and nights out all still go on, just without them involved anymore.

The deployed soldier's clothes in the closet don't get put on by anyone. Their shoes don't get worn. The motorcycle in the garage just sits silently and the guitar in the living room doesn't get played. Those things, the things that belong to a living, breathing creature who's on the other side of the world—those things become nothing more than things. All the books and photos and video games and hats and power tools become museum pieces. The plaques and bicycles and hunting rifles become something from another era. They belong to someone who might reclaim them, but not for a while. All the things eventually turn into mementos of someone a spouse gradually learns to live without. Maybe there's even an old T-shirt a spouse can't bear to wash and which might go in a ziplock bag to keep that deployed soldier's smell around as long as possible.

Once an infantryman is gone on deployment, a partner, a spouse, a mom, a dad, realizes their soldier has become, like Schrödinger's Cat, both alive and dead, or rather, neither alive nor dead.

Yes, they're most likely alive, because, after all, the odds are on their side. Even with a unit that was starting to get as beat-up as Bravo Company, with the increase in IED injuries starting to tick up, only three men ended up dead in combat by the end of the deployment. A spouse also has to plan on their soldier's return home, if for no other reason than to not go crazy.

There are typical indicators that a deployed soldier is still alive, things like semi-regular emails, Facebook messages, phone calls, and letters that arrive weeks after they were mailed. Those all provide proof that the person a spouse packed up and sent to war is still alive and kicking. And while the US Army's efficiency in winning wars isn't so great, its efficiency when it comes to letting families know someone has been killed is second to none. Death in Afghanistan is quickly followed by a government-issued sedan pulling up to a house back in the United States so some dress-uniformed soldiers can knock on the door of the next of kin.

That means so long as no one's knocking on the front door wearing their dress uniform with gleaming buttons and shiny black shoes, the deployed soldier must still be alive.

And yet, the partner, the spouse, knows that despite the Army's efficiency at dispatching those soldiers in dress uniforms, they can't just magically appear at the doorstep a moment after a combat death. It takes time for them to get the call, to look up your address in the dead soldier's service record. They need time to put on their freshly pressed uniforms. They might need to grab a quick breakfast. It takes time for them to drive over.

A spouse wonders when they last talked to their deployed soldier. There will always be time between a death and the dispatch of those messengers of death. That time could be any time. It could be right now, for God's sake. Right now they might be driving over in that sedan.

If that spouse is not on the phone at that very moment with the infantryman deployed in a combat zone, then they can't be completely, 100 percent certain he's alive this very moment. The soldiers in those sharply pressed uniforms might be heading over to knock on the front door right now.

Or now.

Or maybe now.

Nearly every moment of deployment is filled to the brim with that terrible uncertainty. The only thing that provides something resembling relief is when that next phone call comes, a brief respite, empirical proof they're alive. As soon as that spouse in the United States hangs up, though, the *maybe now* thoughts begin again.

Thus, while waiting for those phone calls, emails, or letters, that spouse is left back in the real world with the possessions of a soldier who might, even now, be dead. All that person's things become remnants, reminders, talismans. Quotidian memorials. But over time they stop being lovely mementos and start to get in the way of everyday life. Shoes by the front door become something to trip over when getting the mail. So they get moved, boxed up and sent downstairs to the basement. The guitar in the corner is just something the kids knock over all the time. So up into the attic it goes.

The spouse of the deployed soldier starts going about life without them. The bills need to be paid and dinner needs to be cooked without their help. The kids have to be packed off to school, no help from that person deployed thousands of miles away. At first, it's hard to do anything without them. But then it all gets done and that soldier's existence is not even factored into the calculations. A spouse starts to live as if he's never coming home.

The typical deployment eventually comes to an end and the soldier comes back alive, unharmed. Everyone picks up just as they left off. The guitar goes back into the corner, gets picked up and strummed again. The shoes come up from the basement. And that old shirt, well, that spouse might tell him about how she kept it in a bag and would smell it from time to time, and they'll both laugh and feel a bit silly and sentimental. And then that once-priceless shirt just goes into the wash pile. They're alive.

When that soldier gets back, things to him seem mostly the same. That year of deployment was like a time warp and he expects everything to be just as he left it. He wants things to be unchanged. But the spouse has lived with those *maybe now* thoughts for a long time, a year or more. They've lived with the idea of being a war widow. They know how to live with anticipated grief.

Danica wasn't Allen's spouse, but she had experienced some of this. She'd felt the what-ifs of expecting the soldiers in dress uniforms. Danica already had a taste of the gray area a soldier occupies once he comes back, how he's changed. With the phone call in March that Allen was injured came a plunge into a new gray area. She thought back again to when her brother-in-law had come home, welcomed with hugs and laughs like a scripted event. She remembered how Allen had come home for leave just a few months earlier. It wasn't wonderful, but it wasn't awful.

This time he didn't come back home, back to her like he had on R&R. This time she was told he'd go directly to Walter Reed, the military hospital in Washington, DC. She was told he'd be sent straight to the hospital, something she'd never thought possible even after her initial awakening to the realities of what combat does to people.

Allen called her from the hospital in Germany as soon as the intubation was removed and he could talk. The first thing he'd asked her was "Are you OK?"

The only thing he wanted her to bring once he made it to the States, to the hospital, was fresh fruit, which he craved. That and, of course, his guitar.

Danica arrived in Washington the night he was brought to Walter Reed, but for a host of reasons she didn't go to the hospital until the next morning. His mom had been there the night before.

Before going to Walter Reed she went to Allen's mom's house, only a few miles from the hospital, and she asked Allen's mom, "Is it still him?"

Allen's mom was the type who could get it together and keep it together no matter the situation. She reminded Danica that she, too, needed to get it together not for her own sake but for Allen's sake. And they went to Walter Reed.

When Danica walked into his room and saw him she thought it was still Allen. Kind of.

"First time I saw him it was like somebody snatched my soul," she said. "I felt totally helpless. I looked up to him as this incredible power-house who was untouchable."

To her eyes he seemed to have shrunk. He'd already lost weight. He wasn't able to get out of bed, much less walk, just days after getting blown up.

"He was there and he was alive," Danica says. "That's all I could have hoped for in this situation, I guess."

It was still him, the man she'd planned on being her rock, her refuge. She told herself that one day this would all be done and they'd have a normal life. It was inconceivable that their life could be any other way. They'd have a normal life because normal is always possible when you don't know any better.

Sure enough, it was Allen lying there in that bed, but it certainly wasn't the old Allen anymore. It wasn't just some kind of metaphorical or philosophical difference in his persona. Sure, he'd been changed by his experiences and memories and trauma, but it also wasn't the old Allen in a literal, very visceral sense. The man she'd known and loved had left physical bits and pieces of himself in Afghanistan.

At first he had to use a bedpan and a catheter. He tried to be his old self, but he wasn't. He was missing part of that one lung. And inside his head, after all the rattles and bangs from the blast in December when Johnston died and now this latest blast that had knocked him out, well, it had caused dendrites to unmoor themselves from neurons. Synapses had been wrenched apart, destroyed, or had just started to misfire. The trauma had changed him, shook his head like an Etch A Sketch. Those were injuries Danica would not fully recognize until much later. At this point she didn't even know what traumatic brain injury meant. PTSD was a bunch of letters, just something she'd heard about.

But what was it really? What was *he* really?

"It was just like him," she said of the man she saw at Walter Reed. "But a broken version of him."

* * *

Steve Towery, who lost his foot the day Johnston was killed, was going through recovery himself. He was at Walter Reed for about a month getting his foot cleaned out and letting the stump start to heal. It was a trying time for him and his wife, who refused to leave his side for much of the process. She slept in the hospital room with him rather than in a hotel room despite his protestations.

The hospital became stifling in no time, and he wanted to just get out of there for a bit, to get a reprieve. His first trip off the hospital grounds was over to that hotel room they had but in which she never slept just to get some new scenery. It seemed better to sit around in some new room than to sit around at Walter Reed. Hotels have carpets on the floors, though, and for a guy used to linoleum everywhere it can pose problems for crutches. Sure enough he snagged the tip of his crutch and lost his balance. His body hadn't gotten used to the missing foot yet and his reflex was to stomp down and regain his balance. *Whammo!*—he slammed the nubbin into the ground and broke open barely recovered wounds and had to head straight back to Walter Reed.

Towery still wondered years later, in the back of his mind, if what he did could really be considered a proper combat deployment. His bad day was just the start of things for Bravo Company. He got blown up and went home, but everyone else had to stay and patrol day after day, wondering if they'd end up like him. They had the hard times, he just had one incident.

Years later he was still trepidatious about flaunting his wound. He would never wear shorts to veterans' events, for instance, he'd wear pants to keep the wound a private thing. Even with his young kids he wasn't forthright. They didn't know for a long while that he'd lost his foot in Afghanistan. Whenever they'd ask him about it, he would give them some far-fetched explanation. Sometimes he'd tell them a shark bit it off while he was swimming. Other times he'd say he lost it in a knife fight down in Mexico. *They'll eventually find out but no need to have them make a big deal of it*, he thought.

He was just happy to have them, and to have his wife, and he knew if they were able to keep it together through the stresses of Walter Reed, then they're going to do just fine.

He only lost a foot, after all.

* * *

Meanwhile, in the Arghandab it was becoming spring. The buds on the trees turned to flowers and fruit. Pomegranates grew on those world-famous boughs. The earth softened as waters flowed. Undergrowth filled in. Grasses grew. The Arghandab was becoming a lush, beautiful place again, a great place for the Taliban to hide more bombs.

Agricultural techniques were advanced in the Arghandab, so the farmers could make the most of those sought-after fruit orchards, remembers Carter Malkasian, a longtime State Department Afghanistan specialist and advisor to the US military. The trellises for grapes might as well have been part of a trench system. The dense orchards of pomegranates might as well have been a series of blinds and concealments. It was a marvelous place for an enemy to fight and emplace IEDs, Malkasian remembers.

The fighting season, with the regularity of the calendar, picked up across the country. Over in Helmand, Operation Moshtarak got underway with the Brits and US Marines leading the way. Known to Americans as Marjah—the name both of the area and the key battle—the effort was a high-profile blockbuster where the Marines did as much to win headlines as they did to win battles. That operation was a key effort in President Obama's burgeoning surge, that plan to make Afghanistan—not Iraq—the center of military attention. But the surge was just beginning, and it was kicking off in Helmand.

Kandahar? Well, in Kandahar, as far as the White House was concerned, there wasn't anything major happening and there wouldn't be for months, not until the surge started in earnest. As far as Washington was concerned, Bravo Company and the thousands of Fourth Brigade soldiers Obama sent over in the first days of his administration were just marking time.

Bravo slogged it out with no headlines or pomp. They weren't part of the big fight, to officials in the Pentagon and the White House. No, Bravo Company was still fighting Jenio's War, an essentially unknown and unacknowledged effort, tucked into a corner of Afghanistan. And in Jenio's War, after Johnston at Christmas and after Allen Thomas in March, in the springtime, casualties started piling up.

Foot patrols hit something regularly. Step on a bomb and maybe lose a foot. A concussion from an IED here and there. Injuries like these became commonplace, and since they weren't deaths, they became almost accepted by the men of Bravo Company. Johnston's death and Allen's catastrophic explosion set a macabre standard. Nearly all else paled in comparison, and wounds that would have once been considered major injuries became regular old injuries. A leg here, a foot there.

Every day the men wondered, *Is today the day for me?* But they never seemed to encounter the enemy, rarely got to shoot at anyone, never saw the people they were fighting.

You can't have an exceptional hero without having an exceptional villain. That's at the core of so many stories, especially war stories. How can a soldier be a hero by pulling a dirt-covered IED out of the ground? No, he needs to face an onslaught, a barrage. He needs to know and see the force he's up against. He needs to fight bad guys to be a good guy.

What happens to those war stories when the villain isn't exceptional? When he isn't even there? Who was the villain? Was it the Taliban? Who were the Taliban, anyway? Bravo Company patrolled every day, but there wasn't anyone they could stand up against. It's not like the Taliban were out and about, marching in formation on the battlefield. There were no more Halloween Zombie Massacres, no cathartic fights.

Was that farmer sowing his field also surreptitiously emplacing bombs? What about that quiet villager? Did that Afghan choose not to tell the Americans that there was danger around the corner? That farmer's family who never thought about picking up a weapon but who were indifferent to the Americans' fate: Were they Taliban? Maybe the farmer didn't care either way but just wanted a bunch of strangers off his farmland.

Jared Lemon said he sometimes thought about that, switched up his perspective. What if a bunch of well-meaning Afghans came over to America and tried to impose their will in the United States? No matter whether those Afghans were good or bad, Lemon reckoned there's really only one response: Red-blooded Americans would fuck up foreign troops who occupied their farmlands, even those with the best intentions. It's hard to see someone as a bad guy when they are doing what you'd likely be doing in their shoes.

In the beginning, Jared Lemon remembers, those apparently benevolent locals brought in massive IEDs to the Americans. They hand-delivered bombs right to the base as if to say, Look how much we're helping you by digging up and bringing in this horrible thing before it hurts you!

The locals also sometimes pointed danger areas out to the guys from Bravo, showed where bombs had been buried. It seemed to Lemon that they were just looking to get paid rewards for big-ass IEDs that they knew wouldn't work on dismounted troops. The whole time those locals were watching, watching, watching. They watched Bravo Company to figure them out. They might not have had any formal education, but they sure were smart. And at the same time, Lemon remembered, some of those smart, red-blooded Afghans were helping the Taliban and getting Lemon's friends blown up. There was no good way to parse it all. There was no single, uncomplicated way to feel about it.

Down in the Arghandab, the Taliban buried bombs that maimed and killed, and did so with regularity. But they were never able to provide a definitive blow, and maybe they didn't want to. Maybe they wanted to wear down the Americans like the force of erosion, slow and steady and geological.

Bravo rarely met the Taliban face-to-face. They only met farmers. They met people who had goals and desires and aspirations and who didn't want some foreigners tramping across their farmlands. They met people. Maybe they were Taliban, whatever that meant. But maybe they were just people, heroes of their own individual fights.

As Bravo realized there was no real villain, some of the Americans, likewise, came to know deep down that they might not be heroes.

* * *

At Water Reed, Allen stayed as a full-time resident from March 2010 until August, first as an inpatient, barely saved from death, just like anybody in any hospital after a horrible accident. Then he stayed on, continuing with rehab and tests and trying to breathe deeply again. His one ruined lung and other damaged one made it a trial to breathe fully. It was so much work for him at first to try and just have a big yawn.

Walter Reed is a land of middle ground, a place no one expects to visit, a place no one can plan for. A Walter Reed reunion isn't on the evening news. Life or death are definite, can be labeled, categorized, girded for. But this, Danica thought, looking at him lying in a bed at Walter Reed in those first few weeks especially, this is indefinite and uncertain and like stepping into an abyss without preparation.

Danica still thought that one day Allen would just be better. Once the doctors finished up with whatever it is doctors do, with the inevitable treatments, then the inevitable cure would follow. He'd surely get patched up, he'd get well, and they'd continue the life they both expected for themselves and for the baby growing inside her. After that they'd have a normal life, the one they had just so excitedly been planning and talking about.

Even though she was pregnant with his child, Danica was reticent to swoop in and look like she was trying to take control. When young adults are in a situation like this, there's still an expectation that Mom will be the loving woman who will make it all better, so she many times deferred to Allen's mother.

Danica wanted to be in the room with Allen, to sleep next to him, to crawl right into that hospital bed. He was, after all, her rock and protector, a man who went to war at six feet three inches tall and 250 pounds. Now he couldn't take a shit on his own.

Eventually he was able to get around, move with a walker slowly. And then he could stand up and shuffle off to the bathroom.

The indignities that a wounded man must suffer are legion, and though they seem, objectively speaking, to be embarrassments and insults to his very nature, they are not so. Wounds are the simple wages of war. They are what happens when a man pushes his entire stack of life's chips out onto the table for a bet, to go where others dare not, and the Taliban croupier takes them all away from him. Allen's body and mind there at Walter Reed were the result of an upside-down wager. But he was bold enough to make that bet, goddammit, and that's more than most can say for themselves.

So what are we, mere bystanders at the casino, to think and feel after we see what happens to this sort of man? What are we to think of the night Allen went to sleep and the tubes and drain valves and wires connected to his body got all jumbled and tangled so that when he needed to go to the bathroom, he couldn't move? What are we to think of how he, Sergeant Allen Thomas of the 82nd Airborne, made an accident in his bed? This is not something Allen would ever have wanted to talk about. It is not something Danica ever wanted to talk about. And yet it happened. And it happened to others. It happened in the past and it will happen in the future because this is life, and this is war, and it's enraging and it's pathetic, and it's noble, and it's sad, and it's tragic, and it's life in all its glory and all its shame.

It's life, it's life, it's life.

A grown man messing his bed is something we should be forced to face, unblinking. When we think of patriotism, it's not the Veterans Day parades, the Memorial Day celebrations, the Fourth of July backyard picnics we should focus on. Sure, all those things are well and good, but we should also be forced to think of Sergeant Allen Thomas, and of the many noble warriors like him who come home from war to soil their hospital beds.

For those closest to him, Allen wetting his bed was an embarrassment. For the rest of us, it was and will ever remain an attestation, an exemplification, and even a holy tribute. Do not look away from him in his apparent shame. That this strong rock and steady timber of American youth should be cracked and broken—and piss his bed—is beyond what we can ever hope to understand about what it means to go to war.

* * *

Danica had never had to help somebody eat. She'd never had to help somebody go to the bathroom. The pact they'd made with each other hadn't been finalized with marriage yet, there was no "in sickness or in health" clause binding her to the relationship. But she was growing *their* child and in front of her was the Allen she knew and loved dearly. There was the man she had wished goodbye on his way to Afghanistan. Sort of.

"I guess I feel like I lost a piece of myself watching him lie in that hospital bed," she said. "I'm seeing this grown man who led an entire squad in combat lying in a bed, and I had, a week prior, had this expectation that he was going to come home and lead our family, and then there I was."

There was a part of Danica that believed that if she looked closely enough, if she squinted, she could still see the rock, the foundational Allen set deep within his atrophied, struggling body.

When Allen came home on R&R, she had gotten a glimpse of how a deployment can change a man. She had hoped, maybe foolishly, that things would go back. Allen, the real Allen, would return. But watching him in Walter Reed, Danica had to reconcile with the reality of ongoing change. She had to accept that there was no going back to before the days in the Arghandab, for her or for him. At Walter Reed the Technicolor Allen she knew had faded to a pastel.

So here he was. And here she was. Jesus, that was so depressing to think about on the one hand.

But that meant, too, that there was always the possible. Change always happens. Change *could* happen. Together, Allen and Danica could exert their will on his condition and cause the ever-changing Allen to change again.

The Allen that she knew before deployment was a professional soldier. He was caring. He was lively. He always wanted to be the smartest and best person in the room. He could be something like that again. He would be that again—she vowed it, willed it right there in the hospital.

So here they were, together. In this changed reality, in this new world.

CHAPTER 15

DUSTWUN

In the spring, Jared Lemon finally got ready for promotion to sergeant. He was told he had to go see the sergeant major up on the battalion base a few kilometers away from COP Ware for an interview, what's known as a promotion board. All those hours of studying while they were stuck on the training mission in Helmand would finally pay off. But nobody was sending Lemon an armored limousine or flying him out in a VIP helicopter. No, he had to walk to that promotion board along with the other schmucks who needed to go up there for an interview, too.

Lemon put on a brand-new uniform and everything to look his best, a real special event in Afghanistan, where a soldier wears combat utilities until they fall apart at the seams.

These promotion boards with the sergeant major are notoriously fickle. All hopes and dreams of a new rank might be dashed in a few minutes because the sergeant major doesn't like the way a guy folded his beret, or a potential sergeant might forget, when quizzed, about the distance some obscure weapon is able to shoot. Promotion boards are a painful rite of passage, difficult but unavoidable.

Some things about the Army never change, and to have to wander through a dangerous combat zone just to present yourself to the sergeant major for what amounts to an oral exam was a surreal endeavor. The relentless cogs of bureaucracy, of Big Army, never stop grinding, and that's as true in a place like the Arghandab as it is anywhere else.

There's the fighting and the combat, all the stuff that folks back home assume happens in a combat zone. But then there's the chickenshit stuff that happens by inertia, or if you give the organization the benefit of the doubt, you might just say it happens because it's what's needed to keep a reliable organization humming along. Either way, it means things like promotion boards in the middle of Afghanistan.

Lemon put on his brand-new uniform and joined a few other guys who were all going up for the sergeant selection board just like him. Then they trudged off in patrol formation to the big base a few miles away to see the battalion sergeant major to properly perpetuate the United States Army.

Please remember, though, it's not as though the Taliban respects the promotion schedule of the United States Army, or pauses their insurgency to make way for guys like Lemon to earn a new rank. No, it's business as usual for the Taliban, just as it's business as usual for the Army. That meant Lemon and the others had to manage all the banal threats of a foot patrol in the Arghandab as they made their way to an equally banal promotion board. Poor Lemon and the others had to wade through canals and go through the usual patrolling problems, so he showed up for the board with his brand-new uniform all muddy and dripping.

It was so typically Army.

But then as soon as they got there, the sergeant major told them he didn't have time to see them because he was going out on some battlefield tour. Then he roared off in a Humvee.

What the fuck? Any patrol was a literal risk of life and limb. This guy couldn't clear an hour in his calendar, if not to respect the promotion board interviews scheduled, then at least as recompense to the men for their potentially perilous journey? They turned around and just walked back to Bravo's combat outpost, tirelessly watching for IEDs along the way.

Lemon picked up the rank of sergeant soon after anyway and was in disbelief that he did so without having to face the sergeant major at a promotion board. He'd gotten around the unwavering requirement somehow by happenstance. All that bullshit for nothing. But at least he was a sergeant now.

* * *

Lemon's canceled board interview foot patrol came in the midst of Bravo's other patrols regularly hitting bombs. Johnston was dead and Allen was back home. It was early spring and Bravo was starting to find IEDs by stepping on them—not a lot but enough. Guys from Bravo Company, guys from Charlie Company, and other units in what had been Jenio's 2-508 were getting hurt regularly, racking up injuries for the Purple Heart list: broken clavicle, punctured lung, maimed leg. Other injuries, like a concussion from being too close to a bomb going off, might not even earn a person a Purple Heart.

The Army didn't have fancy concussion protocols, didn't always check a soldier out to see if his head was OK. The Army certainly didn't note in his medical record every time he got his bell rung.

The month of March 2010 saw seven major injuries that sent men back to the United States or to a major base to recuperate. That's not to mention the small injuries that didn't require medevacs or trips to base hospitals. Take for instance Jordan Flake. He seemed unharmed by the suicide bomber, but it turns out he was hit in the forearm by a piece of shrapnel. A couple weeks later it worked its way to the surface and he dug it out with his Gerber multitool. That kind of wound didn't end up on anybody's casualty roster or spreadsheet of injuries. As far as the Army was considered, it never happened.

Enough guys were stepping on things now, getting injured and shipped back home, that Bravo had to start getting combat replacements sent over, new troops here and there who could plug holes in the roster. While a US Army squad of a dozen men can be a force of nature in combat, it becomes nearly ineffective if it's missing even two guys.

For Bravo, this time would turn out to be an interim. Those legiti-mately suffered, Purple Heart–earning injuries would be nearly forgotten in the shadow cast by fighting season. An event that spring, as the ground thawed, marked the dark turning point for Bravo Company. It began as something funny. Of course, no one in polite company would have thought it was funny. It was the kind of thing that's only funny in a combat zone where the darkest, blackest humor is what gets a big laugh. It's funny only to a combat veteran. Or a sociopath.

* * *

A squad was out on patrol and it had along Private Betts, a new guy. Betts was kinda skinny at the time and came in as a combat replacement. Poor bastards like Betts don't get the advantages of training up with a team, building trust or friendships before leaving for a deployment. They don't get the bonding experiences of spending months back in the States with their units, commiserating before sunup on the rifle range, sucking down beers on the weekends, and learning all the inside jokes.

Combat replacements are something the Army doesn't talk about very loudly because of the well-deserved abysmal reputation the practice got back in Vietnam. Back then as guys were wounded or killed, they were swapped out piecemeal with newbies shipped over one at a time or in small groups. It led to disjointed units lacking personal bonds and esprit de corps. Some argue it was injurious—if not lethal—for the mission in Vietnam.

And yet, there have to be combat replacements to plug holes in a roster. Guys like Betts show up and join a unit that's worked up together for the deployment for maybe a year, and then have been out on patrol together for months in-country.

The new guy comes in and doesn't know anyone, and they don't know him. They don't know if he can be trusted and don't even know if he's been well trained. Odds are he's a young soldier fresh out of boot camp and has only just learned the basics of soldiering, and here he comes, thrown into real-life, no-shit combat alongside grizzled troops who lord it over him.

Betts was the real-life equivalent of one of those old *Star Trek* crew members from the old TV show, the guys in the red shirts who got wiped out first in combat with aliens. Old hands just assumed Betts was going to be the one to get fucked-up. After all, the dictates of cosmic propriety should most certainly make it the new guy, the one nobody cares about, who gets the bad luck. If he gets blown up, well, at least it wasn't one of the real members of the team, right?

In March of 2010, Private Betts was out with his brand-new squad. The poor guy had only been with the company for what seemed like a few days. He'd maybe sat watch in a guard tower a couple times, and suddenly he was out on a foot patrol in the Arghandab.

It was the end of a two-day patrol, they were walking back to the COP. Betts was about midway in the patrol formation in the dead of night, around 0200 hours, and hadn't quite yet mastered how to walk right behind the guys in front of him. Those Bravo veterans weren't slowing down for the cherry to learn the ropes. Sure enough he stepped in just the wrong spot.

Bang!

Betts stepped directly on a toe popper, a mine about the size of a hand grenade meant to blow off part of a man's foot. Those toe poppers are real bastards, designed to maim a guy, cripple him so then the squad has to deal with a casualty. They're a quick hit that does just enough damage.

Since they'd been patrolling in near silence, that sudden explosion seemed pretty loud, sounded like it could be bad. Betts started screaming about his foot and Yeske, with his trusty radio, got on the horn right away calling it in, thinking Betts now had a stump and was an urgent surgical.

Yeske with his EMT training was ready to get over there and take care of Betts, calm him down, tell him it's all OK and his dick's still there and the whole nine yards. Most importantly, though, Yeske wanted to make sure he could save the kid's life. All that screaming, Jesus H. Christ, it must be bad. Doc was out there, too, and they scrambled over to him and braced for the worst.

They got there and they looked down at his foot. Suddenly, their fatherly compassion and doctorly urgency disappeared. They started to laugh. No kidding, they started *laughing*.

"This motherfucker just got the best explosion ever, and he's still got his foot," Doc said to Yeske.

The popper was buried too deep, evidently, so the explosion was absorbed by packed earth rather than by Betts's foot, it seemed.

No matter how well the Taliban buried something, how perfectly it's been planted, Mother Nature can always intervene. Some rain might help pack the dirt too hard, so over the course of a few months a perfectly placed bomb loses its pizzazz. It seemed as if that's what had happened with Betts—the bomb just didn't do what it was supposed to.

That and Betts was wearing his new boots. They were some kind of newfangled combat boots with crazy steel shanks to make a soldier's foot into a mini tank. The new guy was wearing shoes custom-made, literally custom-fucking-made, for this precise situation. His foot still looked like a foot, his boot still looked like a boot. No hamburger or anything.

So Doc and Yeske started laughing. It still makes them laugh today. The kind of laugh where they have to shake their head at the same time, nodding "no, no" because they know it's a low-down, miserably mean joke. They know, they admit, that only combat troops or sociopaths would laugh at a guy who nearly got blown up, and they shake their heads "no, no" to prove they're not sociopaths.

Doc and Yeske will admit as much even now that their compassion was lacking. Betts had, after all, stepped on an IED, had been blown up and injured. It must have hurt like hell, could be a permanently disabling thing, who knows? And it had to have been supremely scary and unnerving out there in the darkness, among a group of soldiers he hardly knew. He wasn't being a pussy, he was just someone they could call a pussy, which is the way it often goes with soldiers acting callous beyond their years.

There in the dark of the Arghandab, they weren't laughing the glorious laughter of relief, of finding out the guy's OK. No, Doc and Yeske were laughing at the preposterousness of the situation. This poor bastard private who didn't know anyone and didn't know enough to even stay in line in patrol went and stepped on a mine designed to blow off his foot and it didn't do the job. They were laughing because Betts didn't—couldn't—understand his good fortune. This guy hadn't seen Johnston or Allen Thomas or any of the other injuries, so he had no context into which he could place his current predicament. They laughed because he wasn't an urgent surgical. They laughed because it wasn't them. The sheer fucking luck of this guy! And him screaming like crazy.

OK, granted, his ankle was broken, they'd give him that much. Once they stopped laughing and looked at it, well, it seemed like Betts might have shattered his ankle pretty good. But still, come on, what luck! If he only knew!

Doc gave the hollering kid a shot of morphine because he had probably never experienced pain like that before.

Doc and Yeske were laughing, and Betts was yelling. So they started yelling back at him to shut the fuck up, what's all this racket about, et cetera and so on. Another Bravo guy who was there actually slapped Betts, they said, as if he were a hyperventilating damsel in an old 1940s movie. It was still the black of night out there, but they sent the metal detectors out front, as usual, and swept out a landing zone for a chopper to come pick up this loud, supremely lucky SOB.

By the time all that was done, they were totally wiped out from the last couple days of patrol. Hill, along with Third Squad of First Platoon, came to help them out, add a little support for the squad that had just taken a casualty. Once Hill arrived he said everybody was going to hunker down for the night and figure out things in the morning when the sun came up and shed its light on the circumstances, making everything easier.

So they set up a defensive perimeter and lay down on the ground for some sleep, with the usual guards and sentries. Setting up a defensive perimeter isn't so hard, but it takes time and effort and has to be done. Teams of men are spaced out to give a unit maybe a few dozen yards of space between each other. They all face outward from the rough square they've formed and they wait to see if anything comes.

Adios, Private Betts. What a laugh. Thank goodness that was all over with.

* * *

But when the sun rose the next day, they realized it wasn't all over with. And it wasn't so funny anymore. Sure, Betts got relatively lucky with a dud of a toe popper and an uneventful chopper ride out. But the Taliban were really, really good at burying things in the ground, and once the sun rose, Bravo realized they were surrounded by bombs.

Patrolling at night pretty much guaranteed the Taliban couldn't take potshots or snipe at a patrol, and it allowed the Americans to move under cover of darkness, but it did prevent them from seeing everything. As they scanned the terrain, with the cold morning light spilling over the dirt, the soldiers began to notice little indicators, visual cues easy to miss in the dark, but in the daylight all too obvious. Over there some disturbed ground, and also over here, then all around them. Holy shit, they realized they were in the middle of what seemed to them a minefield, camped out in the GD middle.

No matter how much Bravo Company had learned to this point, they still made plenty of mistakes. And now they found themselves in a minefield.

* * *

Memory is fragile. It shows its cracks from the very beginning, at its very inception. As soon as an event happens, there's an imperfect memory of it formed. From there, it starts to crumble. And yet, at the same time, memory is adamantine. Memory, once formed, cannot be shaken and becomes indisputable to the one recalling it.

Memory is a paradox. And remembering an event as it was becomes at once impossible and indubitable. This is a human burden, to try and reconcile these truths that are not self-evident. And this is the soldier's burden. It's a burden for everyone who remembers Staff Sergeant Scott Brunkhorst.

Brunkhorst's team of about a dozen came out to help identify problems and figure out how they'd deal with the minefield. A handsome and strong guy, Brunk was a respected leader and a dude who knew a hell of a lot about soldiering. He was one of those soldiers who looked the way a soldier should look, acted the way a soldier should act, and had the experience of a few deployments under his belt.

Brunkhorst certainly should have known what he was doing when it came to operating in the middle of a minefield, and that's why he'd come out with his team, to help everyone navigate their way out safely. One of his team members, one Sergeant Lee, was walking around out there and accidentally found another of those toe poppers by stepping on it.

Bam!

The same thing that happened to Betts happened to Lee—the toe popper broke his foot but didn't blow it off. Yeske and Doc acted, this time without uproarious laughter. Brunk then set his squad into positions so they wouldn't move around anymore, wouldn't foolishly step on any more bombs.

Nobody really remembers what happened after that, but at the same time, everyone remembers it with crystal clarity. According to one telling, one that seems most believable, Brunk told his guys to hold fast so they wouldn't get themselves blown up and then he kept walking to take a look around, confident in his own abilities. He found some kind of exposed wire that didn't need to be pulled hard to be triggered, even though it looked like it did. It was hooked up to a delicate mechanism that made it go off as soon as he messed with it in any way.

Another telling is that one of the guys from his squad took a knee. The guy knelt right down on a pressure-activated trigger hidden in the ground with cords that traced their way back to a big, big bomb that Brunk happened to just then be standing on top of. While not every mine goes off as intended, this one did. And it wasn't a mere toe popper.

According to another telling, Brunk got out there and was carefully pacing around, inspecting the ground for telltale marks of an IED in the dirt, using his finely tuned experience to scout out danger and eliminate it. And then, simple enough, he accidentally stepped on the IED.

A fourth telling goes back a bit and has Brunk finding out bad news from home that broke him up something horrible, and he went out on that patrol with anger and despair boiling inside him. Out there among the IEDs, some remember Brunkhorst was nearly stomping around and it was in that way he triggered the explosive.

Yet another telling has it that Brunk pursued some unnamed and unidentified Taliban fighter, forcing the enemy to detonate an IED he was wearing or carrying or something, thereby saving his squad from the bomber's payload. This final telling is what made it into the newspapers, cementing its status as "official" and Brunk as a selfless hero.

In any case some kind of explosion went off.

Boom!

When the dust cleared after the explosion Bravo realized they had no idea where Brunk went. There was no more Brunk. The blast was so big, his body—his being—just sort of . . . disappeared. He wasn't *anything* anymore. Brunk was just missing. Gone.

All the different memories of the event, many of them spoken in hushed tones because they shouldn't be spoken aloud, don't really matter in the end. The end result is always indisputably the same. Brunk was no more. The IED was so large, Armendariz remembered, when they found the spot where the explosion went off there was nothing but a hole in the ground. No trace of the sergeant. A life atomized.

It's hard, in the moment, to come to the determination that a guy has just ceased to exist because of an explosion. They looked for him. No Brunk. They found his plate carrier, parts of his rifle and his helmet, but nothing else. So they got on the radio and called in a DUSTWUN, which stands for "Duty Status Whereabouts Unknown." Translated into regular English it means someone's been lost in a combat zone. Captured, kidnapped, walked off unknowingly, or just straight up missing: It's one of the most dreaded things to hear on a radio.

The entire area of operations nearly ground to a halt, and about every resource available, including top-tier secret stuff reserved for Special Ops, got rerouted to help find the DUSTWUN. The Bravo guys thought Brunk might have been blown up, but who knows, he might have gotten snatched. He was gone, that's all they knew.

It took more than an hour of looking until someone found some part of him big enough for everyone to realize that Brunk wasn't DUSTWUN. No, he'd been all but obliterated by that bomb.

* * *

While the men in the minefield came around to realizing that most of Brunk had been turned into nothingness, there was evidence that some parts still remained, so Armendariz's entire platoon was told to get in a line and sweep the area anyway. They had to find whatever pieces of Brunk they could.

There's something known as a police call on the rifle range, something every soldier knows well. Ranges on military bases are always exceptionally clean, no shell casings left lying around, no scraps of metal or trash.

To make sure that's always so, at the end of a day of shooting everyone gets in a line and sweeps the grass or dirt between the firing line and targets looking for every single, tiny, spent cartridge to make sure the hundreds of meters of grass and dirt are spotless. Nobody can go home until the place is spick-and-span, a whole outdoor area that looks as though it's been vacuumed.

That's what they did on that day in March in the middle of Afghanistan. They lined up next to each other, almost shoulder to shoulder, and started walking slowly, picking up whatever they could find of Brunk and putting it into regular old garbage bags brought up from the COP because that's the best thing they could find to use. Other guys put Brunk into their assault packs because they didn't have a garbage bag at hand. They had to put pieces of their friend into their backpacks.

One guy picked up a piece of Brunk's scalp. Armendariz picked up Brunk's shoulder. Or maybe it was his hip? It looked like a ham hock that had been charred around the edges. To this day Armendariz, a guy who saw some crazy stuff in his time in the military, remembers that police call as being one of the worst things he ever had to do in the Army.

Armstrong was on the radio and heard the guys wondering whether they'd found Brunkhorst or a piece of a roasted goat.

"It was a fucked-up thing to do," Armendariz said. "I was picking up pieces of my buddy."

Getting back to the COP that night was when things set in for Bravo that something else had begun, a new phase of dread and death and dismemberment. It had been one thing when Johnston was killed, that had been real enough. Now they had spent the night among mines expertly laid by somebody they never even saw or got to shoot at. They had to tiptoe out of it and then go around picking up scraps of their friend. And if Brunk, an excellent and experienced soldier, could get blown up, what did that mean for the rest of them?

Lieutenant James Harris, the company executive officer, was at the COP for the whole Brunk event, following it closely on the radio. He was set to go on mid-deployment leave and flew home soon after everyone got back to the COP with their bags full of body parts. He went back to the States, to Washington, DC, to stay with his cousin. She lived in the nation's capital, and that seemed a good place to spend some of his R&R.

Harris was there when he found out Brunk would be buried in Arlington. He decided he should go, since he'd be the only person from the deployment who'd attend, even though he didn't really know Brunk and didn't know Brunk's family. Heck, he wasn't really even in Brunk's chain of command, just an officer in the same company who had respected the sergeant and who listened in on the radio to the events following his death.

How would he act at the funeral? Would he step forward as an officer and represent Bravo Company? Represent 2-508? Would he just stand back? He didn't even have his service uniform, the dress uniform. By that point in Afghanistan he'd earned some new ribbons he needed to add to his uniform for it to be in regulation. Maybe he could order a new ribbon rack and have it shipped overnight or something? No, that would be dumb, because he didn't even have a uniform to wear.

How could he handle this? he wondered. Thankfully his cousin's boyfriend was about his size and had a suit he could borrow. So there, at Arlington, for a funeral of a man in his unit who was killed in combat, Lieutenant James Harris—a man on his break from the shitstorm in Arghandab and soon to reenter it—wore a borrowed civilian suit to mourn the death of a man who'd been vaporized.

He wanted to tell the family the story. Not all the details, mind you. He just wanted to let them know the basics, a vague general outline, because surely the family wants that. Needs that. The Army never really gives any details on these matters.

When the time came he decided he'd just stand in the back and only say something if someone approached him. No one did. He was unrecognizable in his generic suit. They buried Brunk, and he stood at the grave site looking like a nervous salesman. He said nothing, nobody seemed to notice him.

He left Arlington without saying a word to the family.

In a few days, he was on a flight back to the Arghandab.

CHAPTER 16

PINK MIST

By April, it didn't seem things could be any worse. After Brunkhorst, some guys in the battalion refused to go out on patrol—said no way, and stayed ensconced in their combat outposts. Other guys came up with excuses so they wouldn't have to go.

The modern Army can be cruel and unforgiving. Back in the United States, in garrison, there are all sorts of draconian measures commanders can use to compel troops to do things. If a guy doesn't hop to it when tasked with something he can get an informal physical training session—push-ups and squats all by himself—that drills him into the dirt. He can get an official counseling, paperwork that means his career can be derailed. He can have privileges like leave and liberty taken away, seemingly at a whim.

Despite the idea that Hessian discipline pervades the military, at some point—oddly enough, it mostly applies on a deployment—there's no power a commander can bring to bear that can make a cowering soldier go out beyond the wire.

In the Army, men and women ultimately follow combat orders because they want to. There's an internal motivation at work compelling them to go out there into harm's way. All the discipline and terror instilled back in the States is supposed to build up a team of soldiers who just do what they're told on deployment because they've internalized their duty so deeply. Punishment only works if someone fears the trouble they'll get into for *not* doing something more than they fear the thing they're supposed to do. And for some soldiers, going into the Arghandab on foot patrol was the thing they feared most on this planet, and they could avoid it if they really wanted to.

No matter how crappy conditions were for them at COP Ware, the Arghandab was not the British campaign of the 1800s, a bunch of troops marching through Afghanistan with no bases and no logistics. Those Brits had to keep going or get left behind in hostile territory with no supplies or support. By the year 2010, there was no march-or-die reality. Bravo had an outpost to live in where things felt safe enough.

The American style of war in Afghanistan was to establish bases—big and small—and venture forth from them and back again. A soldier may spend a night or two out on a lengthy patrol, but then he went back to the relative comfort of a base, even if it was a COP as bare-bones as the one Bravo Company occupied.

If a lowly soldier put his foot down and refused to go, he was safe and secure on a COP. He was safe from the immediate exigencies of war. A guy who did something like that wouldn't even get hazed by his fellow soldiers, because if he was the type of shithead who refused to patrol next to his fellow soldiers, he'd definitely be the kind of shithead who would rat out fellow troops if they hazed him for refusing to patrol. And what other soldier really wants a piece of shit like that out on patrol anyway? Some unreliable sad sack is more trouble than he's worth.

Sure, a goldbricker who won't patrol will get an Article 15, get officially disciplined and busted down in rank, and maybe even thrown out of the Army. But all that punishment comes later. In the here and now, a guy who doesn't want to patrol can't be forced to go out, and there were some guys wouldn't leave the wire. What could commanders or vengeful fellow troops do to them?

Sometimes the shirkers stood guard duty on the base, something that requires little more than a warm body willing to stay awake and watch to make sure bad guys don't sneak in. Guarding a base was for their own good, they knew. An Article 15 and the shame of being a coward is better than getting blown up, they figured. Other shirkers were savvy and figured out injuries or excuses to not go out. Malingerers, that's what injury-fakers are called in the military.

That means a command was left with guys who wanted to go out of the wire. Or maybe they didn't want to go out there, but felt, instead, a duty to go. Either way, it came from a place within them. Yes, they went because they knew that's the mission that the Army has given them because someone, somewhere, has decided that's the best way for them to fight the Taliban or help the Afghan people or whatever the end goal is.

Sure, in the modern Army, there's all kinds of external pressures. There's peer pressure, and threats, cajoling. There's commanders and senior sergeants breathing down their necks. There's a threat of a bad discharge from the Army. But nobody's going to shoot them for disobeying.

And so it's actually more surprising that there's so many guys willing to go out there, into harm's way. Who choose to do it. When you really get down to it, it's a blessed miracle that there aren't more shirkers. At any given moment the whole edifice of discipline would crumble to dust if everyone said, "Nope."

Soldiers go out there day after day even though they may say they don't want to. In Bravo Company they bitched, they moaned, they grumbled. They complained and, to a man, made threats of never, ever, ever going back out. It's second nature for an infantryman to complain. But most of those dumb, beautiful, marvelous bastards stepped out on patrol every day into the Arghandab, even after everything they'd gone through.

Early April saw more injuries, two major IED casualties. More reasons not to go out.

Yet the vast majority of them went because their friends went. They went because deep down they needed to do it, because it's what they had prepared their whole lives to do. It's ultimately a free will decision by guys in a volunteer army. Rest assured, they decide to go out of the wire. Don't let them ever fool you on that one.

Every day, then, every patrol, became a testament. What kind of testament? Well, who can really say? Perhaps it was a testament to how supremely stupid they all were. Perhaps a monument to the carelessness of youth. An edifice of soldierly idiocy? Maybe it was a testament to the fact that some of them had few other options in life other than drawing a paycheck by walking around minefields with rifles? Perhaps it was a lamentable proof of how meager the alternatives were back home. But goddamn, so what if that was the case? So what if they would be nothing without going out on these stupid patrols day after day after day? Those daily affirmations proved their worth as soldiers and as men.

And yet, let's not fool ourselves that it's all altruism and call of duty. There's something else that draws a man out on patrol, something that's only available out there where it's scary and hot and dangerous.

That's the place where a young man who might not have anything else in this entire world has the full faith and credit of the United States government. He can shoot at someone and not get in trouble so long as that person is trying to kill him. Out there on patrol, with a rifle, the soldiers of Bravo knew, to a man, that as long as they weren't stepping on a mine, they were masters of their own universe, striding across Afghanistan with guns.

In those moments, a soldier learns that—as long as he doesn't die or get blown up—he's invincible and unstoppable and omnipotent. He's a panjandrum of war living out fantasies tattooed on his brain since the first time he watched *Full Metal Jacket* on TV. And all of the might of America is there behind him, cheering him on and telling him he's a hero.

Bravo Company knew something most people never will. They knew what it's like to do something because they took an oath to do it. They knew one of the most wonderful and horrible truths possible: the pure aesthetic experience of knowing what it's like to have life and death balanced there on the edge of every moment.

They had the morbidly titillating defiance of the odds every day. There was the knowing—just knowing—that something will eventually happen to someone out there in war—whether it was them or the bad guys.

Oh, dear God, it was a shitty place to be. But there was nothing else in the world like it. And the motherfucking shirkers could never know that feeling. They'd never have the rapture-like orgasmic feeling that comes with stepping out of the wire to defy the odds, to fulfill their oath. And that, in and of itself, was why they kept going out.

* * *

It got to the point for Bravo where they'd joke before every patrol about who it'd be that day to step on an IED. They joked because they had to.

They'd say to each other, "Look man, if I get blown up and lose a leg, don't try to save me."

It seemed funny in the moment, but there was no way to know how serious a guy was when he said that. They never imagined the weight it heaped on their buddies, the guys next to them. What if a guy did lose a leg? What's his buddy supposed to do?

Is he supposed to honor that jokey pledge that some nineteen-year-old kid said as he stepped out on patrol trying to sound tough? Was that a real request? Or is his buddy supposed to realize that it's just a leg, man, and that joke was just a joke? Does he let him bleed out, or does he save him? Of course when the time comes he saves him!

Either way, after a while that conundrum solved itself as more and more legs were lost. While legs were lost, lives were saved, because of course that's what a buddy does, joke pledges be damned.

As legs were lost, guys started reevaluating things. Pledges and promises evolved. They started to say, "Man if I get blown up and lose *both legs*, don't try and save me." But after a while two legs gone didn't seem so bad. So they'd say, "Man if I get blown up and I lose my dick, don't try and save me." That one never changed. The dick is a sacred piece of Army gear that no soldier can imagine losing. Even the balls are somewhat expendable. A guy would prefer to keep those, of course, but losing nuts isn't in the same league as getting his dick blown off. Fuck that. No way. You can always joke about losing a ball or two. But dickless? No, Sir.

If a fellow loses a leg—even two of them—he could still get some carbon-fiber blades and run around like Oscar Pistorius, that South African Olympian. He might even stay in the Army if he wanted. That was a real option. Back then you'd see soldiers on fake legs, still on active duty, walking around base, some looking like they were trying to Hula-Hoop while balancing on a waterbed. By 2010, a legless soldier could get prosthetics with a set of flippers attached if he wanted to go scuba diving. Cinch a cleat on a separate one if he wanted to play some softball. All of them free through Walter Reed!

Truth to tell, down deep in a place only a soldier himself knows, he might even say . . . no, there's no way he could even say it, not out loud. He'd think quietly to himself: *Shit, a missing leg would be rock-solid proof of my bona fides, would prove I've been there. Man, it might even get me some free beers at Applebee's.*

That fantasy beer would then lead to dreams of getting laid. It might be easy pickings with the ladies, using that peg-leg badge of honor for everyone to see at the bar. Free beers, maybe a couple of appetizers, and everyone at the bar staring at that leg of his, just imagining how he lost it. Let them imagine the worst, civilians and rear echelon motherfuckers. Oh baby, how they would stare at it!

(PTSD, TBI, all the rest, that doesn't often register in a young soldier's mind when thinking about the consequences of war, but who's got time to worry about all that?)

On top of all those free Bud Lights and tater skins would be that holy grail, a pension from the Department of Defense, health care from the VA. Now, that would be living.

And he might think to himself, pants. He'd never have to wear pants again! He could be like that double-amputee veteran senator who rolled around Washington in her wheelchair, or the guy in Congress, walkin' around in a suit on Capitol Hill, but with no pants. The guy wore shorts with the suit, which meant that everyone could see his prosthetics as he limped around the Capitol. That was the way to do it, man! Pants would hide from the goddamn civilians that glorious carbon-fiber prosthetic at the bottom of his stump that he was already dreaming about.

In his mind's eye, some crusty Vietnam vet at one end of the bar would give him a knowing nod of the head. Same time—in his mind's eye—at the other end of the bar there would be some other veteran having a drink, a pussy-ass POG veteran who would just stare ashamedly at that sweet stump. Hahaha, no free wings or jalapeño poppers for that asshole!

But wait, this dreamer might think, a guy might lose more than a leg. It's not like he's got it *in writing* from the Taliban that they'll just take a foot or something. Yeah, maybe on second thought it's best just to not step on an IED at all. A fellow can't guarantee it's just a leg, after all. He might get killed. Or worse, a blown-off dick and balls. And a dude like that isn't picking up chicks at the bar, no how. Not a good trade-off for the appetizers.

A soldier, if he has to make a deal with the cosmic reality—make a deal with God—well, a lost leg is the deal to make. And no way an arm. Shit, losing an arm would be awful. A missing leg looks cool, but a guy missing an arm just looks like some charity case out of a World War I scrapbook. A guy can't do basic shit without an arm, right? Can't even wipe his ass properly. Besides, how would you get an arm blown off anyway, with IEDs buried in the ground so close to feet and legs? Well, it can happen. Anything can happen in war, because there's no dealmaking with the Taliban. There's no dealmaking with cosmic reality. There's no dealmaking with God.

* * *

Sergeant Jared Lemon was a team leader by April, one of the guys who wouldn't—couldn't—dream of sitting out a patrol. He was in charge of three other soldiers now, a typical fire team size, which included one of his best friends, Specialist Joseph Caron.

Three of those fire teams make up a squad, and the squad Lemon was part of was out on patrol on a hot night in April in the middle of the deployment with all the leaves and greenery and cover and concealment that had been growing throughout the spring, the things that made it ever easier for the Taliban to stick IEDs in the ground and harder for Bravo to find them. The misery and fright was ever-present by this point. Every step of every patrol.

Sergeant Alex Jauregui was the squad leader. He was good, everyone agrees. He didn't cut corners and he knew his stuff. He was in the business of daily caretaking, making constant checks and adjustments. As always, the squad of just over a dozen people had planned the patrol route ahead of time so they wouldn't walk where another patrol had walked recently. They did their best never to cross the same area twice in the same way, always to make the routes a little different.

Armstrong had even assigned a soldier at the COP to plot out patrols on a map, keep track, so they'd know who'd already been that way and when. But this night, in the middle of a patrol, Sergeant J turned to Nick Armendariz, a veteran of combat, with a sickening realization. Sergeant

J said he suddenly worried that maybe another squad had patrolled this route a couple nights ago.

But Jesus, by the time he realized that, half the squad had already walked across a tricky area with walls and things to climb over, so it wasn't so easy to tell them to backtrack. Sergeant J wasn't about to have them return, that would put them all at risk. With half of his soldiers across already, there was no way to go but forward. He told them to keep going, and he hoped he was wrong about the route. And he hoped to God that the Taliban hadn't been paying attention if another patrol had been through there. Because if they'd been paying attention, they'd know right where to put a bomb.

The Taliban always paid attention.

And it turns out a Bravo Company patrol had apparently gone that way a few days ago. How had they not taken note of that? How had they not noticed? With so many things to keep track of, at some point something slips through the cracks.

Something has to slip through, right? Doesn't it?

And here Sergeant J's squad found themselves with half the squad that still had to get across all that treacherous ground. The patrol had found a spot to cross over a wall—of course they'd always go over walls instead of through gaps in the wall, those gaps were easy pickings for the Taliban. Shit, there were trees everywhere, too. Trees here and there, walking in and among orchards that could get so dense so suddenly. Overpowering and oppressive.

Over the wall the squad had been going, one after the other after the mine sweeper first cleared a path everyone was obliged to follow.

Caron and Lemon were trudging just behind Armendariz, who remembers hearing them bitch about this and that, complaining in true soldiers' fashion as they walked along.

Armendariz was carrying the M240 machine gun, a hulking beast that gets heavy as hell out on patrol but can be decisive in a firefight. A 240 isn't always part of a dismounted squad's weaponry, but on foot patrol in Afghanistan the 240 became a staple because of the firepower it could bring to bear in a moment. He hopped the wall, then helped his assistant gunner hop over. That poor A-gunner, Armen can't even remember the guy's name now, was still green as hell. He had just arrived as a combat replacement, and this was one of his first patrols in the Arghandab.

The men of the squad made their way over that dangerous area and soon enough came Lemon's fire team. Over the wall Lemon went. He went carefully, carefully.

Joey Caron came next. He was a SAW gunner and carried his light machine gun. "Light machine gun" was a misnomer. Caron had so much shit, about a hundred pounds, with the gun and the belts of extra ammunition. So Lemon grabbed the SAW from him to lighten the load as Caron prepared to get over the wall. Caron made it over, and Lemon reached his arm out to hand back the SAW. He stuck his arm way out there to hand him the gun, and . . .

Ping!

Explosions make all kinds of sounds. It's not just *ka-boom*. They can go *pop* or *pow* or *bang* or *boom* or *BOOM* or *crunch* or *ka-RUNCH* or *KA-runch*. Sure, every explosion sounds a bit like every other—there's a family resemblance of sorts. But each one has its own signature, depending on a number of factors. Was it buried shallow or deep? What kind of soil was it in? And was it close?

Was it really close?

Lemon was really close. He was right there, holding out the SAW for one of his best friends to take out of his hand. And when you're really close like that it can sound like a *ping*. Metallic, high-pitched, and ringing out like a bell.

Ping!

Lemon knew only one thing for certain and immediately, before he even thought about himself, that Joey Caron from Tacoma, Washington, who had wanted nothing more than to be a soldier, was no longer Joey Caron. He was gone.

Joey was even closer to that explosion than Lemon. He was at the very spot where that IED went off. He was standing at the one place, there in the middle of Afghanistan, where he shouldn't have been. But he couldn't have been anywhere else. After all, he'd practically been bred to be a soldier.

His dad, Jeff, had been in the Army, 101st Airborne Division, and his granddad had done two tours in Vietnam. Caron had always played

Army out there in the woods of Washington State, which is a wonderful fantasyland for a kid to play soldier. On September 11, he was just a young teen. But that day he waited for his dad, Jeff, to come home, and he made his dad come out to the porch with him.

He wanted to talk to his dad away from the rest of the family, away from his siblings, to tell him that he was going to join the Army as soon as he could to keep the people who were responsible for 9/11 from ever coming to the United States. His dad, a military man himself, agreed. He said that would be just fine. And from that moment on, Joey Caron spent his time becoming a soldier.

Joey joined Air Force JROTC because, hell, it was the only ROTC program at his high school. It was a great program, and he got his Cessna pilot's license through JROTC before he even had a driver's license.

Joey was an all-state wrestler and played varsity football. He was soft-spoken and disarming, despite his soldierly proclivities. And he had a way with the girls, yes he did. Girls just felt comfortable with him, his dad recalls. "It was almost uncanny how he was with them," Jeff said with a laugh. "After he passed, so many girls said they could have been my daughter-in-law."

On the day he was blown up by the IED, Caron had been hauling that M249 squad automatic rifle, the light machine gun, in part because he could flat-out shoot.

His dad started taking him into the woods when he was about three years old. Joey and his sister went out with Dad to shoot as soon as they could heft a .22 rifle up to their tiny shoulders. Jeff was right there and helped steady his children as they learned how to let loose a round.

Before long, Joey Caron was going out in the woods whenever he could. He spent plenty of time there with his father. They might walk into those great Pacific Northwest forests, or they might drive out there in a pickup truck. Sometimes they'd go out to just watch the awful majesty of loggers clear-cutting. Or they'd go big-game hunting. Caron was just a teenager, but he was a helluva shot with the .30-06 or the .300 Win Mag rifle, knocking targets down as far out as he'd want. Still, when they hunted, Joey would go out with his dad and Jeff Caron would often take the shot to fell an animal. Then Joey Caron, wrestling and football star, would pack out all that dressed—and heavy as hell—meat. He was the best partner his father could have asked for.

That true aim, that love of guns, put Caron in good stead once he hit boot camp and then joined the 82nd Airborne Division. It didn't take long once he was with Bravo Company to prove his mettle with a medium machine gun. Hell, those things shoot just about the same size round as a deer rifle, just a lot more of them.

Before the 2009 Afghanistan deployment, lowly PFC Joey Caron was out with the rest of the company on a live-fire night shoot on a range. He was just an assistant machine gunner, helping feed ammo to the machine gunner on the 240. An instructor came by and tapped the gunner to tell him that some pretend bad guy had shot him. It was part of the training, knock out the gunner and see whether the assistant gunner would be a complete nincompoop behind the gun.

Caron was no dunce on that gun. Ready to go, he grabbed that medium machine gun and started hammering away at a target in the distance. The battalion commander came by and saw a PFC he didn't recognize jamming away with the machine gun.

"Who the hell is on that Bravo?" the CO yelled out, referring to the machine gun.

"PFC Caron, Sir," came the reply.

"How'd you learn to shoot like that?"

"My father, Sir!"

"Well, how come you're not in my Ranger Battalion?" asked the CO, a veteran of the elite Ranger units.

"I'm working on it, Sir!" came the reply in between bursts from the gun as he kept pouring automatic fire onto the target.

The next day the CO presented Caron with a challenge coin, a token of appreciation typically stamped with the CO's name and rank. It's one of the military's informal bestowals of merit.

Caron couldn't wait to tell his dad the story and to give him that challenge coin as a token of thanks. Joey Caron wasn't one to keep trinkets and mementos like that. He'd rather share them with his dad.

Same thing with his Airborne wings. As soon as he graduated jump school he gave his original wings to his dad. And he made sure to tell Jeff that they were Blood Wings, just like Jeff earned back in the day when he was with the 101st Airborne Division.

You weren't allowed to get Blood Wings anymore. It was against regulations, but Joey found a way to get them.

Jump wings are a small, metal insignia with a pair of pins on the back to attach to a cloth uniform. To get Blood Wings, you take the safety backings off those pins and smash the insignia onto a newly minted Airborne soldier's chest, drawing blood when the exposed pins go through the uniform and into the skin of his chest. With a really good blood-wing pinning the badge actually sticks in a guy's skin and he has to pull it out. The pins on the back of the badge make a little *pop* sound as they're pulled out.

That kind of Neanderthal behavior simply isn't allowed in today's Army. But Joey Caron told his Airborne instructor that he had to get Blood Wings, same as his dad did back in Vietnam days. He just had to get them. That instructor nodded quietly, knowingly, and walked around a corner with Caron so nobody could see and—*smash!*—slammed his hand on the wings and drove them into the skin of Caron's chest.

Joey Caron gave those Blood Wings to his dad, Jeff. He just had to give them to him, to let his dad know how much it meant to give something back to the man who'd helped him become a soldier. Who'd helped him become a man.

Joey Caron called his dad as soon as he could after he left the States for this deployment with Bravo Company, his first deployment. On that first call, he said he couldn't tell Jeff where he was, but that he was staring at the Hindu Kush and, man, he wished his dad could see it.

His reports back to Jeff were often about the landscape. He marveled at the scenery, the flora and fauna of Afghanistan.

"Dad, I think I saw a snow leopard with my night vision!" he reported back one day.

That was Joey.

He came home just before Christmas on mid-deployment R&R leave, and he was talkative, caring Joey. He borrowed the family car and took his sister to the mall one day, bought her new bedding, a nightstand, all the fixings for an adolescent girl's room, and then helped her set it up.

Then he made her promise that it would look pristine for his home-coming from Afghanistan in a few months. She promised.

And he busted his dad's chops, that old veteran of the 101st Airborne Division. Joey told him he knew all about the 101st's long history, from Bastogne to Iraq. But, he said with a smirk, he'd come to realize the 82nd was actually better.

One day on that leave, Joey was in the living room playing *Guitar Hero* with his sister, but Jeff noticed that his son kept looking over at him. When Jeff walked into another room, Joey followed along.

"Hey, can I see my .45?" he asked his dad.

The 1911 model .45-caliber handgun is about as classic as a handgun gets and can be modified and tinkered with to make it almost a work of art.

"You don't have one, that's my .45," Jeff replied, knowing that his son didn't own one of those classic automatic pistols, only he did.

Jeff also knew his son coveted that handgun.

"What if I reenlist? Can I have it?" Joey asked his dad.

And Jeff, proud father and former soldier, said Joey certainly could have it as a reenlistment gift.

That sent Joey scurrying into the bedroom. He emerged with a crumpled-up piece of paper and a mischievous grin. He'd reenlisted in Afghanistan around Thanksgiving. Here was the paperwork, right here in his hand.

"Can I see my pistol?" he asked his dad. Doggone if Jeff wasn't snookered into giving him that peach of a Springfield MC Operator model 1911-style pistol that had had some custom work done to it by an armorer Jeff knew from the Ranger battalion.

Man, that was a pretty handgun, Jeff remembered. And it was now Joey's.

Despite the laughter, the grins, the jokes, Jeff knew the Army. He knew deployment. He knew war. And he knew there was probably something buried deep inside his son at this point—here on R&R—that needed some release, and he was determined to get after it.

Joey told goofy stories about deployment, jokes and funny observa-tions about this or that, but nothing heavy about what he'd seen so far. Jeff, a veteran himself, had been around law enforcement and the military his entire life, and he knew what kind of stuff guys brought back home. So one night, Jeff bought a bottle of Patrón tequila—Joey's favorite—and he proceeded to get his son good and drunk.

The young soldier broke down under the weight of the deployment, the stress, the knowledge he had to go back. And, of course, the Patrón.

Joey wept.

And Jeff, the father, held his son in his arms.

A burst emotional dam is a thing to behold, to watch feeling flow through a reserve that seemed impenetrable. An old soldier understands something like that when he sees it in another.

"It was the best night with my son," he said. "It was a beautiful moment."

Joey told his dad he still wanted to be a career soldier, but he'd be happy if he never again had to see some of the things he'd witnessed in his short time in Afghanistan. Death and pain and, well, war.

After that night, they never talked about it. The needed catharsis was over and done with. There's a certain bravado a soldier requires to do the job of a paratrooper, and Joey needed that. Jeff would never want to imperil that swagger by bringing up the crying. That night, though, had proved his son's innocence was gone, replaced by something else. Was it manhood? Was it callousness? Had he become someone different? No, it was just life. Joey was changing, as all people do. It was life, as such, intruding on that dear boy of Jeff's who used.to walk beside him in the woods and once needed help to shoot a .22 rifle.

One of the things Joey told his dad was that he had a dread in the back of his mind. He said to his dad during that leave that if he were to be killed in Afghanistan he wished it to be from a bullet shot. He did not want to be blown up. Dear Lord, not blown up, anything but that.

"Unfortunately, Buddy, you don't get to pick your poison," Jeff told him.

A couple days later, Jeff packed his son up and sent him back to the Army.

He sent his beautiful boy, Joey Caron, back to Afghanistan.

* * *

Back in the orchard in the Arghandab, Lemon handed that SAW back to Caron there over that wall when the *ping!* went off. In less than a split second, much of Joey Caron was pulverized. There's no other way to say it. Nearly all of him had been transformed into a pink mist, Lemon remembers.

With an IED it's not dust to dust. It's to pink mist, the result of a violent and horrible cancellation of a person's parts and pieces.

Nick Armendariz was just paces ahead of Lemon and Caron that night in the Arghandab. He was about as close as you can get to an explosion like that and not get hurt. But he was close enough that when the bomb went off that his hearing just went away. Erased by the explosion.

"It's all matter of luck," Armen said. "It was like playing Russian roulette out there."

* * *

Armen suddenly had total silence in his head. He couldn't hear anything for a few seconds, maybe. Who knows how long, really? Time loses its shape in those moments. This became one of those where Armen comes unstuck. He revisits it even now whenever he chooses to, and sometimes when he doesn't.

After those few moments, who knows how long, Armendariz's ears started working again, and he heard screams.

As he hustled back through the orchard, it was dark as could be in there among all those branches and leaves and burgeoning pomegranate fruit. He didn't want to use a flashlight because that would make them all perfect targets. Instead, he was looking around, using his night vision goggles, but that was like looking through a soda straw. He couldn't see much other than what was right there in that glowing green bit of light in the goggles.

Armendariz got to the two men and he saw Caron. Joey had been split open, legs gone, and everything that was left inside of him just sort of spilling out onto the ground. There was still some life in his eyes but he was fading.

Eyes don't just get sleepy and close when a man dies like that. They go distant, looking at something Over There. And a fog comes in, settles right into the pupils. The fog was coming in over Caron.

Lemon remembers that he, him, didn't feel any pain at first. But there was something odd about his right arm. And he examined the source of that oddness.

He looked down and saw that it was just sort of hanging there, the arm dangling by a sinew or tendon or something. He really didn't know what all those parts were because it was stuff a person's never supposed to see. It was stuff that is nearly always hidden when the muscle and skin and everything is intact and doing their anatomical jobs correctly.

Next thing Lemon remembers is somebody sort of handed him his arm to hold on to, just passed it to him like a parcel. It was really heavy, he remembers thinking. And since an arm has all sorts of joints and bendy places, things like wrists and elbows, it was also all jiggly when he tried to hold on to it. That's what he says he remembers so well, that it was "jiggly."

Armendariz grabbed a few guys who were close to Lemon and ordered them to form up in a kind of defensive circle and point their rifles outward, to make sure nothing else bad happened.

Then he looked up into the trees. Pieces of Caron hung from the branches. He said it was like a scene from a Rob Zombie movie, like a campy horror film.

Armen recognized that sometimes the only way to make sense of reality is to compare it with fiction. In combat, troops often use metaphors and similes to explain what it was like, as if the starkness of the real situation, paradoxically, is too much to believe. It's probably because the only place a guy has ever seen pieces of a person dangling from trees is in something as patently ridiculous and improbable as a Rob Zombie movie.

Yet there it was, right there in the Arghandab.

Armen only looked at the trees for a second, then he grabbed that new assistant machine gunner who had stuck beside him as they went back to check on Lemon and Caron. They took off at a good clip to set up a landing zone so a chopper could get in there to medevac whatever was left of Caron and to get Lemon. Armen set in some security and then gave his 240 to his newbee A-gunner, taking the kid's lighter-weight M4 rifle in exchange so he could run around and coordinate the medevac.

The A-gunner looked at Armendariz, lost and anxious, and asked what he should do, where he should go. Armen threw down his assault pack, pointed to it, and said, "There. Right there." The kid stayed right there.

Armen ran back into the orchard and helped Lemon walk out to the LZ, the landing zone for the helos, they'd set up. Armen remembers it was impressive that Lemon walked out there on his own, carrying that jiggly arm attached by something-or-other he couldn't identify. Armen put his arm around Lemon's waist to kind of steady him as he walked and toted his arm, which was shredded from elbow to shoulder, pulled clean off the bone.

Lemon kept saying, "Goddammit, goddammit, it fucking hurts," Armen remembers.

"I'll see you when I get back—save some of the good drugs for me," Armen said to Lemon as he dropped him off at the LZ next to the poor assistant gunner.

He ran back into the orchard to carry out Caron.

There's all kinds of litters and stretchers the Army has for carrying casualties. Most of them are way too heavy to get taken out on a foot patrol, so what often gets used is a simple poncho, the kind you might see at any surplus store.

That's what Armen used for Caron.

"For being half a man, he was still heavy as fuck," Armen said.

He and a couple guys rolled Caron onto the poncho and took him to the LZ. Armen turned on his flashlight to look into Caron's eyes. Fog. He was gone.

Armen said goodbye and loaded the half a body onto the helo.

After they loaded Joey Caron's body, Lemon got aboard. The flight medics laid him down and cut off his uniform to check out his arm, then started cutting off just about everything else he was wearing to check for unseen wounds they might have missed at first. As they cut, he thought to himself, *Not the boots.*

He was wearing brand-new combat boots, really nice and hardly broken in. And dammit all, the bastards cut off those pretty boots.

As they cut away at his uniform, as he was stewing about the loss of his boots, Lemon had his first out-of-body experience. Lemon left his body. It was just for just a little bit. He didn't soar up and out, go to the light or anything like in stories in the *National Enquirer*. No, Lemon went down instead, felt like he'd been sucked down. He went down two or three feet and was underneath it all, looking up at everyone in silhouette. Backlit, everyone had a sort of orange tinge about them.

He came back to his body somehow, doesn't know how, and was back in himself. Things were so crazy he can't really say what happened or how. It was all kind of disjointed.

The next out-of-body experience he had was different, though. That time he floated up. It might have been drug induced, sure, he'll grant you that much. It was a couple days later in Germany as he was going into surgery, and a hospital tech was working his damnedest to get an IV into Lemon's arm but wasn't having any luck. Lemon had just one actual arm you could use for an IV at this point, so that poor technician trying to stick him had 50 percent of the options he had with anybody else.

Lemon floated up this time instead of sinking down. Up and out of his own body he went. There was some kind of life force or energy or something that he could feel, thrumming and humming around him.

The energy, the life force of his spirit or whatever, was connected to his body by some kind of a rod, at least that's the best way he can describe it, and the rod stretched as Lemon drifted from his body. The rod of energy kept getting thinner and thinner as he floated farther away. Would it snap?

Then success! The medic got the IV in, and just like that, Lemon was sucked back down and into his body.

* * *

For the soldier like Lemon, who gets wounded, the excitement doesn't stop. He flies out on a helo, then goes into surgery and it's action-packed for hours. He's at the center of everything for a while. Even though he might be unconscious, there's plenty going on around him. For the wounded, a marvelous story of combat trauma keeps unfolding with them as the protagonist.

But back on the ground, as soon as the medevac chopper's gone, things get eerily quiet. The story has moved on and left them behind. For the soldiers in the wake of it all, suddenly there's absolutely nothing happening. Lemon's up in the air, having a wicked-ass out-of-body experience, cheating death and high on adrenaline and fancy drugs while his buddies left behind in the Arghandab lie on the ground and wait for an unlikely follow-on attack, for that rare instance on the deployment where they could exchange fire with someone. His buddies lay there in the dark and quiet, prone on their bellies, worn-out and sleepy, and still something like a couple of hours by foot from the base.

Sergeant J and his squad stayed on-site for about two hours after Lemon and Caron's helo left because they had to wait out the possibility of the follow-on attack. They also had to make sure everything had been cleaned up and they weren't leaving behind any gear or pieces of their buddies.

After the excitement and the cheating of death, the parasympathetic backlash sets in. Everybody knows about the fight-or-flight response when senses and energy are heightened. But the parasympathetic backlash is what follows. The aftereffect. After the adrenaline goes away, the body is left with a bone-deep weariness and sleepiness. That's what Sergeant J's squad felt.

They eventually made it back to the COP and dropped their gear. Armstrong wanted to talk to the patrol, but Armen didn't have time for some officer to yammer at him, so he walked out. He went to his bunk to try and sleep. But even though he was so, so tired, how could he sleep after something like that? Armen lay there trying not to think, but he hadn't yet mastered such a talent. Eventually, finally, sleep started to come—it was well into the next day by this time.

After Armstrong finished talking to the squads, he decided to take another patrol out to inspect the site where Caron had been killed, to see what they could learn from the Taliban's setup of things.

As Armen finally drifted off to sleep, he heard an explosion. He was awake again. He woke up the rest of the squad. They got ready in case they needed to go back out and help whoever tripped that explosion.

The boom came from the patrol Armstrong led out to the site where Caron was killed. A guy named McNamara had walked over an area that they'd trod all to hell during the medevac, a place boots had trampled dozens of times. A place that seemed to be as safe as you could get outside the wire in the Arghandab.

Somehow McNamara stepped on the one perfect spot where no one else had stepped, which had an IED trigger.

Another leg from Bravo Company gone.

* * *

Back in Tacoma, Washington, Jeff Caron was sitting at home on what seemed like a regular old Sunday. His wife, Joey's stepmom, looked out the window and told Jeff two soldiers were coming up the front walk. They were in dress uniforms.

Jeff's first thought was to send his daughter to play in the other room. First things first. He knew what was coming and was ready for it. Then he went to the door.

"I'd hoped never to meet you," he said to the female officer at the door in her well-pressed uniform.

"We'd hoped never to meet you," she replied.

Everyone was all business. There was hardly a need for the soldiers to tell Jeff the news at this point. They told him anyway. And then the officer asked him if he wanted to let the media know about his son's death. Jeff told them Joey hadn't just been his son, he'd been America's son. So, please, by all means, let the media know about it.

Jeff already knew he'd have to go to the Air Force base in Dover, Delaware, the port of entry for the remains of the war dead of the United States of America. He was already making plans in his head. Jeff realized later that he'd all but ignored his wife and Joey's sister during this because he wanted to be professional about it. He wanted to handle it like a soldier. Looking back on it, he was too professional. Almost cold. After all, Jeff himself wasn't a soldier on official business. He was a father learning about the fate of his son.

Jeff flew to Dover, took along Joey's grandfather, and they stayed on the third floor—the top floor—of the Holiday Inn Express there by the base. This was back in 2010, back in the middle of the wars in Iraq and Afghanistan. At the time, the third floor of that Holiday Inn was reserved for family members waiting for their loved ones' remains to arrive at Dover.

It must have been a helluva thing for folks staying on the first or second floors of that Holiday Inn, just regular paying customers, Jeff said.

Imagine, you're just trying to enjoy your trip to Dover while all these weeping, sad people shuffled around above you. It was a hotel with an attic full of ghosts, he said.

Then they headed over to the base to wait for Joey's plane. The hangar they waited in was the oddest thing, Jeff remembers. The massive space was filled with all these living room sets in different styles and configurations. It was like a furniture showroom. Grieving families could pick out the spot where they'd feel most comfortable sitting and waiting for a dead son, a dead daughter.

Do we want modern and sleek couches, maybe? Perhaps something more traditional?

They sat in their airplane hangar living room. An Army general showed up and joined Jeff. She came to pay her respects as the high-ranking representative of the Pentagon there for the families, for the fallen soldier.

She walked over to Jeff, introduced herself. Jeff said she should take a seat, put herself at ease, and let him tell her about Joey.

Well, the general had some major with her, an aide, and for a second that major thought Jeff had given the general a command, had told the general "At ease," and that major sputtered and about swooned from the perceived impropriety. Jeff still laughs when he thinks about it.

Asking the general to have a seat was extraordinary enough. It wasn't often that parents extended such an invitation. Most of the time parents cried, they yelled, they blamed the general for the soldier's death. The general was typically the punching bag for a family's grief, Uncle Sam incarnate. But with Jeff, the general did find herself at ease. And she sat. Jeff wanted to introduce her to his son, their soldier.

"I said, 'There's no blame for this,' " Jeff remembered.

Soldiers die. Even if they're your son.

About 1:30 in the morning, Joey's plane landed. The brass told Jeff they'd wait until he was ready to start the ceremony, to bring Joey off the plane.

Quick like, Jeff said he wanted to get it done. Let's go.

The honor guard in their fresh cammies and crisp white gloves carried the shiny casket, flag draped, off the back of the plane.

Jeff saluted his boy. Then Jeff and Joey's grandfather headed back to Tacoma to wait—again. The body still had to be flown out to the West Coast.

Jeff got back home in Washington State and started preparing for Joey's final trip home. Joey remained there at Dover for four or five days as the mortuary affairs team prepped his body, dressed him in a new uniform, and then sent him via a Gulfstream jet across the country.

They buried Joey in Washington State.

Jeff and some friends went up to the casket before they closed it up and put some stuff in there that Joey surely needed for the afterlife.

That beauty of a Springfield pistol went into Joey's waistband, as best as they could find a waistband. It was Joey's pistol after all, gotten fair and square after his reenlistment. They put a fishing pole in the casket next to him, and a fellow needed a new pocketknife, too, so one of those went in, and, of course, a bottle of Patrón.

Then he was buried, and all that had remained of Joey Caron in this world was gone.

Now, Joey and Jeff had always promised each other that whoever died first would report back from the great beyond somehow, some way. Jeff always said if he went first he'd make his way to Joey's attic and clink some chains like the Ghost of Christmas Past or something. Joey never really said how he'd do it. But he had told his dad to rest assured, he would.

Soon after the funeral, some friends came to visit Jeff and he took them to Joey's favorite bar. They all had shots of Patrón, ordered an extra one in Joey's memory, and let it sit there on the table for a while until the bartender came over and she asked with a laugh whether someone was going to finally drink that last shot.

Jeff told the bartender it was a shot for his son, who'd just died in Afghanistan.

That nice bartender started to cry.

She said she was very sorry, she didn't know.

Jeff told her not to be sad. Don't be sorry. Joey's death was just something that happened. Ashes to ashes.

He handed that nice bartender the shot and told her she should drink it at the end of her shift, it would be a fitting tribute to Joey.

She thanked him, saved the shot for later, and handed Jeff his bar tab.

It was 101 dollars exactly. $101.00.

That's the first time Jeff Caron started to see the number 101. And he realized, damned if old Joey just might be clanking those ghostly chains from the great beyond. He was the type of guy to have the last laugh on his dad, the old 101st Division Army veteran, by screwing around with him like this.

And that number, 101, began to pop up all the time.

When Jeff and his wife did the calculation, they realized Joey died on the 101st day of the year.

Soon after that, Jeff went to check out a house he was thinking of buying up in the woods. He'd be using some of Joey's life insurance money for it, and when he parked the car at the front door of that prospective new house, the trip odometer read 101 miles. Jeff decided to buy the house then and there, he didn't even need to look inside.

Jeff's happy to talk about 101 following him around ever since Joey's death, but he's sure to explain it so it doesn't seem like he's become an astrologist or some kabbalistic numerologist. Jeff will give a little laugh, like he knows there's no way it's real. He won't say he takes it as conclusive proof Joey's still around in some way, but finding those little 101 bread crumbs scattered through life makes him feel as if Joey's still here.

"It's comforting to me," he said. "It doesn't matter if it's scientifically real or not, it's just a comfort."

But shit, who's to say it isn't Joey?

After all, the father and son made a pact to report back from the afterlife, and Joey was never one to break his word.

* * *

Every war story has some details you just can't make up. Stuff that would be silly and downright unbelievable if somebody tried to put it into a novel.

Jared Lemon had been a right-handed jeweler before the Army. How about that? Have you ever heard of a soldier who was a jeweler before going into the service?

It had been the thing in life he was best at, intricate work with those steady fingers placing precious stones in tiny settings. But in the Arghandab, in an instant, that right arm of his had been turned into a jiggly thing. He said it was like God himself came down and punched that arm clean off his body. The only guy on that deployment to lose an arm and it was the dominant arm of the former jeweler? You can't make this stuff up.

At first Lemon thought, hey, maybe doctors could save it?

They did try their best with surgeries, treatments, all kinds of medical stuff. He was about two months into his stay at a hospital in Germany as doctors did their best to keep that mangled arm of his alive and to make it once again a working thing rather than a jiggly mess. Then, one day, his entire medical team came filing into his room.

Uh-oh, he knew it must be bad when all his doctors shuffled in looking like a bunch of sad-sack penitents on a doleful pilgrimage.

One of them said in apologetic tones that it seemed best to just amputate the arm. It wasn't healing correctly and, in their respectable and varied medical opinions, they thought if they somehow were able to save the arm, it would be quite a drawn-out process. The best they could do probably wouldn't be too good anyway. In layman's terms, no matter what, that arm was going to be a real piece of shit.

Lemon figured the doctors knew better than he did about this stuff.

Fuck it, he said, take the arm off. So they did.

Hey, on the bright side, it was better than a guy losing his dick and balls, right?

* * *

Those four months between arriving in the Arghandab and when Lemon was hit by the IED were crazy. Crazy busy and crazy scary. It seemed every hour of every day was filled with some task or another and one terror on top of the next.

The enormity of it all, the sheer pandemonium, didn't hit Lemon until he was lying in a hospital bed and had time to consider the injury, the deployment, and his Army career. It was only in the calm of a hospital he could recognize how bonkers that brief time in the Arghandab truly had been.

He flew back to Walter Reed soon after the amputation, and they worked on the nubbin that remained of his arm after they chopped off the useless stuff.

Over time they grafted what seemed like dozens of pieces of skin to the stump to help it heal correctly.

"You know where they get the skin from," he'll ask people, deadpanning.

"Baby dicks!" he then yells out gleefully. "No shit."

That's true. Doctors make a patchwork of skin from circumcision leftovers, which is good as gold for fixing up the working end of a mangled stump.

CHAPTER 17

FUCK IT

It was only after that damnable patrol where Caron died and Lemon lost his arm that Nick Armendariz realized that he'd said to himself, *Fuck it.*

He'd come to understand there wasn't any rhyme or reason to who got blown up and who didn't in the Arghandab. He came to understand that it was a cosmic crapshoot as to whether today would be the day he'd get blown up.

So, fuck it.

In the military there are all sorts of ways to say fuck it. There's the give-up-on-life-and-do-nothing fuck it. That's when a guy blows his mental fuse and can't do anything at all. That's when a guy is messed up on a *Catch-22* level, lying in bed until the doctors get called and they pull you out to take you down to the ward. That doesn't happen too often.

There's the do-nothing fuck it—the version that doesn't include giving up on life itself. That's the goldbricker, malingerer, shirker move, when a guy decides that he isn't going to do a damn thing and nothing that anybody does to him as punishment will change his mind.

There's the hold-your-nose-and-complete-a-crappy-task fuck it. This particular flavor of fuck it is the most common in a soldier's repertoire. Every infantryman experiences it. Its most common incarnation comes when some jerk-off officer assigns a preposterous task, typically requiring hours of backbreaking labor. There's little else a grunt can do but say fuck it and power through the task. The idiocy of the thing typically remains at the forefront of the grunt's mind, so he says "Fuck it" regularly to stoke the embers of anger down deep in his belly and to make him forswear any thoughts of reenlistment.

And then there's a metaphysical fuck it. That one is powerful, indeed. It's defined by resignation and a sense of inevitability, maybe even of fate, that can only be truly known to a person who has signed a contract, is in the middle of the shittiest place imaginable, and now has to figure out how to deal with all that. The metaphysical fuck it allows a Zen-like acceptance of one's lot in life and the knowledge that there isn't a good-goddamn thing to be done about it.

Bear in mind, that abbreviated catalog is just a few of the fuck it variants available to your average soldier, but arguably the most popular among them.

The fuck it Armendariz chose was a combo. His was a mix of the hold-your-nose fuck it along with the metaphysical fuck it, which is actually a spot where a lot of honorable guys end up finding themselves on the fuck it spectrum.

To say fuck it in the way that Armendariz said it doesn't mean he gave up on doing his job and doing it as best he could. No, he was still a good soldier who was ready to take care of the men around him and complete whatever was asked of him day or night. Instead, it meant he was ready for death or dismemberment in a way he hadn't been ever before and yet he was going to do his job as best he could despite all that.

It was a true existential reckoning.

And that reckoning, once made, becomes very hard to shake even once a man goes back to the civilian world.

Fuck it.

Armen began that 2009 deployment in Helmand as a machine gunner, on the M240G, and for those first few months he was as bored as everyone else on the deployment—maybe more so, because he had a prior action-packed deployment and knew what a fair fight was and he wanted one bad. He wanted to earn his paycheck, wanted to do his job, especially after all those firefights on the previous deployment. That was fun. And it never happened when he was with Bravo Company.

They began the deployment with that dumb training mission in Helmand, where there was no getting into a firefight of any kind. And then they were sent to the Arghandab, where the Taliban were too damn chicken to come out for a fair fight. The Taliban didn't have the balls. At least, that's what so many American soldiers like Armen told themselves.

Except an American fair fight really isn't too fair if viewed objectively. Firefights like those Armen remembered from his last deployment might begin with the two sides shooting rifles at each other, the steadiest hands and truest aim winning out. That seems about as fair as it can get. But as far as the Taliban were concerned, the Americans were always cheating. The Americans got their bullets delivered to them in convoys, bullets with brass cases that never rust, while the Taliban's rounds might be steel-cased, get all rusted to hell, having been buried out back in a court-yard so the Americans with their dogs and metal detectors and drones and who-knows-what-else couldn't find them.

Those supposedly fair fights often ended with American artillery raining onto the Taliban position or American helicopters and jets fir-ing rockets, dropping smart bombs. Maybe an American drone inter-vened with its multimillion-dollar, ever-present eye in the sky looking down at some Talibs armed only with AKs, machine guns, and maybe some mortars.

It's so easy to be cocky out there and talk about fair fights when you've got A-10 attack jets on station ready to swoop in with cannons and rockets and bombs. It's easy to be cocky when you've got encrypted radios that can talk to everyone on the battlefield, to planes, to artillery, to medevac helicopters—all with the touch of a button. The Taliban were often work-ing with Icom-brand radios or something like you'd find at Radio Shack. They were little better than what an American kid might find under the Christmas tree. Everyone on the battlefield could listen in.

It wasn't uncommon for Taliban commanders to say hello to the Americans they knew were listening in on their conversations.

"Hello, Lieutenant! I hope your family is well and you get to return home to them, *Insh'Allah*."

The Americans always talk about wanting a fair fight, mano a mano. But the Taliban know there's no fair fight and the Americans are a bunch of assholes for thinking combat is some gunfight at the OK Corral, all fair and square.

Nuristan was fun for Armen because it was an American-style fair fight.

On the Arghandab deployment he discovered that there never is a fair fight. Someone always has an advantage in a fight, usually an incredible advantage. This Arghandab stuff seemed a fair fight for the Taliban. Armen's fun stopped with the IEDs buried in the ground. It wasn't fair anymore. Not fair for the Americans, at least.

The Taliban had figured out the way to eliminate the American air superiority, the drones, nearly all of it. They planted bombs at night in the thick overgrowth of pomegranate trees and elephant grass and mud of the Arghandab Valley.

Oh shit, Armen figured out, *this is what fair looks like when you're on the other side of it.*

* * *

The realization that it wasn't fair, that it was awful, was right about where Armen's fuck it began. That meant he wouldn't even think most of the time when he was on patrol, he'd just walk. One foot in front of the other. If he didn't think, then he wouldn't hope. He wouldn't pray for each step to be OK, to not be the one that would lead to amputation or death. No, he couldn't hope or pray about every next step. So he stopped thinking about it. He put the whole thing on autopilot.

That big old 240 wasn't worth a damn anyway until a firefight started. And since machine guns are heavy as hell, his job was essentially to just carry the thing like a pack mule on patrol, trudge along until something happened. As soon as something happened, he'd be ready to snap to it, drop to the ground, and lay automatic fire on target. Until that happened, he didn't have to think too much. And because the Taliban fought via IEDs rather than firefights, nothing worthy of the 240 machine gun ever happened. Therefore, Armen's task lent itself to turning off his mind, to not thinking at all.

The only thing he had to do was walk in the footsteps of the guy right in front of him, because that footprint was the only safe spot he knew of in Afghanistan. That little footprint in front of him was Shangri-la, the most beautiful and only certain spot on the planet.

But even then, if he thought about it, even that footprint didn't seem like a sure thing. So Armen had to not think.

It was a Zen-like experience, purging the brain of all thoughts, making each footfall a little karmic victory unto itself. "Fuck it" became a koan of his very own. Sometimes it takes a little something extra to banish thinking, so Armen would push the metaphorical play button on a cassette stored in his brain and let a Metallica or Katy Perry song blare away in his mind. That passed the time better than not thinking of anything at all. But every once in a while, even with the soundtrack blaring, he'd accidentally think.

When that happened, he'd just repeat over and over his silent mantra. *Shut the fuck up, shut the fuck up, shut the fuck up*, he'd think, like some Transcendental Meditation, which helped all things fade away.

Halfway through the deployment that new assistant machine gunner arrived to be Armen's load bearer, the low-ranking soldier who carries ammo, the poor guy who was there when Caron and Lemon got blown up. When the new A-gunner got to the Arghandab, Armendariz had just gotten off a mountaintop observation post duty and was introduced to this new kid, one of the mid-tour replacements for all the guys they'd been losing to IEDs.

Then, like from some movie, Armen greeted the kid like a jerk. Even as he was doing it he knew it was a dick move, but sometimes that's the way he was.

Armendariz said to this poor cherry, "Welcome to the suck."

And on the first patrol, this kid who knows little more than what he's heard through the grapevine about how dangerous and shitty it is out there, he was walking real cautious and slow and using a stage whisper to yell forward to Armendariz to slow down.

"Hey, wait up!"

And, like from some movie, like a real asshole, Armendariz told this guy to shut the fuck up and come on, man, you'll be fine. And let's get going, goddamn cherry bastard.

What the fuck was this new guy thinking, anyway? Why was he still thinking?

* * *

For Armen, fuck it wasn't all that big a cultural or ethical leap. But for Tyler Koller to start coming around to that was something indeed.

Even saying the word "fuck" was something he wasn't able to do for so long because of the strictures of the Pentecostal church and the uprightness of his faith.

"I had friends offer me money to say 'fuck,'" Koller says of the olden days when he was in uniform, when he refused to cuss no matter what.

He never said that filthy word, or any other nasty heathen thing like that, the whole time he was in the Army.

Even on long deployments, he had his faith. He'd make sure to get the men from his squad together before stepping off on patrol so they could bow their heads in a nice prayer, take a moment to reflect on God's glory and goodness and all that. Sure, it was nice to have M4s, but he needed God's shield and buckler, too.

Koller never cussed while in uniform. He passed up on plenty of cold, hard cash from guys who pleaded with him to say something raunchy. It would have been some easy money for him. Guys would hold the money out right there under his nose and practically beg him to take it. There was no way, though. He remembered as a kid his mom said a dirty word one time in front of him and his brother and they asked her why she'd say something like that. It broke her heart to have said it, to have disappointed her sons. And in the Army it would have broken his heart to do the same.

On his first deployment Koller was gone for more than a year and then he came home to train up for that 2009–2010 deployment with Bravo company.

And on that Arghandab deployment, he saw some fucked-up shit that shook his faith. Yeah, sure, there were all his fellow soldiers who got hurt and blown up and all, but it was the other stuff that really got to him.

Afghan kids got hurt for no reason, because they were born in a country at war, or were blown up by some IED not meant for them. Kids got molested by Afghan police. Horrible shit that the Royal Rangers doesn't teach you how to deal with. Horrible shit that the Royal Rangers couldn't imagine happening.

When they were in Lashkar Gah he met a little Afghan boy who'd gotten a broken leg trying to get away from some Afghan soldiers who were into *bacha bazi*, making boys dress androgynously and then molesting them. And seeing stuff like that makes you wonder about how a great and loving God can allow some of the shit that he allows here on earth.

Koller always wanted to be a family man, wanted to have kids of his own, and what he saw in Afghanistan was a direct rebuke to the life he'd want for his kids. What once would have been mustard seeds of doubt cast on rocky ground were nurtured by atrocities and perversions. Those seeds finally started taking root.

Those seeds got plenty of fertilizer from the constant threat of getting blown up. One time Koller was back at the main battalion base, had to go there because he picked up sergeant on deployment and needed to get a new ID card printed out. He ended up chatting with a Navy shrink who he and another Bravo guy happened to run into.

The doc, she asked them what unit they were from and where they were stationed, small talk. And when she found out they were out in the Arghandab she said she'd heard about what it was like out there. She didn't know how they did it day in and day out.

And the Bravo guy Koller was with told her, "Well, you just realize that every day you go out, you are going to die or get messed up."

And that was as starkly put as he'd ever heard. He realized then that things were not normal and not OK out there.

Ye of little faith.

All that stuff he was seeing, he might not be able to say "Fuck it" just yet, but jimminy flapjacks, he was getting close to it.

CHAPTER 18

NOT MY ARMY

Once at Walter Reed, Sergeant Allen Thomas spent long weeks recovering from the immediate injuries, the things that almost killed him, just getting himself in a place where he could walk again, breathe again. Then he moved to the Warrior Transition Unit (WTU).

The units, found at many Army facilities, were first established in 2007 with the simple concept that injured soldiers needed a place where they could get support, care, and understanding while they were still on active duty and recovering from injuries. Initially the units were designed for troops who needed six months or more of rehabilitation and complex medical care. But like other things in the Army, the reality was far different from the idea. Allen hated it from the start.

To begin with, not every soldier in the unit had been injured in combat. A guy recovering from a suicide bombing might be in the same unit as a soldier who had broken her legs in a mechanical accident. Some soldiers were there for car wrecks that had happened stateside. It fostered division among those admitted and set up a sense of anger among the combat wounded who'd felt they were the only ones who had really earned being there.

While at the WTU, Allen had to show up to formation every day. The staff, the officers, and senior enlisted Army personnel who were assigned

to run day-to-day operations, weren't wounded warriors. A number of
them weren't even combat veterans. They were just soldiers who had been
assigned to a managerial job at the unit. And even though it was a unit
dedicated to medical assistance, the people in charge often didn't know
about medicine. Hell, they weren't doctors—they were just Army officers
and senior enlisted.

Allen, the person, had changed the moment he was injured,
and he was also coming to find out that in that moment his Army had
also changed.

The Army he had known, of infantrymen and airborne operations and
combat and honor, had changed. He was now in an Army that he'd never
seen before, hardly knew existed. It was an Army of people who weren't
preparing for deployment to a combat zone and who didn't ever want to
do the things he had so loved. This Army was full of people who didn't
make sense to him, soldiers who might have never deployed to combat
and who couldn't care less if that were the case.

In the WTU he didn't have Army peers anymore.

Allen had come home to a pregnant girlfriend, a misplaced identity
as a paratrooper, and the fallout from his serious brain and lung injuries.
Danica was there for him at all times when he got back. She was there
when he took his first steps away from his hospital bed. She was his new
rock because the Army wasn't even the Army anymore.

After a few months at Walter Reed, Allen and Danica went back to
Fort Bragg, where another Warrior Transition Unit awaited him. He had
gone from being a squad leader on a COP in Afghanistan where he was in
charge of a dozen paratroopers to being just some lowly sergeant in this
new Army he'd landed in. He'd become another cog in the Army wheel.
He felt small and he felt lost and Danica felt much the same way.

They didn't really have any friends to connect with. All their friends
were still deployed. Their best mutual friend, Jason Johnston, had been
blown up in front of Allen. Allen still swaggered when he could, talking
shit to his squad leader every so often, but what kind of swagger could
he muster? He wasn't physically what he used to be, and he wasn't a
paratrooper anymore, not really.

Neither he nor Danica knew who to ask for help. They didn't even know what they didn't know. They were two young kids, really, didn't know how to advocate for themselves, to fight for themselves or to push for things they needed even though they had gotten married and were awaiting a child. Allen and Danica were alone as a couple, navigating the system, but each of them also felt alone, in a way, in the relationship. Sure, they were reunited and together, but Allen was struggling with his recovery. Danica was struggling with the exhausting realties of being very pregnant and the uneasy expectation of becoming a new mom.

It was more of the same when they got back to Fayetteville, but, unlike at Walter Reed, Allen was now close enough to see the paratroopers who could still run and jump and breathe and didn't have horrible headaches. He saw what he used to be. What he now wasn't.

For a painful few months, he was at Bragg while the rest of Bravo Company remained deployed to the Arghandab. It was all further complicated by his relationship with his squad leader at the Warrior Transition Unit.

She was a female staff sergeant who'd broken her leg, and from the start she barked at Allen that she was in charge. For a paratrooper in those days the idea of a female soldier telling him to do anything was a shock in itself. Allen always griped to Danica about how the staff sergeant was out of regs all the time, didn't even tuck her T-shirt into her trousers. Basic stuff that paratroopers have to do.

One day he told her, "You're my squad leader? No, I was a squad leader."

That didn't go over well.

So she had no leniency for him. Even when he couldn't sleep because of the pain or anxiety and maybe he'd get three hours of shut-eye, making him groggy sometimes and late to morning formation, she had no sympathy. She'd write him up.

Allen was surly, he'd just gotten back from combat, almost died, had his second Purple Heart, and now they were making him stand in formation to get yelled at by somebody who hadn't the first clue about leading troops in combat. Couldn't even tuck her shirt in. Granted, his attitude toward her from the start probably didn't endear him in any way.

They were supposed to show up to formation in standard Army patrol hats, the things everybody gets at boot camp. But he'd show up with his paratrooper's beret, the biggest fuck-you to this new Army he could now muster.

* * *

That wonderful first child promised invigoration and love, and when Danica gave birth it started a new phase for their family, a phase, paradoxically, of closeness and separation.

It started badly. That squad leader Allen had been tangling with always gave him a hard time when he was scheduled to go with Danica to prenatal appointments. Even on Danica's due date Allen's squad leader wouldn't let him leave formation to go to be with her for an appointment. When she finally went into labor soon after, he was allowed to go, but only after he went through all the paperwork to sign out for the day.

He made it and Danica had their new child. They now had a family.

Oh, but their new daughter gave Allen remarkable joy! He loved being a father from the beginning, everyone said so. There were flashes of happiness in his life, in their life, and when it clicked it was fantastic. It was what Danica had expected.

But then he would have headaches that would require him to lie in a dark, quiet room for hours at a time. And sometimes he'd just have to get away and be alone, maybe ride the motorcycle that he bought while on deployment and let him escape in so many ways from day-to-day concerns, or he'd retreat to the comfort of his guitar.

Danica tended to their new daughter and dealt with her own feelings and anxieties—the stresses new moms deal with. Changes in life, in what she expected from a partner.

And now that he was in the transition unit and she had their daughter to take care of during the day, Danica couldn't be a full part of his recovery. She didn't know what he talked about in his sessions, she didn't know what he was doing or not doing during the day to get better.

* * *

Allen's body recovered soon enough so that he no longer *looked* as if he'd been injured. That his wounds were now all but invisible to other people sent him into a topsy-turvy Alice's Wonderland.

Soldiers who'd broken their legs doing something stateside like getting in a car wreck or falling during a basketball game clearly looked like wounded warriors, wearing walking boots or using crutches while in uniform. Yet Allen, blown up in combat, seemed to an outside observer to be just fine, even though his lungs and brain were irreparably damaged.

One time a major pulled Allen aside and told him to stop being a pussy and there was no way he had PTSD. Was that some misguided form of tough love? Was it callousness? Disregard? Ignorance? Who knows, but it made Allen feel small. The major minimized Allen's injuries and maximized his anxiety. The incessant pressure made Sergeant Allen Thomas believe that, yes indeed, he was being a pussy and just needed to get over it.

When the troops of the Warrior Transition Unit talked among themselves, they mainly talked about how bad it was. They all complained about stagnant care, they all complained about how much they hated the system. It's a God-given right for a soldier to bitch and moan, but in the operating forces there's payoff. There's great live-fire ranges. There's the camaraderie and commanders giving them a sense of purpose. There's deployments! At the WTUs there seemed to be just formations.

Bravo Company was still in the Arghandab, but there was none of that for Allen now. Broken men and women left the unit when they were discharged from the Army or got better. More broken troops came to replace them in the unit. It was like an entire army made up of combat replacements. There was no way for the men and women to gel with one another. It was an inherently lonely endeavor. It was designed to be a place where the wounded could go to recover properly, but instead it was a vicious cycle of misery and feeling lost. It felt to men like Allen the opposite of what was intended when the unity was first conceived.

Danica didn't know how to deal with it all. With new motherhood, with Allen. Sometimes he tried to get her to come to his appointments or to learn more about what he was going through, but usually Allen didn't seem to care that much about her coming along, so she didn't prioritize it. Sometimes he tried to keep up the bluff that he was still a big-chested,

burly freedom fighter, and he didn't seem to want Danica to have to come
in and hear the truth.

In retrospect, Danica wishes she could have just seen the whipsawing
for what it was: Allen figuring out his new reality and trying to figure out
how to manage it with Danica.

She still has some of his clinical memos from back then, with the doctors' notes on them that she didn't see at the time. In some instances, the
notes show Allen told his doctors that Danica didn't understand him, that
he was trying to make her understand what he was going through. Some of
the notes say he just couldn't figure out how to make her understand. She
didn't know he was trying, though, she didn't see. All she knew was that
she had a newborn to care for and that Allen sometimes seemed more like
a second kid she had to manage rather than a husband. It was all so hard.

CHAPTER 19

WHO TO BLAME?

After Allen's return home, Brunk's death, Lemon's lost arm, Caron's death, and everything else, it felt like more of same for the men of Bravo. They patrolled and hit IEDs. Captain Adam Armstrong redoubled and redoubled and redoubled his efforts until it seemed as if he had nothing else to give. He sat in front of his operations computer and typed reports, munching on junk food. When he wasn't doing that, he was out on patrol with one or another of the platoons, inserted into some squad, undertaking activities that seemed far below his rank. But he had to be out there, on patrol, to be there along with the men. Something burned within him. With the unrelenting pace of patrols, reports, and nearly obsessive worry, Armstrong grew skinnier and skinnier, gaunt, with sunken cheeks, despite the junk food.

Other men were as dedicated, though they said little about the toil.

Lyle Pressley, the soldier who'd broken his ankle on a training jump even before his first deployment and whose back had started to hurt him, never wanted to be thought of as a shirker. He remembers when they got to Afghanistan on that advise-and-assist mission in Helmand, it was sort of boring, but it was the life. They had great internet and would sometimes just sit out in the motor pool all day in the sun, waiting for the next mission.

Such are the ways of a lowly specialist. Lyle didn't know any better, since it was his first deployment.

Then came the Arghandab. Lyle had been expecting to patrol cities in Iraq, not to hump through canals and over huge walls in Afghanistan. And it was after they got to the Arghandab that the pain in his back really started, turning from something he could just grit his teeth about and into something that caused the kind of pain that concerns a man, that makes him scared of what could possibly make things hurt so bad.

Turns out the disks in Lyle's back were degenerating the whole time, but there was no way to really know. Too many jumps from airplanes, too many miles under a full pack. The life of an airborne infantryman, really, is the life of someone whose body starts falling apart in training, even before he deploys for the first time.

Then came those Arghandab patrols. Lyle was a big guy, so he did what seemed like interminable humping of that SAW light machine gun and all the rounds a machine gun needs, all the gear, all the pounding on his back and legs. The SAW itself weighed about seventeen pounds. Then there's the ammo that came with it, the same cartridges that an M16 uses, but all linked together in something resembling a chain so they can feed though the gun at a rate of maybe one thousand rounds a minute. When all is said and done the SAW gunner of the time carried a load of seventy-nine pounds, according to the Army. A guy like Lyle, built like a Clydesdale and relatively junior in rank, was the perfect person to carry that gun and its load.

Then the numbness began. It crept down a leg and caused a nauseating mix of pain and nothing. That right leg would go numb to the touch, and yet there was also blistering pain all down it. How was such a sensation even possible? But he kept patrolling, over walls and crashing down on the other side, because that's just what you do if you're not a shirker.

He started getting some injections of Toradol to make the pain subside. But it never went away, it just receded a bit.

In February, Lyle had gone home for his two-week R&R and his back hurt so bad that when he landed stateside, he had to lie flat on the back seat of his girlfriend's car for the hours-long drive home. Once home, the pain remained so bad, he went to the emergency room. There was no way he was going to complain about it in the Arghandab. He wasn't a malingerer and he didn't want to be thought of as one. It's a second-order effect of actual goddamn malingerers that the good soldiers who are really, truly hurt just keep pushing because they don't want to be thought weak, or fakers, or not devoted to the cause and their brothers.

The ER doc at home told Lyle his back was all messed up and they needed an MRI to confirm the diagnosis of degenerative disk disease. They hopped him up on some painkillers, and he told the civilian docs he'd have the Army check him out as soon as he got back to base. He doesn't remember what he said or how he convinced those medical professionals that he'd be real responsible about it, seeing as how he was on serious painkillers and all foggy in the head. One thing he most certainly didn't do was tell the civilian docs that he'd just gotten back from Afghanistan and was set to return in a few days. Sure enough, the MRI images would show he'd been royally fucking up his back for months. Herniated disks, real bad stuff.

He could have just thrown in the towel, probably didn't even have to go back to Afghanistan if he didn't want to. If he had just flown back to Afghanistan and handed the docs his MRI results he could have stayed at Kandahar Airfield on light duty, heading over to the boardwalk in the middle of base, maybe. Just eat some donuts at the Tim Hortons and watch the Canadian troops play deck hockey on the rink they had built in the middle of the base in between shifts.

Lyle could have just gone through rehab, gone home to rest those damn disks, maybe have an early surgery to intervene before things got really bad. But no, back he went, back to the Arghandab after R&R anyhow. He left the MRI result at home and went back because that's what he thought a man should do. Perhaps it's what a foolish man does, or a man unknowing of what it might bring him in the years to come, but it's what he did. He got no medals or commendations for it, no Purple Heart—a soldier gets nothing for that sort of thing.

But it was a supremely noble and brave and generous and loving—and perhaps stupid—thing to do. He made the decision to go back and keep doing it all. It was a real-life version of *The Song of Bernadette*, that movie about the girl who becomes a saint, in part because she's suffered her entire life and never complained about it. Bernadette Soubirous saw visions of the Virgin Mary, experienced the ecstasy of religious enlightenment, and was eventually sainted by Pope Pius XI. Lyle just humped a fucking SAW through the Arghandab.

Was it worth it? Was it worth all the pain just to get back to more patrols? The question is moot in hindsight because it's done. He did it because it was the thing he had to do.

They were out on yet another painful patrol in June with Matthew Kinsey, whom Lyle remembers as another one of those soldiers who's friends with everyone, an all-around great guy. Lyle had gotten up on one of those mud walls that seemed to be everywhere in Afghanistan and was watching Kinsey, who was using a metal detector down below, scanning away.

Lyle knew Kinsey was good, that he would find something if something was buried down there.

"Too bad he found it the way he did," Lyle said.

He found it by stepping on it.

The explosion took off Kinsey's foot, and the dried-mud wall Lyle was sitting on crumbled. He came down with it and was knocked out for a few seconds.

When he came to he jumped up, because that's what a soldier does. That's what Lyle did. And he tried to help carry Kinsey on the litter someone had gotten out, but he couldn't do it. Something important and necessary had gone out in his back. It was no longer just pain and numbness, the whole damn system had malfunctioned. He couldn't pick up the litter. He had done all that he could possibly do. That's what Lyle did. And now he was totally broken, even though his body looked fully intact and it wasn't him who'd stepped on an IED.

Lyle, who had always relied on his body as a truism and constant companion, realized that body had now betrayed him. His body had failed him.

After that, Lyle had to sit out a couple patrols because he could hardly walk. The doc injected him with Toradol, about the strongest non-steroid you can use to keep swelling and pain down without resorting to narcotics.

Fucking malingerer, he worried they all thought of him.

Half the guys did think he was being a pussy, the other half seemed to understand. But either way he felt like a jerk. He didn't feel like Lyle and had to get back out there to help out. There were so many patrols in the Arghandab, if one person didn't go out, it just added the burden to the rest of the group. So he went out again, this time with more pain. Every patrol a struggle, a testimony to Lyle's saintly and silent suffering.

Seeing the death and dismemberment around him just made him want to do more, to be ever-present. He'd joined the Army because he knew deep down he would be able to bear more than most men could. Now he was proving that to himself.

Armstrong, too, kept enduring. If the troops were to be out on patrol, he had to be there on patrol. If the troops were exposed to IEDs, then he had to be exposed to IEDs. And when he wasn't out there, he was in the Tactical Operations Center, the TOC, planning and researching and eating garbage food and sucking down energy drinks. He had to do everything possible to prevent mistakes, oversights, or anything else that would lead to more injuries and deaths.

Nevertheless, the truck bomb happened.

* * *

Bravo Company had COP Ware, the base there in the middle of the radish field that they'd built from scratch and fortified over time. And in the midst of everything else the company had to do, they built a second base just a few thousand yards from the radish field to exert more control over the valley, to try and bend it to their will. They called the place COP Brunkhorst.

This new base wasn't as hard to build as the one in the radish field.

COP Brunkhorst relied in part on existing compound walls, those dried-mud affairs that tower into the sky, a marvel of engineering. Part of the COP's reason for being was to sit right there along a ratline that stretched from the river to COP Ware. And in order to do that, and to use existing walls, the COP was positioned close to other compounds, compounds that were inhabited and that saw traffic from trucks and tractors and people.

It allowed Bravo Company to extend its presence and send patrols into IED-infested lands from different angles and paths. The ever-extending presence kept squeezing the Taliban, cauterizing supply arteries, and preventing free movement. That new base was close to a road, though, and even while Armstrong planned and planned, he couldn't plan away the fact that cars could drive near that new base—too near.

Armstrong still can't forgive himself for not pushing back the COP's edges from some of those other compounds, from roads accessible by civilians. And he still blames himself for what happened that July day so close to the end of the deployment.

Lyle Pressley remembers the truck bomb well. It wasn't long after Kinsey's foot had been blown off, and Pressley's back became a god-awful, unending pain, that a bongo truck—a local version of a pickup truck—drove up close to the COP. Before the men on guard could do anything about it, the truck blew up, collapsing some of those mud-brick walls.

Lyle was in the COP when it happened. He frantically dug through all that collapsed mud and dirt, with the dust swirling all around after guys had been buried alive in the rubble. Lyle remembers reaching out toward a mouth he could see in the dust and dirt.

He couldn't see the rest of his fellow soldier's body because it was buried, but there was a face that he could just make out in the mess. So he stuck his huge finger right into the mouth and swept out the dirt and debris that filled it so some air could get in.

A few men were buried wholesale, and the others scrambled to exhume them from their potential graves, but none had died, thank God.

Dave Abt remembers that he was at Kandahar Airfield when that explosion went off. Every so often teams made their way back there for one errand or another. Abt rushed to the base hospital when he heard from someone that Bravo had been hit.

He got there as a Bravo soldier came in, ears bleeding from the blast. As the soldier sat there, dazed, the brigade commander, Colonel Drinkwine, arrived and started talking softly to the soldier with bleeding ears, nearly whispering because he seemed to be entranced by the sanctity of a hospital. He asked the soldier how he was doing and threw out a few more questions and that soldier with the bleeding ears just nodded his head earnestly but he didn't reply.

Drinkwine got annoyed and asked the soldier why he wouldn't respond to any of his questions. When the top-ranking officer paused, clearly wanting a response, the soldier hollered out, "I can't hear a fucking thing you're saying!"

The exasperated colonel promptly halted his questioning and left, Abt remembers.

* * *

Over the course of twenty years in Iraq and Afghanistan an untold number of patrols and bases were targeted by suicide car bombs, so many that there was no way to keep track of them and get a comprehensive tally. Many bomb attempts were thwarted by luck, attentive troops, adequate security measures, or some combination thereof. Every time a bomb successfully found its mark it was due to a fault in one or more of those factors.

When the enemy succeeds against you, there's always a reason. Yes, sure, they will always find a way to get one over on you, and in war, losses and injuries will occur. It's inevitable. That's the truth at the macro level, the 10,000-foot view. But when examined at the micro level, focusing in sharply on a single enemy success, on a single instance of loss or injury to one's own forces, you can find a way that you could have prevented it. Nothing is inevitable at that level.

On a macro level, truck bombs were understood as a given in Iraq and Afghanistan, something that most certainly would affect US forces in-country. But on a micro level, every single truck bomb could have been prevented.

Armstrong knows this one could have been prevented, and he still blames himself. The walls could have been rebuilt, the base could have had its perimeter extended or shrunk. The men could have been better drilled on how to deal with vehicles approaching the base. The road could have been closed, or traffic diverted.

Each decision that might have changed the outcome there at COP Brunkhorst, though, would have had other effects. If the base had been rebuilt, then it would have meant more time spent by Bravo Company troops building walls instead of being out on patrol.

If traffic had been diverted, it might have made the locals mad and paradoxically made things less safe because they'd be more inclined to help out the Taliban. Preventing a truck bomb here could have meant more IEDs dug in over there.

There's no single right answer in war, not even for a company commander with a physics degree from West Point who tried to come up with every answer for every variable. War yields loss, no matter how hard a captain tries.

Self-forgiveness is a necessary and laudable part of post-deployment recovery, but when a soldier pushes into the territory of self-exoneration, it rings hollow. Men with earned guilt know this much. Mistakes are made in war, but someone is responsible for making those mistakes.

Armstrong would come to forgive himself, as much as a man can, for things like the truck bomb. But he also fully blames himself for it and will continue to do so as long as he lives. These two things he can do because he understands the tensions, the countervailing forces, that coexist in war. Armstrong knows that the thesis and antithesis of combat does not yield a neat synthesis. It yields a slurry of paradoxical truths all competing against each other. Armstrong, deep in his own breast, cannot be exonerated for the truck bomb's devastation because it's his fault. He is culpable. But at the same time, the factors that caused this bomb to go off where it did might have prevented IEDs elsewhere. The factors favorable to this bomb might also have shut down a Taliban ratline that prevented an IED from being implanted, then detonated—hundreds of miles away, even.

Armstrong accepts the blame that is due to him because he knows it can't be shrugged off as survivor's guilt or some such other mumbo jumbo. The survivor should feel guilty, because he survived. That guilt can't disappear, but it can be managed and understood. The survivor's task isn't to accept none of the blame for the things that happened, for all that he might have been able to affect differently. The survivor's task is to find mastery over that guilt, keep it at bay by accepting the paradox of war. He will never find true forgiveness in this world for what he did in a combat zone, and to know that for certain is at least a foundation upon which he can build.

Lyle Pressley, though, was there, too. And as far as foundations go, physical foundations, his was crumbling. After the truck bomb, with that deployment so close to being done, his back was kaput. He felt like he'd been through a twelve-round fight, that deployment, and then gotten knocked out at the last minute.

And then everyone came home, and that was that. The deployment was over.

PART III

AFTER

CHAPTER 20

WHAT ARE YOU GOING

TO DO NOW?

A few square miles of territory in the Arghandab had become everything to Bravo Company. Those daily patrols had come to define them. Then, just like that, those daily patrols became something they had once done, became a thing of the past.

Just like that there was no more combat outpost, no more patrols, no more IEDs, no more Afghanistan, no more pomegranates. To be sure, that stuff was still there in Afghanistan. It all got turned over to the next unit, while Bravo Company headed home. Over the course of a couple weeks the men left the valley, many of them convoying in vehicles, some of them walking out, taking a final awful patrol out of that bomb-laden land.

After deployment, once the plane with the bulk of the unit landed at Fort Bragg, everyone who hadn't been medevaced back to Walter Reed walked on their own two legs across the tarmac in the United States to be greeted with hugs. Then the whole pre-deployment preparation process immediately began again. Within days, if not hours.

Experienced soldiers left the company, heading to other units, maybe, or even to begin gathering the paperwork to leave the Army altogether.

New men joined the unit to replace those who had left. Officers and senior enlisted took on commands elsewhere, sometimes at different bases entirely.

Bravo Company was still Bravo Company, but it was also completely and totally different. It was the same, but it wasn't.

At West Point or ROTC, in boot camp and throughout the professional training courses soldiers are forced to endure, there are all sorts of ways that men and women are prepared to deal with the realities of combat and its aftermath. They read books about war: what it's like, how it affects the human body and the human psyche. They prepare for the wreckage that happens in battle by dehumanizing the enemy and learning how to be empathetic to the civilians caught up in the maelstrom. They learn down in their very bones to be ready to sacrifice everything for the man next to them. They are taught that they're responsible for the well-being of those under their command.

But nobody ever teaches them about how something like walking through an IED-laden minefield day after day will reverberate through their very being, how it will affect them for years to come. Nobody teaches them about how dehumanizing the enemy and finding empathy for the civilian who gets mangled and killed can bounce around in their heads once they get back home to the United States and can keep bouncing around, gaining momentum year after year, the entropy taking over.

Sure, West Point and ROTC teach an officer like Adam Armstrong to care for the troops and tell them they're like kin. But there's no class or lecture that teaches the young officer-in-training about the enduring debt undertaken when he leads men in a place like the Arghandab. There's nothing that explains the unbreakable bond that they are responsible for. An officer, senior enlisted, and each and every man take on a debt that lasts for life. A debt to the Army and to each other.

Nobody tells a young man that.

And nobody tells a young man that as he's getting ready to leave the Army, process out when he's fed up with all he's had to endure, that he will miss that uniform every single day of his life from the moment he takes it off for the last time.

That's not taught. Instead, it has to be learned on the job, in real life and often without the help and resources of anybody else, because all the men you've fought with and had these experiences with, well, they all go someplace else as soon as you land back home after deployment. They become free-floating individuals, and there's no clear physical bonds to hold them all together.

* * *

The transition from active duty to veteran status hit them all hard. It's good policy in life to never, ever say every person in a group is affected by some event or another. There are always outliers, there are always exceptions. One should not speak in definites. But for Bravo Company, every man was hit by the return home from that deployment.

The Department of Defense (DoD) and the Department of Veterans Affairs (VA) are two very separate institutions. Although politicians have been trying for decades to streamline the transition process, it is especially difficult for soldiers leaving the military who expect it to be easy to just jump right into the VA system. Allen Thomas found the experience jarring and confusing.

There was no singular, simple process when Allen left the service for troops to learn about their benefits and what to expect when they took off the uniform. Each branch of the military transitioned troops out a little bit differently, and each base did it a little differently. Yes, there was a system that was supposed to be in place, something like a week's worth of classes for a soldier to teach them about taking off the uniform, but the classes were irregular and inconsistent. For most soldiers, their commanders could choose when and how to let them go take the classes. And those commanders could always say, Tough shit, I need that soldier in my unit until the bitter end and I can't afford to let them attend those classes.

The classes themselves were hit-or-miss, sometimes they'd have a teacher who led troops through what to expect, other times, hours could be wasted with a civilian teaching troops not how to cope with the outside world but instead how to game the system, how to apply for unemployment benefits as soon as they took off their cammies. Sometimes in these classes, experts from veteran service organizations such as Disabled American Veterans (DAV) would look at troops' medical records and help them fill out the paperwork to get disability benefits and sign up for health care. But sometimes not.

Either way, the transition from military service member to veteran wasn't like taking a freeway off-ramp smoothly onto a side road. A service member might be handed his medical record as he left the service and be told to hand carry inches-thick stacks of paper to his local VA medical center to enroll there.

Those paper files might have to be scanned in by hand into a digital record in the VA's electronic health system. But sometimes the files would sit for months or years in a backlogged system where stacks sat waiting to be entered.

A veteran like Allen who had been getting treatment through the military's health-care system found himself going through an intake process at the local VA, starting all over again from the beginning, it seemed. New doctors, new hospitals, new medications, new treatments, and new waits for assistance.

A decade after Allen went through his transition process, the VA and DoD were still trying to get health-care record systems that could be interoperable, to create one health record that could follow a soldier from boot camp through the rest of their lives. And somehow only a fraction of veterans who were eligible for VA benefits and health care had taken advantage of it. By 2015, only 62 percent of veterans from the Global War on Terror had used the VA for health care, according to the VA.

Many troops getting ready to take off the uniform had no idea about any of the complexity and confusion they would face when they were ready to draw on their benefits. Most American citizens have no idea about all of this. It contributes to the confusion and the dread and regret troops have when they leave the service.

For someone like Allen, there's another level of confusion to the whole thing, because when someone gets medically separated, he relies in part on the military's health-care insurance program known as TRICARE, and he also relies on the VA for some things. It was all inscrutable to Allen, and he had been away from the loving bosom of the Army for only a few weeks.

Danica remembers his frustration and anger when he'd visit some new doctor and complain that his chest was hurting. The doc sometimes asked Allen if he felt as if he might be having a cardiac episode. Allen would reply, no, it wasn't a heart attack, his chest just hurt because a ball bearing had recently ripped through it.

* * *

Jared Lemon, the now one-armed jeweler, found 2010 to be a dark time. He was soon out of the hospital, medically retired from the Army. Unlike a guy who has lost his legs, Lemon didn't have to relearn to walk and go through all that, so despite the supremely shitty deal of losing an arm, he could still walk around fine. There was just a fat chance he'd be able to be a jeweler ever again.

Lemon's wife came to visit him when he got back to the States, the wife who'd told him she didn't want him to join the Marines or Army or whatever it was. A month after the visit, she told him she wanted a divorce. The one person he could trust just left.

Now he was alone and wondered to himself, *What girl has grown up thinking,* I want to marry a dude with one arm?

Thus, Lemon's wife was gone, and their two kids were often with her. He wasn't a paratrooper anymore. What the hell, he thought, and so after Walter Reed he'd sometimes just sit in his truck with a gun, he said. Suicide typically happens when a number of factors all come together at the same time. A person has to have the inclination to do it, the tool to do it, and the knowledge of how to use that tool. Suicide isn't a spur-of-the-moment thing, it's thought about and mulled over and plans are made. The actual event itself might be sped up by drugs or alcohol, by a sudden despair, which makes it seem spur-of-the-moment. It should instead be thought of as a chemical reaction just waiting for a catalyst to set it off. Sitting there in his truck, Lemon never found himself catalyzed to action. One or more of the things needed to make him proceed wasn't there, thank God. Instead he just sat there thinking whether he should use that pistol on himself, be done with it all, but he never did.

Lemon had a few friends at that time, but he didn't have too many people he wanted to hang around with. One of those friends, an Army buddy, just stopped calling him. The guy was about to deploy to Afghanistan and Lemon guessed his pal didn't want to get bad vibes from a dude who left an arm there. If a soldier's getting ready to deploy, then those good-luck reservoirs have to be filled to the tippy-top.

That's the sort of limbo where Lemon was for years. For *years*.

When a soldier gets medically retired from the Army, there's a pension, enough cash to get by month to month. So if he doesn't want to get a job, or if he can't get a job, well, he's not going to go broke. And all the medical care he needs is free. Well, it's not free, that shit was paid for with deployments and an arm, but he doesn't get a bill in the mail.

A fellow can just bump along for a quite a while without having to get his shit together, and that's what Lemon did. It wasn't until he started talking to some nonprofit veteran organizations like Ranger Road, which organizes activities to help veterans transition into the civilian world, that things started to change for him. He went and climbed the Grand Teton with a veteran outdoor group, a nonprofit meant to help veterans find purpose.

That mountain was a real accomplishment. It was when he realized it's really something to climb a mountain even if you've got all four limbs, but when you're missing an arm? Well, that's an entirely new transcendental sort of experience.

On that Teton trip he climbed with some Special Forces guys and they all talked during the trip, got to know each other. At the end they asked Lemon, "So, what are you going to do now?"

What, indeed?

* * *

If his deployments had proven anything to Rob Musil, it was that he was good at fighting. He was adept when the shooting began.

After the Arghandab deployment, when he was a sergeant, Musil didn't want to leave the Army and pursue some horseshit civilian career. No, he chased whatever Army posting he could get that would put him in the place where he did the thing he was best at in the world. The only logical course of action for him was to do whatever he could to deploy again and again. He moved from unit to unit, always making sure he was in position for another trip overseas. It was where he was at his best. It was a kind of home for him, and deploying doubled as a strategy for avoiding the civilian world.

WHAT ARE YOU GOING TO DO NOW? 255

When a veteran gets introduced at some event in respectable society, maybe a banquet or a professional ball game, the emcee might note how many times the soldier has deployed. Then the assembled crowd will swoon, shake their heads solemnly at the immense sacrifice. How horrible it must be, that poor young man forced to deploy again and again, they think.

Well, save your sympathies when it comes to Rob Musil. No matter how many deployments he was able to tally, he wanted more, more, more. Only grumble and groan for him when he's forced to settle down and live the quiet life. God only knows what he'd do with himself with a pipe and slippers!

Musil grew up in a pious world, a kid from an evangelical household. Back then, he thought he could wish away, pray away, his bad behaviors and thoughts. He thought there was some big guy in the sky who could swoop down and save him. In the Army he watched his faith in an evangelical God disappear, replaced by a faith in combat and war. He once thought his vocation was to be a minister, but he came to realize his vocation was violence.

It was his calling. It was what he was good at, and that Arghandab deployment and the losses of friends and of his youthful mooring forced him to retreat into the depths of war.

After the Bravo Company deployment Musil tried to reconcile the joy of violence in the here and now as part of a bigger philosophical picture. He knew it was odd for a kid to go from wanting to be a pastor to wanting combat, and he drew upon his education in the church to try and answer that paradox. In other words, he wanted to know if his new vocation fit into Living a Good Life, in the Aristotelian sense. Musil is one of the few soldiers you'll meet who will put it in those terms, of seeking the Aristotelian Good Life.

In the Army Musil jettisoned the Bible for philosophy and has been trying to pin down Truth ever since. Don't worry, he doesn't talk to his family much about these changes, these questions, this new philosophy of his. He doesn't tell them about realizing his actual calling in the world is to kill other men efficiently. He doesn't tell them that his faith has gone and been replaced by the Army and the wisdom of the East and philosophical systems that might have gotten him burned at the stake a few hundred years ago or, more recently, ostracized at a church potluck.

The Arghandab completed his transformation. That particular deployment did it. As a persistent seeker, he would hesitate to say it helped him find the Good Life, but yes, that transformation improved his life.

He rejected not just the faith of his childhood upbringing but also the whole Christianity thing, which he came to figure is a sham. It makes his stomach turn even now, to think anyone would try to clothe the violence of war in a mantle of religious piety. That's no better than what the fucking Taliban was doing, what Al Qaeda did, for God's sake.

The paradoxes of war, of the Army, of society, all dwelled within Rob Musil. He wanted to go to war but wasn't so happy about what much of war means, why it is fought. That Bravo deployment, for instance, what was that for? Musil loved Frank Jenio, a warfighter and a fine commander. Jenio wanted war and he got it for his battalion, but what the hell did Jenio really gain by busting his hump to get Bravo into the Arghandab? Into Jenio's War? Soldiers died, and a bunch more came home missing limbs.

It was a giant chest-thumping exercise, as far as Musil is concerned. They didn't even get any really good firefights out of the deal. The tension of war thrums in every conversation with Musil, especially when it comes to that deployment. How can a man love war so much but hate the fact he was thrust into such a deployment?

Did they need to be there? They didn't, says he. And yet both Jenio and Musil had to be there because it was in their very marrow.

Those poor Afghan farmers, he thinks now, they grew their poppy down there in Helmand because it paid the bills and it got them infamy in the United States. Like Jared Lemon and so many other soldiers who have seen real-life flesh-and-blood human beings on their deployments, Musil knew these people, their enemies, were indeed people. They were just going about their lives. Some American assholes at some point told those farmers in Helmand to grow some wheat worth a fraction of poppy crops. They were told to do it, and when they asked for a reason they were told, well, because America, that's why. Everyone did what they had to do just . . . well, just because. Musil was compelled by the Army, not because he believed in the mission broadly, but because he believed in the mission narrowly—the here and now of being in a deployment.

As Musil worked through the calculations of war, he figured on a purely operational level some unit eventually had to go in there and do something about the Arghandab. So that might as well have been Bravo, might as well have been Musil. Why not? But that doesn't seem to be a good cosmic reason to go over there, a Big Reason.

If you're trying to live the Good Life, you really ought to have a Big Reason if you're making such sweeping sacrifices in your life to find a way to travel abroad and legally kill bad people. Without a Big Reason, war is just murder.

So Rob Musil needs to know that the Arghandab deployment, and by extension all of his deployments, had some Big Reason. He wants to know he wasn't just murdering people on behalf of America. He needs to know he was part of a global force for good. That would make him feel better, it certainly would. But he's worried that there is no Big Reason to it all. He started to worry down in his bones soon after the Arghandab.

Musil was just part of a large and very flawed decision to deploy his unit in accordance with very flawed policies that really hadn't done anything worthwhile in Afghanistan. But that's OK, too, right? It doesn't mean he can't be proud of what he did there on that Bravo Company deployment.

Hell, maybe that's the thing, maybe that's the Good Life, to achieve perfection in combat. Like a Greek warrior whose deeds and heroism live on forever in an epic poem. If Musil has no control over the big picture, then perhaps he just needs to be concerned with his singular contributions to War with a capital W. Yes, his contribution to the concept of War, the metaphysical and ontological thing that was and is and always will be the biggest thing a human can do.

Maybe it's not worth the Jesuitical casuistry to figure out if it was all worth it. No, maybe there's just the simple aesthetic purity of being in the mind-numbing, violent here and now of war that makes it worth it. Maybe it's that Zen-like moment, fully present to the immediacy of life and plugged directly into the transcendent—which amazingly enough can sometimes be every moment when you're in war—that makes it worthwhile. Yes, it's worth it for that moment in combat when you slip the bonds of earth and touch the fucking face of God. Yes, the promise of that moment should be on every Army recruiting poster. But it would scare

the ever-loving bejesus out of those fundamentalist parents who should
be good and goddamn worried their son will drink deep from the pure
artesian spring that is an infantry deployment and come back changed.
Come back a professional, like Rob Musil.

When Musil accepted the sanctity of war, he chose to make it a true
profession. No, it became a vocation, a higher calling. Maybe it's a good
thing the God's honest Truth of it all is not on every recruiting poster.

What does that make him, a Romantic for violence? Perhaps he should
have lived in fin de siècle Europe, been part of the vanguard of soldiers in
World War I who wrote paeans to violence, macabre poems, and courted
death for death's sake? War for war's sake.

And now that you mention it, why would anyone in their right mind
want some warmonger like him serving in uniform? Well, you see, you
have it all wrong, he'd say. Indeed, he is the exact person we most want
representing America in war! What you should ask, dear citizen, is why
you would want deployed on your behalf anyone other than a high priest
of violence who respects, loves, and cherishes war more than anything
else in life?

Should his stark honesty and embrace of violence scare the Christ
out of his civilian countrymen back home? Instead, should it not comfort
them? If a man loves and cherishes war, then would he not do everything
he can to honor it in all its manifestations, in sickness and in health, 'til
death do they part.

"I treat it as a profession," he says. "Not a nine-to-five job, it's a way
of life."

OK, sure, he actually enjoys getting into gunfights and killing other
human beings. It's even fair to say he loves it and, he even admits, there is
something distasteful in that. It's a bit odd, as far as polite company goes,
for him to acknowledge it's calming to have someone shoot at him, because
it means a gateway has opened for him to step into that transcendental
purity that is maneuver warfare.

Since he is a priest of war he must care for every punctilio of the
violent arts. So that means it is he, Rob Musil, who thinks it's horseshit
that some poor Afghan farmer had to suffer because of a morals-drenched
poppy eradication mission dreamed up in Washington. It is Musil who

actually gives a shit about that farmer. The loveliness of war should not be despoiled by causing some poor civilian to suffer. A high priest of war doesn't have to think everything that happens in war is justified, does he?

It is he, Rob Musil, therefore, who 100 percent supported drawing down in Iraq and Afghanistan, because the wars became a waste of resources and people and money and life on both sides. It is he, Rob Musil, who finds the profession of arms so very sacred that to employ the devastating violence of an Army paratrooper on anyone but a legitimate target is pure blasphemy. Who gets to say what's a legitimate target, though? Surely the purity of war, to paraphrase, is too important to be left to the high priests, it must be left to the generals and politicians. Only a high priest of war can love it enough to not want the country to waste such sacred actions on profane cockamamie schemes like motherfucking poppy eradication. Therefore, is it an understandable paradox that Rob Musil is the very person peace-loving American people with pure hearts and true intentions want serving our country in Afghanistan!

Well, either way, he's the guy we got because he couldn't stop himself from going and we couldn't stop sending him. He deployed again and again to these wars that he didn't even support because he didn't want to miss out on the violence while it was happening because it's what he was good at and what he knows. And like an interminable prison sentence or Sisyphus pushing his rock to no end, Musil kept going back to war.

* * *

As a high priest of war, Musil knew there was one pure, holy, and most supreme thing that all his many deployments had yet to reveal to him, a warrior's grail.

Some select soldiers or Marines will admit—sometimes when they're sober, sometimes only when blinded with drink—that the most great, the most gracious, and the most Godly way to leave this Earth would be getting killed while in the middle of actions that win them the Medal of Honor, the grandest military decoration the United States can bestow on a service-member. That's the only thing that would be really righteous.

Musil caveats any discussion of medals of valor by saying he's never wanted one, never sought one out, and never hoped for one. It's blasphemy to even seek such things, and anyone with such hopes is not a soldier for the proper reasons, he argues. Accepting the possibility of death, even preferring to die in a gunfight rather than from natural causes, elderly and alone, is a more accurate depiction of his stoic approach.

That being said, while even talking about getting such a medal is improper, profane, and verboten, there is still the reality of it all that should be examined.

A few things to begin with:

First of all, there are too many people who have read the Associated Press style guide, that paragon of proscribing rather than describing the English language, who will tell you the Medal of Honor is not won, it is awarded. Scolds will get indignant and remind a fellow that to talk about "winning" the Medal of Honor is an insult to all who have been awarded it.

Well, anyone who knows anything knows sure as shit that a medal like that is won. And it's a great and glorious prize for the one who wins it.

Too bad the odds of ever winning it are stacked against the lowly infantryman dreaming of glory. It's a crapshoot roulette game of chance that even gets you deployed to the right place at the right time to get into combat. Yeah, sure, you can join the infantry and will likely get yourself a deployment, but you could get the shitty end of the stick and get stuck for months on some training mission in Helmand. Hell, if you're a Marine you can get stuck floating around on a stupid ship for an entire deployment. If you're in the Army you might get stuck on the DMZ in Korea picking your ass for months at a time.

It's a minor jackpot just to get out on patrol in a combat zone in the first place. Then you have to roll the cosmic dice just right to get to where there's fighting. Plenty of people go through a combat deployment and never get to pull the trigger. It's always possible that one squad out of a platoon will get in a marvelous shoot-'em-up firefight and the rest of them won't see anything worthwhile.

Ah, but you might have royal flush–type luck and find yourself in a place where the odds are stacked against you, the enemy is coming in a wave, and you have a chance to do some shit that they'll read about in books for years to come. You might have the great and good fortune to be in a situation where you know you're probably going to die as the enemy advances and as you mow down a few in the meantime. That might be bad news for most people, but for true high priests of war, that would be fantastic. That's the biggest jackpot of all, as far as the odds go, to put a guy in position to win The Big One. The Medal of Honor.

Yes, it's true in those defining moments there's no luck involved or random chance. During those frantic minutes such a medal is purely earned. That singular moment of glory is yours, hard-earned, no question about it. If you do some stuff that's top-notch, grade A, movie-caliber glory, it's all yours. Maybe you advance on a machine gun, maybe you smash a guy's face in with your boot. In that few minutes, maybe a few hours, everyone can agree you've done what it takes to earn The Grail.

But after that fight, then what? It's not like you automatically get the Medal of Honor. The soldier in the fighting hole next to you can't pin a medal on you. Your great and good luck must continue in order to cash in your winnings. Who knows if anybody saw what you did. Or maybe your staff sergeant thinks you're a cocky asshole and won't testify on your behalf even though you saved half the platoon, including his sorry ass.

Maybe your CO hates your guts or the XO is a bad writer and can't describe well what you did, or maybe he's just too lazy to do the paperwork. And who knows if the generals and the chief of staff and the secretary of the Army don't care about you or simply have other stuff to focus on. Maybe they don't want to spend their political capital on some Medal of Honor nomination right now. Maybe they're worried about getting a budget approved.

And the secretary of defense and the president, well, either of them might be turds. They both might be turds, and in that case you've rolled snake eyes at the big casino of valor. In that case, you don't win jack shit.

Yeah, maybe you'll get a Bronze Star with a "V" for valor or even a Silver Star. Maybe a Distinguished Service Cross. But you don't win The Big One.

You don't win The One that gets you a lifetime stipend from the federal government and trips to presidential inaugurations and Fourth of July celebrations and speaking engagements. You don't get the medal that dictates even four-star motherfucking generals should salute you! No kidding, if you've got the Medal of Honor everybody has to salute *you*, no matter your rank, according to tradition.

The stars must align for it. What you earned in those moments of unknowably awful and valorous glory is just the ante put on the table in hopes of the big win.

And high priests, whether they'll say it out loud or not, they want that medal. But maybe they don't want to be aboveground when that medal is awarded. It's much easier for the Pentagon to give that thing to a guy who was blended into bits while saving his buddies than a guy who survived the ordeal.

"Say, how'd that guy make it out of all that alive if he gave it his all? Sounds kinda fishy, don't it?" the washed-up assholes down at the VFW bar who were fucking engine mechanics back in their day will mumble into their beers.

And, Jesus, have you seen some of the guys who are still alive and have the medal? Have you seen the guys who don't even have The Big One, the poor saps with Distinguished Service Crosses? Some of those guys have wispy holes in their heads in lieu of eyeballs, a stare that goes somewhere, maybe back to that place where one of them maybe clubbed a man to death with an entrenching tool.

It's no good to be a broken ex-combatant, a museum piece. It's no good to end up some drooling old fart they lash to a gurney and put out on the street for all to see on the Fourth of July. No, the way to do it is to go out and be remembered. Just. Like. That. Then you win, and you win big. The AP's style guide can kiss both cheeks, because that's the reality of it.

And that's what a guy like Rob Musil wants more than anything. Not only do you get glory. Not only do you win big. But you never have to deal with anything anymore. You're out, you're gone, you're in Valhalla, welcomed upon your arrival as a true and proper high fucking priest of war.

CHAPTER 21

WOMACK

There were those among the high priests of war, and there was Wendi Sheets, who worked among those considered to be its lepers.

Wendi had been a physical therapist in the civilian sector for a half decade when she began a new job at Womack Army Medical Center at Fort Bragg. This change plunged her into a whole new world of military lingo and combat trauma. It also gave her a front row seat to watch as the Army groped its way to understanding how to treat a generation of broken soldiers.

Or rather how *it tried* to treat a generation of broken soldiers. It also introduced her to defrocked high priests like Sergeant Allen Thomas.

Wendi grew up in Jefferson, North Carolina, the daughter of an Air Force veteran, but she wasn't steeped in military culture. She trained in nearby Hudson, North Carolina, in physical therapy, and as soon as she finished her schooling in 2004, she began working at hospitals and outpatient rehabilitation programs.

She did standard rehab stuff, helping people recover from hip and knee replacements, mostly mechanical things. She also worked on neurological rehabilitation with people who suffered from dementia, strokes, multiple sclerosis, cerebral palsy, and Parkinson's disease. It was mostly the elderly, or people with long-term diseases that affected their brains, which in turn affected their bodies.

A few years into the profession, around 2009, Wendi became interested in something different. She saw a posting on Indeed.com, the massive online job board, for an open position at Womack. A colleague happened to know the colonel in charge of the vestibular rehabilitation clinic there, which would involve helping soldiers who had balance issues or other problems related to concussions.

"I applied," she said. "It was a shot in the dark."

She got the job.

Wendi began her job at Womack around the time Bravo Company deployed to Afghanistan. The clinic's staffing and funding reflected the attention the Army gave to traumatic brain injuries, which wasn't a hell of a lot. Wendi's team consisted of herself and her boss, the colonel. Two people for the entirety of Fort Bragg.

Bragg was one of the Army's premier bases and was home to about 57,000 troops, 11,000 civilians, 23,000 family members, and one Wendi Sheets.

At any given time, thousands of those troops were deployed to Iraq or Afghanistan, and thousands more were rotating to or from those combat zones, any of whom might require the services of someone like Wendi.

Womack is one of the Army's largest and best-equipped hospitals, accommodating the 82nd Airborne Division and many of their dependents along with military retirees in the Fayetteville area. As far as head trauma went, Womack was considered second-tier. Walter Reed was the nation's premier military hospital, where the worst overseas or stateside injuries were treated.

Wendi quickly realized she was seeing soldiers who had finished up their time at Walter Reed and had come back to Bragg in order to try and rehabilitate themselves to be able to stay in the Army. Either that or they were about to leave the Army and were putting in the time to get better while they had easy access to military medicine. That, and there were a lot of active-duty guys whose heads hit the ground during parachute jumps.

With a division full of paratroopers, training jumps from aircraft happen all the time. But the standard parachute jump for airborne infantrymen isn't the sort of thing you see at Super Bowl halftime shows where fancy fellows in satin warm-up suits glide down to a feather-gentle landing underneath a square canopy. Airborne troops typically use a round-canopied chute made to take a lot of the guesswork out of the process. A dumb grunt can't screw things up with a chute like that. He—and back then it was almost all men doing the jumping—pretty much comes straight down from the plane he jumped from. And it allows them to jump with a lot more weight than the typical sport skydiver.

When an infantryman jumps out of a plane, he's in a bulky uniform with his rifle, magazines filled with rounds, a backpack full of gear, and God only knows what else. Those parachute canopies slow him down, but he still hits the ground descending at maybe ten miles per hour if he's lucky. An infantryman doesn't try to stay on his feet when he lands, instead he's taught to sort of crumple once he hits the ground and let his whole body absorb the shock of the landing. This unglamorous landing means he frequently hits his combat-helmeted head on the ground as he crumples. On grass if he's lucky. But parachutes bring a paratrooper straight down, not allowing for much steering. Some wind or a bad jump might land him in a tree or on asphalt, maybe even hit a building if he's had real bad luck.

All that's to say that when hundreds of infantrymen jump out of an airplane, some might end up with broken ankles or smashed knees. And a good number of them will hit their heads on the ground. One of Wendi's first jobs with the 82nd Airborne was to be ready after a big jump for the inevitable flood of guys with concussions coming to Womack to get checked out and make sure they didn't have anything beyond a basic concussion.

These air-drop concussions were like small head-on collisions, with a paratrooper's brain sloshing against the inside of his skull, leaving it bruised and swollen. Wendi helped the paratroopers cope with inflammation, headaches, and the irritability that came with them. It was the same type of thing a sports-medicine doctor might help football players deal with after a bad hit. It was something the 82nd had been dealing with since the first day a soldier jumped out of an airplane.

But Wendi also saw troops come in, mainly guys who had deployed, who had suffered a totally different type of brain injury, one that the military establishment was just starting to learn about at the time. In a few years it would be one of the signature injuries of the generation of soldiers who fought in Iraq and Afghanistan.

Wendi saw traumatic brain injury.

For outsiders—civilians and people whose everyday lives don't expose them to high explosives and IEDs—TBI can seem just like a really, really bad concussion. But it's not just a really, really bad concussion. Wendi understood this as a clinician, as someone who'd trained for it, and who quickly gained experience treating people with ordinary—albeit serious—concussions. But she hadn't seen firsthand the full extent of what TBI meant for the young men affected by it.

"A blast injury is much different," compared with a concussion, Wendi said. "It's not like blunt-force trauma."

Blunt-force trauma, like those jump concussions, typically means the head is hit with one kind of force, often a direct hit to the head. The brain is injured by the initial impact, and also suffers from the contrecoup, when it hits against the other side of the skull. But when an explosion goes off, a shock wave might be the first thing to hit a person's body. That shock wave, a sudden increase in pressure, finds its way into any open orifice in the body: mouth, nose, ears. The force of energy enters the open portholes and then continues, by the path of least resistance, throughout the body, usually finding its way into the air-filled areas.

Imagine a shorefront building during a hurricane. A huge wave from the ocean hits the front of the building. The walls stop the wave, but windows and doors get immediately pushed over as the water rushes into any gaps it finds. That's sort of the way a blast wave acts on the human body. The nose, the ears, the mouth, are ways for the wave to get in. Once inside, the wave keeps on going through air pockets. The blast wave is an invading force, it's a violent external thing entering the sanctum of the body.

The airiest bits are the lungs. They get overinflated, like balloons with too much air. That's called blast lung.

Similar things happen to the brain. The pressure of the shock wave squeezes the brain tissue, then leaves just as suddenly as it arrived, creating a vacuum, and all those bits go from being compacted to suddenly being expanded and pulled apart.

"All that pressure pulls your brain apart and then slaps it back together," Wendi says. "It changes the entire wiring of the brain."

In other words, the complex network of synaptic physical connections gets pulled apart like taffy. Yes, the strands of taffy contract to what might appear their old shape, but the state they return to is fundamentally altered. Wendi had worked with the elderly, people whose minds were fading. What she saw with the young soldiers reminded her of those Alzheimer's patients and stroke victims. It was a sickening realization.

"There was one guy who was only twenty-five and he was having a really difficult time with fine motor skills and balancing," she said. "He'd been to combat and his brain scan showed lesions, like it was a Parkinson's sort of dementia."

To know this twenty-five-year-old was unlikely to get any better left her depressed and deeply saddened. She knew his trajectory forward. He would only get worse. That poor brain of his had degenerated, in effect, by decades due to his combat trauma.

And when she was first seeing all this back in 2009, the Army hadn't yet decided to focus on funding and treatment techniques or even to push for institutional acceptance of these types of injuries. She was, in other words, working on the leading edge of combat medicine with little institutional support. She had no funding to speak of, compared with what the Army could provide, and the rehabilitation equipment was rudimentary at best. Hell, even the way Wendi treated these guys was rudimentary, because she didn't know any better at the time. She groped her way through, always on the lookout for practices and protocols that might help the soldiers under her care.

Wendi remembers one soldier with a brain injury whose job required him to walk out on a ledge every so often, but his head had been damaged so his balance was poor. He had little confidence in his ability to ever get out on a ledge again. But he had to do it, just had to, in order to do his job. So Wendi pushed some tables together, grabbed a few chairs, and set up an ersatz obstacle course. She threw a couple pillows here and there to provide unstable footing, and then she played follow-the-leader with the soldier, making him learn to walk on a ledge just a few feet off the ground.

She pushed him beyond his comfort zone, like any great coach. Back then her prevailing mindset was to push these soldiers, drive them. She was trying to get them back to their jobs. She hadn't yet accepted that pushing them back to their jobs might be too much to ask. Helping them simply walk might be enough. Teaching them to walk would be the therapy needed to improve their well-being. She needed to let them adjust, but not too quickly. She needed to nudge, not push. It was delicate.

Every few months Wendi would ask up the chain of command for this or that piece of equipment to add to the clinic. She needed more than chairs and pillows, but she only had the budget to make a few supply requests at a time.

In retrospect, Wendi sees clearly just how much she was winging it in those early years, as were the injured men with whom she worked.

Active-duty soldiers didn't typically go in to get checked out or even admit they were having problems back in 2009. There was a definite stigma to these injuries, a shame. Their commanders, fellow troops, and even the Army itself didn't encourage these injured soldiers to seek help—didn't clear an avenue for them to walk toward support.

"We did not see so many guys who needed to be seen because they were afraid they'd lose their position, they'd lose their jobs," she said.

TBI wasn't yet recognized as a signature problem of the Iraq and Afghanistan Wars. Even an official diagnosis wasn't a sure way to get good treatment. No, it was often just a sure way to get medically separated from the Army, or to be seen as a shirker by other soldiers. A goddamn malingerer.

The Department of Veterans Affairs wasn't much help at the time, either. In 2009 the department's annual budget was less than a quarter of what it would be a decade later. The VA's research arm wouldn't mark any major milestones in TBI treatment for a few years, and it wouldn't be until 2013 that the VA and DoD jointly established a consortium to study PTSD and TBI.

As with Agent Orange issues among Vietnam veterans and recognizing the effects of burn pits on veteran health, the VA would spend billions on the effort, but not for years after the problems were first identified among those affected by it.

Less than a decade into the Global War of Terror, troops were even getting TBI from too much training. Nevertheless, few had it documented in their records. Troops who shot things like shoulder-fired rockets didn't get it noted in their records that they'd fired those rounds. Each one of those bazooka-type shots can feel like a punch to the head. During a day at the range, some troops could fire a half dozen or more of those rounds. Someone assigned that weapon might prepare to use it for a few deployments, get time on the range while in-country, and who knows whatever else. In combat, they'd shoot them without hearing protection and sometimes near walls, which reflected the shock wave back at them. A soldier might shoot dozens—hundreds—of rockets in their career, each one a punch to the head.

Some of them went to the Department of Defense and VA years later to try to get compensation and treatment, but no records existed—there was nothing that documented those everyday small traumas their heads experienced, so they couldn't get benefits.

The Army didn't even extensively research concussions until 2007 when a bill sponsored by Senator Daniel Akaka, chairman of the Senate Committee on Veterans' Affairs, passed that established the Psychological Health and Traumatic Brain Injury Research Program, allocating more than a $1 billion for TBI, PTSD, and other psychological health research over a decade. The program was born of congressional concern about increasing reports of TBI and mental health issues among those returning from war.

At the same time Wendi was getting a crash course in military treatment of brain injuries, officials at the Department of Defense were trying to standardize treatment. In 2008, programs for mental health issues were, for the most part, localized at bases and within the different service branches, says Kim Hepner, a military medicine researcher at the RAND Corporation. That meant a Marine at one base and a soldier at another might undergo dramatically different treatments. Research from RAND shows that in 2008 there were some two hundred different TBI treatment programs that were poorly integrated and inefficient.

It wouldn't be until 2017 that Congress mandated a centralized defense health system. Years after, that was still a work in progress.

By 2021, the Department of Defense estimated there had been more than 430,000 TBIs reported by members of the military. While some 80 percent of those were concussions, thousands were the kind of injuries that Wendi was seeing more and more of and that she realized the Army needed to do more to address.

While she was working in the trenches to recognize and address these problems, some Army leaders began a parallel effort pushing the Department of Defense to act. General Peter Chiarelli, the vice chief of staff of the Army, was one of those early leaders. He began drawing attention to statistics the Army had only recently begun gathering in earnest.

"I want to change the stigma linked to these wounds," Chiarelli said at the 2009 meeting of the Association of the United States Army. "They are in fact real. These are not phantom issues made up by weak soldiers. They are as real as if you fell and broke your leg or lost an arm."

Chiarelli noted the increasing percentages of soldiers suffering from these wounds, and in 2008 he was put in charge of looking at the Army's suicide rates. The numbers were stark for him. The rates were tied to the fighting the soldiers were doing, as far as he was concerned. "Some of the studies say it had nothing to do with war," he said in an interview. "I think that's bullshit."

He spoke openly to subordinates about the need to change the military's approach to TBI and PTSD, which he estimated at the time affected about one-third of deployed troops. But even with the second-highest-ranking officer in the Army publicly advocating for the issues, changing an institutional mindset and policy takes time.

* * *

Around this time brain injuries were getting more attention among the general public as the National Football League began taking greater official actions to address brain trauma. In 2007 the league hosted a concussion summit and issued an informational pamphlet. Two years later, in 2009, the front page of the *New York Times* featured a story about dementia risks to football players.

At Womack's brain clinic where Wendi worked, the big breakthrough came from members of the special operations community, the Green Berets and Navy SEALs who began seeking help.

When a Humvee gets a flat tire or a smashed fender, it's not sent to the junkyard, it's fixed up and sent back into the fight. Even a few bullet holes or an explosion or two doesn't mean it's done for. A broken Humvee isn't fixed up for the intrinsic good of fixing up a broken Humvee, it's repaired because it's often cheaper to fix it than it is to procure a new one.

Humvees that really need help are sent back to a repair depot to get fixed, far away from where they were broken. During the Global War on Terror, it was the same with troops. When a man or woman was physically broken in war, that soldier didn't stay with the frontline unit. They were typically shipped off to Walter Reed or someplace similar and taken out of their units. This took them away from their support network, stripped them of meaning and purpose.

Special operations troops know they're more valuable to the Army when they're rehabbed and sent back into the fight than left to fall apart. Special operations troops also know that when they're not operating at full capability, they're a liability to themselves and their high-performance unit. Troops in those units also tend to be older, more mature. They also know they've proven their worth, their mettle, and they don't have to worry about seeming like shirkers.

Special operators take a pride in their bodies, as does the military, providing them with trainers like a professional sports team might. Visiting the doctor can be something that prevents catastrophic injury rather than something to be avoided at all costs. And it's likely to be done in-house, keeping them part of the community rather than scrapping them, kicking them out of the unit outright.

Sure, at the time people from the defense secretary on down the chain of command told troops to reach out for help if they needed it. This messaging was equivalent to—and about as effective as—a high school principal telling the freshmen to report bullying from the seniors and not worry about repercussions. A soldier in a regular Army unit like the 82nd Airborne who spoke up would most likely get mocked. If they did get care, they'd get shifted to someone else's unit, some hospital or clinic.

When a Humvee broke down, it got pulled from the unit's books and became the responsibility of the maintenance depot. From the perspective of the original unit, the problem now belonged to someone else. The same was true for a broken soldier. Such broken soldiers went to a hospital and then proceeded to Warrior Transition Units or to a medical battalion, where the intent was to give them treatment and get them back into the force, but too often it seemed their experience was like Allen Thomas's in that they felt they sat in a heap along with the other broken parts.

Special Forces units were different. During the wars in Iraq and Afghanistan, the community figured out that counseling and prescription medication wasn't indicative of worthlessness but a sign of maintenance. Just as a Humvee needs oil changes and regular tune-ups, so, too, do soldiers need maintenance, and mental health became part of that program. The prevailing sentiment among special operators was that they should look out for their own, appreciate the toll the job takes, and, above all, get operators back in operation. After the years of specialized training a Green Beret's gone through, it'd be a damn shame to see them sent off to the rear to fester in a hospital when they could be kept operating in a unit.

Nevertheless, it remained a tricky thing, getting mental health care. No matter what, there would always be a stigma of some sort surrounding it. And while the special operators had begun to come around to accepting treatment, a decade into the wars in Iraq and Afghanistan, it wasn't all that prevalent. These guys were more likely to come in, but still not all that likely.

Wendi remembers in 2011 a Navy SEAL came into the Womack clinic. The guy knew the head of the clinic, so he decided to try some treatment. It worked for him. Word started trickling out through the special operations community that the TBI clinic could help.

"A guy would call and say, 'Can I come in? Do you have to put it on my record?'" Wendi remembered. It was like she was getting a phone call on a secret line in a spy movie or something.

"We can find a way around this," she'd tell these special operators. They'd come in one or two at a time as word spread through the community that the clinic would take care of them and do it quietly. Those guys still had to warm to the possibility of treatment.

As treatment became more acceptable among the special operators, it started to become more acceptable among other troops. And as acceptance of treatment grew, so did the budgets and staff at Wendi's clinic. More therapists joined them, and Wendi was able to pick up increasingly specialized equipment. She'd ask for a piece of gear here, a new contraption there, and they slowly built up the clinic. She retired the pillows when she got specialized balance devices. She got some scanning machines that could tell, definitively, when someone had objective signs of brain trauma. She was learning more about treating these young men as well, learning to push them—but not too hard. She was understanding how not to overdo the treatment.

On top of acceptance of TBI there was the simple, horrible truth that the numbers of those suffering from brain injuries kept rising the longer the United States was in overseas conflicts. The more that companies like Bravo deployed and were blown up, the more troops came home needing treatment. Wendi's colleagues at the clinic gave seminars and taught commanders and soldiers that they needn't fear losing their jobs if they required help.

Soldiers from units like the 82nd Airborne who were getting ready to retire also had to go to the clinic to get a signature required on paperwork for separating from the military. It could be a check in the box, but the Womack clinic took advantage of the situation. Wendi and her colleagues used the highly effective "Since you're here anyway . . ." strategy, and it worked. With little else on their agenda, a number of those older troops consented to treatment. And these older guys recognized they had some issues, saw that treatment worked, and believed in its efficacy. They became evangelists, praising the Gospel of TBI. Then those older guys went back to their units and passed along the word that it was safe to go to the clinic. Acceptance of treatment further spread.

Wendi loved the job, she loved that each soldier was like a puzzle to be solved. They were individuals with individual illnesses. She came to feel uniquely qualified to help each of them. She basked in what might seem like small successes, like helping a soldier learn to drive again. Maybe helping him learn to walk straight down a hallway and not bump into a wall. She got used to the military, learned the ranks and the never-ending lists of acronyms. She had pride and fulfillment in the job. She was doing good for these troops.

She also got used to the locker-room talk, the cursing and trash mouths. It was a regular occurrence for some guy to say something foul and then follow it up quickly with a "Sorry, Ma'am." Some guys went through quite a few "Sorry, Ma'ams" in a session. But that vulgarity and coarseness cut both ways. It meant she could be brutally frank with these men to help them accomplish their goals. She didn't have to worry about offending them or hurting their feelings.

"Get your crap together and stop acting like this," she'd say to a recalcitrant patient. No way she could say that in a civilian clinic. And the soldiers would respond to it. They'd cut their crap. They'd get things done.

In the midst of all this, Wendi met Sergeant Allen Thomas.

* * *

After his stay at Walter Reed, Allen went to the Warrior Transition Unit at Fort Bragg in late 2010 and soon showed up at Wendi's clinic for treatment. He was larger-than-life, she remembers, a big guy with a bigger smile. He had charm and arrogance, but he was able to play it off in a way that wasn't obnoxious.

As soon as he walked into the clinic Allen commanded the attention of the whole room with his jokes and attitude. Wendi, the expert, saw that despite the swagger he was hiding serious underlying injuries. She saw he could probably fool most people, but it's just about impossible to hide those kinds of injuries from someone like Wendi, who was attuned to sense even the smallest signs of larger problems.

"It was very frustrating for him. He didn't want you to see it even though it was there," she said.

Allen often had double vision. He couldn't walk down a hallway without veering toward one wall or another. If he was on uneven ground, he'd stumble all over the place, even walk off the edge of a sidewalk.

Wendi knew right away Allen probably wasn't going to get any better. Yes, sometimes those brain connections find new ways to patch and mend themselves, like a subway train that has to reroute to bypass a wrecked station. But there's seemingly uncountable numbers of connections in the human brain, and a lot of Allen's had been ripped apart.

Wendi wasn't naive about her work. She knew "healing" was, in a case like Allen's, out of reach. She came to accept her role as that of helping a young, strong, cocky soldier learn how to cope with a painful new reality, a reality that would be there for the rest of his life.

Allen wasn't the only soldier she was helping. And the goal for so many of these men, like Allen, wasn't getting cured. That simply wasn't possible anymore. She couldn't help them fix something unfixable. No, Wendi's skill soon became helping people learn to cope. She helped people adjust to and live in their new normal.

She wasn't a psychologist or psychiatrist, but she was still doctor-esque to many of these men, so they'd often open up to her and talk about things they might not even tell their doctor. Hell, they talked to her specifically because she wasn't a shrink. She didn't carry the taboo of being a mental health professional, so distrustful soldiers came to trust her.

Her office was a safe space where they could admit their problems, their concerns, their worries, a place where they could just talk. And in those safe spaces where Wendi was just supposed to be treating physical trauma of TBI, she ended up also helping them work through the other traumas of combat, like PTSD.

One young soldier used to send her a text when it was time for his appointment so she could come meet him at the front door to the clinic, hold his arm, and help him walk into the room. The door's threshold was a damn near carbon copy of a threshold he remembered from a building in Afghanistan, and he simply couldn't get across it without her.

Another guy would casually ask Wendi if she ever saw the dead bodies in the corner, the ones right over there? She'd say no, she didn't, and ask him to describe what he was seeing. She helped him process it. She listened. She steered these soldiers toward follow-on care.

The men and women who came to the clinic had random and unpredictable triggers, and she had to prepare for eruptions at any moment. When the reactions came—the emotions, the fear, the vigilance, the stress, the anxiety—she would take on some of their burdens and help them. That was her job. No, that was her vocation. In her office they were able to get away from everything else and focus on themselves, on the quiet.

She treated female soldiers, too, but far fewer than male soldiers, who make up much of the military and especially combat-specific units. Over time, Wendi saw greater numbers of women come in for treatment and she remembers they were often more accepting of their injuries, more willing to face the emotions. Men had a tendency to bury things, to fester.

The independent activities of daily living that the uninjured think nothing about become torture to someone recovering from PTSD and TBI. Balancing a checkbook. Going to the grocery store to pick up a few things. Giving the kids a bath. Mundane activities can cause setbacks for men or women with blast injuries, with those changed brains.

"They didn't need to do a lot of tasks that we do every day," she said. "They needed a quiet area to decompress."

They also needed to find space to fit back into a world that they no longer knew and didn't want to be a part of, a world where they were no longer able to be soldiers in combat. Allen would let down his guard sometimes. Sure, most days he'd bound into the clinic with that outsize personality of his. He'd even joke about his new normal, giving Wendi a hard time for getting in his way as he careened down the hallway in a crooked line.

Other days, Allen would come in defeated. She might set up a balance exercise for him, and he'd just say "No."

But Allen loved his music, so she'd tell him he could pick the playlist, whatever he wanted while they worked together. And he'd choose some Stoney LaRue or Jamey Johnson. He loved to introduce her to something new.

Then they'd work together, guitars blasting, helping drive him toward his new normal.

Wendi worked with Allen for about six months. He came in a few times a week and she'd push him to get to a place where he could cope with the balance and dizziness. Then he'd relapse and have to adjust all over again.

He was learning to cope. But still, it was so hard, so frustrating to be a bad-ass soldier stuck with a body that was doing things he didn't understand and a brain that was so confused. He could name every man from every squad he'd ever been in, so why couldn't he remember where he put his wallet that morning? Nothing bad had happened that day, so why did he feel so sad? Nothing upsetting had happened, so why was he angry?

Wendi started absorbing Allen's trauma, taking it on as her own. It was with him as it was with others—she came to know these young men on a deeper level. Even by assuming a fraction of their pain, Wendi began to strain under the load herself. Her vocation began to weigh greatly upon her.

She and Allen remained connected after he left the Army, and he would sometimes come back to Womack, where he knew he could always find a refuge and a chance to readjust.

Allen had gone through fundamental personality, mood, and cognition changes. These would likely intensify as the years progressed, she knew. She knew he'd have good days. She knew he'd have bad days. And she was certain that the bad days would outnumber the good. But she was also hopeful.

Allen and Danica had a second child, another daughter. They hadn't been trying to have a child, but they also hadn't been *not* trying. Allen had always wanted a larger family, and Danica, while well pleased with their first daughter, had been open to the possibility of a larger family.

But she worried about their family, worried about some of the problems they were already having. It wasn't anything violent or scary, but they were having issues in their marriage. When Allen had a bad day, he would just check out on her, retreat to the safety of his guitar and all but abandon her to deal with life.

For people like Wendi, it seemed that Allen might be able to cope with those bad days because of that outsize personality and the will to project strength. Allen loved his kids, loved them more than anything, Wendi remembered, and he wanted to be with them.

But being with his children, a wonderful task, was also an everyday task. It was mundane, and while it was a thing he loved, it also caused turmoil in that damaged brain of his.

And the holy task, that of donning the vestments of a paratrooper to go to work out in the field, that thing he loved more than anything, was gone. His biggest obstacle was trying to figure out how he could still be the man he had been in the Army before he was blown up. He had been identified by his rank, by his prowess. Now what?

* * *

That erasure of identity cut across every patient in Wendi Sheets's clinic, especially those who had been injured in combat. Those soldiers, when they'd been injured, had all been in the very heart of the place that had come to define their very selves. They'd been doing the sine qua non of soldiering, the thing many of them had been dreaming of doing since childhood.

Then they came home like this.

They came back to the Army base they thought they'd known so well, but now they were going to parts of that base they might have never known existed. They'd all found themselves, like Allen Thomas, a part of a new and unknown Army, in the medical underbelly of Fort Bragg. Instead of being soldiers going to training areas and firing ranges, they were going back and forth to clinics, trying to walk straight down a hallway and not fall over while their friends, their brothers in the operating forces, went to those training areas and ranges.

Once it had been torn away from them, even the men who had hated being soldiers felt the power of nostalgia set in. Their service was imbued with a sweetness that might not have ever been present.

There were many soldiers at the clinic, but they were all there as individuals. All discrete molecules adrift. They no longer had their unit around them. They no longer had the pride of being fully functioning soldiers.

Even if they hadn't loved their time on deployment and their unit, even if they didn't look back on things with rosy glasses, their time in service still often took on a gravity that it might not have had before. Suddenly decisions and events from that deployment became memories incessantly plaguing their conscience. *What if . . . ?* was a nagging load to bear.

And *Why?*

Why me?

They were also going through it all alone at the clinic, torn asunder from their units and from their friends and even from their spouses—if they had spouses or partners. That was one of the things that tore Wendi apart, that spouses rarely came to the clinic to see things, to check in.

She could never tell if it was because the spouses didn't give a shit or if they didn't know it was something they knew they needed to do. Or maybe the soldiers never told their spouses to come in, maybe they gave them mixed signals. Wendi tried as best she could to get the spouses to come in. She sent pamphlets and packets home with injured soldiers. She sent brochures and notes and told them to share these things with a loved one.

Those spouses, they were in a similar situation as their husbands. They were suddenly dealing with a new normal themselves, something they hadn't signed up for.

Their strong husbands were now too scared to walk into a clinic by themselves. They had a hard time going to the store, balancing a checkbook, giving the kids a bath. A spouse might think to herself, *Why can't this lazy son of a bitch just help give the kids a bath?*

And the spouses got stuck doing all that stuff themselves, not unlike how they did during deployments. The spouses were so very alone, too. If the soldier didn't know what had happened to him—what was still happening to him—the wives often knew even less. They didn't know how excruciating it was for their husbands to try and walk straight down a hallway.

All they saw was a guy who used to be a paratrooper and who now seemed, well, much less than that. Any existing strains on a marriage were exacerbated. Communication faltered. Wendi heard all the time about wives accusing their husbands of cheating on them because they weren't around. But they weren't around because they didn't want to be around anybody! They didn't want to get laid or go to the strip club, they just wanted peace and quiet! They'd wonder aloud to Wendi, "Why can't my wife understand?"

Many of the wives were angry because they felt like they'd been sold a bill of goods by their husbands, by the Army, by life. Wives wouldn't understand, would call bullshit on their husbands when they got home. It's not like these men were perfect angels, though. It's not like these guys were paragons of clear communication. They'd mumble something and maybe holler in anger, explode in rage. How can a wife be blamed for giving a guy grief if he can't explain himself? How can you blame her for being mad at him?

Wendi would beg her patients to bring their wives in, just once, to see the clinic, to talk to a doctor or to a therapist so they could begin to understand things. Sometimes they would.

One time she remembers a spouse came in, and the woman said after that trip it all suddenly made sense to her. The scales fell from her eyes. That wife saw definitive, clinical proof that her husband couldn't do some simple tasks because—well, because he couldn't do them. That wife saw all these professionals helping her husband, coaching him through the simple, silly-looking exercises that could help him become a better person, a better husband.

She understood.

* * *

Wendi asked Allen what seemed like a million times to bring Danica into the clinic, to have her come by just once to see things, to understand things, to talk.

Wendi pleaded with Allen to bring her.

But Danica never came in. She never saw.

Wendi was never able to explain that Allen wasn't as strong as he tried to look. She never explained that he was trying to get better but that it would take time and understanding. She never got to explain that he had become a different person. She was never able to help Danica understand that it was OK for her to be frustrated with Allen, but to please understand.

Wendi was never able to tell her he wasn't Allen anymore. At least not *that* Allen.

* * *

Allen was discharged from the Army and fell into the whirlpool that other troops like him feel that they're in when they leave service. Their health care is guaranteed, but it's not a part of their daily job or a routine. Once they become civilians, they have to navigate the twin health care systems of the Department of Defense and the Department of Veterans Affairs. The integration is not seamless, and the two systems were, and remain, disconnected in many ways.

He no longer had the hated squad leaders, but he also no longer had the all-encompassing and warm embrace of the Army. Even though as a wounded warrior he was pulled away from being a paratrooper, at least he was still a soldier. The medical separation took that away from him. Now even the very uniform was gone. He was a civilian.

CHAPTER 22

THE CITY OF ROBOTS

Sergeant Alex Jauregui finished the 2009–2010 Bravo Company deployment and came back from the Arghandab without a scratch, at least no physical one. Back in the States he had fourteen months back home, plenty of time to get ready for another deployment.

A civilian might think a soldier just goes from one deployment to the next, hopscotching their way through a career. But deployments are followed up with preparing for the next deployment. For J that meant more than a year of going back through many of the same training evolutions he'd gone on in the past. The training is often the very same training. For a sergeant in the 82nd that meant the dreaded OP 13 evolution, that training exercise all paratroopers hated, had to happen all over again with a new group of soldiers.

In 2012 his battalion went back to Afghanistan, to the Zhari district in Kandahar this time.

It was only two months into the deployment, April 8, 2012—how could he forget the date when something like that happens?—when Sergeant J lost his legs.

Some of the platoon already found an IED, and his squad escorted the EOD techs out to the site. He set his guys in and went to take some photos and brief the EOD tech when one of his guys called him on the radio to say they'd found yet another one. So he went to take a look, and that's when he stepped on something.

Boom!

After all those convoys as a mechanic and that horrible deployment with Bravo to Arghandab, he knew full well from the moment of the explosion what it all meant. He knew the sound of an IED and the feeling of being on your feet when one goes off close by. He knew the physical feeling of standing near a bomb when it blows somebody else up.

This was a new feeling. And not a good one. J wasn't on his feet after this one, and his ears were ringing something horrible.

He knew it had happened to him as soon as it happened.

The first thing he remembered was his buddy dragging him. He was getting dragged through a grove of pomegranate trees. Why were there these damned pomegranate trees in his face on every deployment?

He didn't feel any pain at first.

He'd also seen so many IED blasts and so many injuries and so many medevacs that he knew, immediately knew, he was going to live.

For starters, he figured if he wasn't dead already, he was likely going to live because of the wonders of combat medicine. A tourniquet or two, a medevac chopper, and a guy like him would be in surgery within a half hour. It's one of the things the Army does really well, he knew because he'd seen it multiple times.

His next thought was, if he was alive and he was going to live, then the rest would be gravy in the sense that he wasn't dead. And for an optimist like J, not being dead was a pretty good deal.

His buddy, after dragging him off the X, started working on him and telling him over and over that he was going to be OK.

But that much was obvious to Sergeant J already.

"I know, motherfucker, just say how bad it is," he said to his buddy as he tried to sit up and take a look to see if there was a mess down there around his legs, but his buddy wouldn't let him sit up so he had no idea.

By now his hand was starting to hurt, so he took a look at it. Two fingertips missing. *That's going to suck,* he thought. By this time he could have really used some morphine, but there wasn't a medic on this patrol, so he would just have to wait for the medevac.

Thankfully a Special Forces team was in the area and swooped in with their helo to get him. Only took twenty minutes from the explosion to him getting to urgent surgical at Kandahar. Not bad at all.

That flight to Kandahar sure was foggy, though. On the helo, at first, J was able to say to the medic that he was doing all right. Then he couldn't talk anymore, could just give a thumbs-up. Then he couldn't respond at all. The medic had to give his leg a hard squeeze. Sure enough, that got a response out of him, got him to give a little yelp and show he was still with them.

J went from Kandahar to Bagram to Germany to Walter Reed. The whole trip and all the initial surgeries took five days. Five blurry days. When he arrived at Walter Reed, his family and some of his best friends were already there waiting for him.

The final tally: He'd lost one leg below the knee and another above the knee. But the family jewels were still there, unharmed. Everything was gravy.

Jauregui was oddly contented, even without legs. He wasn't thinking about the glory of it or what it might get him. He was thinking about what he had *already* gotten from the Army, from the United States. It wasn't so bad, he figured. Heck, at Walter Reed there were guys just like him walking around on their new prosthetics. It didn't take long for him to start surveying the various fake legs guys had on and deciding which kind he wanted to ask for. Like a Christmas wish list. As an immigrant from Mexico, he knew the US Army was going to take care of him. And the Army did.

It took J only thirty-eight days after getting blown up to start trying to walk around again. Carefully. Slowly. Goddamn painfully. But overall it took him two years to recover, much of it at Walter Reed in the amputee ward. He and the guys called it The City of Robots because everyone looked like a cyborg with their fake legs, walking around all haltingly and jerkily as they got used to the new reality.

A lot of guys he knew at Walter Reed were pissed off because they'd lost limbs. A lot of them were low-ranking enlisted guys who blamed their leadership for getting them into the mess they were in. Well, Staff Sergeant J wasn't low ranking. He was leadership, a noncommissioned officer, the type of guy who got some of these guys into these messes.

The type of guy who got Lemon and Caron into their messes. So how could he bitch?

He had seen these leg injuries before. He'd seen guys recover. He had it good—after all, he was still alive. Men like Joey Caron of Tacoma, Washington, were gone. Plenty of guys who stepped on IEDs didn't live. He accepted it right away, didn't want to blame anyone. Some days the US Army got the upper hand, some days the Taliban did. That's just life, man.

Walter Reed is an amazing place, with people coming in and out all the time. Politicians thanking them for their service. Doctors, nurses, therapists scheduling stuff for them all day long. There's an entire community of support right there.

It's what comes after Walter Reed that gets to a lot of guys. And J saw it coming and was determined not to let it get to him.

The simplest difference between Walter Reed and the real world is a damn fine metaphor for the whole business. When a guy learns to walk again at Walter Reed, it's in a physical therapy room with level floors and gentle slopes. It's the perfect conditions for recovery. It makes a man feel good about himself. But as soon as he steps out into the real world trying to walk around, there's gravel and curbs and shit. Potholes. Lots of stuff to trip you up. It can make a man feel pretty bad about himself.

CHAPTER 23

THE CUL-DE-SAC

That Saturday in late September 2013 started out great. It was like Danica had the old Allen back, the man she'd known before the Afghanistan deployment.

He was the man she'd known before he'd been injured by the suicide bomber, before those tedious months of recovery at Walter Reed. He was the man she'd fallen in love with, married, and had two daughters with. The man she'd been watching slip away.

Allen had pulled away from her and their family, taking refuge elsewhere or just escaping from the realities of his life by playing his guitar. The guitar was a constant for him, something that had been there since before the drastic changes in his life and which could always be relied on. In some ways Danica came to detest his guitar-playing, it meant that he'd checked out on her and the girls. The guitar, though, is an instrument that relies on muscle memory. Complex strumming patterns and difficult chords can be mastered through practice, sheer force of will, and can't be easily erased from memory. They can get imprinted in the mind in ways that overcome even neural pathway damage. The certainty of even a delicate task can thus be vouchsafed, can be certain. To be able to delicately master the instrument was a residual comfort to a man for whom few physical or mental certainties existed any longer.

One of the other things that relies on muscle memory and which is not easily erased is the effective and efficient use of a firearm.

Oh, that Saturday was wonderful. Earlier in the afternoon they'd gone to get pizza for lunch with Dave Abt, his old Army buddy.

At lunch the two friends reminisced about the Old Days, drinking and girls and country music concerts they'd snuck out to go see. The Allen that Danica loved so much was back, thank God.

She'd been so scared for the past few months as the changes seemed to accelerate. But what could she do? He wasn't threatening anyone, he wasn't violent. Or at least he hadn't been violent with anyone other than her. With her he'd shown signs, troubling signs, like threatening her. Signs that she never wanted to share with anyone else because they struck at the very heart of her hopes and of what she believed him to be fundamentally.

But there was the Glock.

She never told anyone, not even close friends, that he had threatened her recently. She kept that buried, because she had no idea what to do. She didn't know if that was Allen or if that was someone else, someone she didn't know. Just as those who have never been to combat can say with certainty what they think they'd do in an extraordinary situation, so, too, can those outside such a relationship.

His paranoia had deepened recently, with him saying stuff like they had to have bags ready to go in case they needed to get away from the city. His obsession with his handgun had also increased. He had to have it. Allen would pack the Glock just to walk out to the mailbox, ready for whatever might come, even though they lived on a sleepy cul-de-sac in suburban North Carolina.

Maybe he thought some bad guy might show up midday somewhere between the shrubs and the mailbox? He never really said. All he seemed to know was that he had to be prepared to protect his property and loved ones, and that gun was about the only dependable thing he had left, the ways and means of its proper and effective use burned into the recesses of his mind and body in places no suicide bomber could get to.

Allen's body wasn't the paragon of strength it had been in the Army. His lungs weren't worth much because they'd been nearly destroyed by shrapnel. His head wasn't worth much because of the migraines and traumatic brain injury.

So if he had to fight, who knows how well he could actually do it? He did know he could still shoot, and shoot well. But he wasn't living in Iraq or Afghanistan. He was living on a cul-de-sac.

Earlier that week he'd broken down and asked Danica to take him to the local VA hospital emergency room, where he begged the doctors for a psychiatric evaluation, telling them he wasn't right in the head, that he needed inpatient treatment. Danica had their new baby—their second daughter—with her, so she couldn't go in with him. If she'd just been in there with him, she's certain she could have been his advocate, forced the doctors to do something. She knows down in her bones everything would have been different had she been able to explain it all and get him admitted.

But she wasn't there with him.

The doctors didn't admit Allen. They said they had no beds available, and no immediate appointments, so they gave him a prescription and sent him home. A few pills and a promise he could come in for an appointment later, not to worry. It calmed him at the time, to have a doctor, a professional, tell him he could come in later. It seemed enough.

Three days after that emergency room visit, the kids were at her mom's and she and Allen spent Saturday with their longtime friend. Dave and Allen hung out, the two friends who went back years, who had met so early in Allen's time in the 82nd, who had absconded together to go to country music concerts and who had shared deployments and a house together back in the Bravo Company days. Then Dave headed home.

Evening fell and Allen was watching TV. Danica was in the other room reading on her Kindle. His parents called him and said he just had to tune in to this classic car show they were watching. Danica heard him flipping through the channels, trying to find it, then she heard him suddenly rack the slide on the Glock and burst out of the door.

She heard a round go off out in the driveway. Allen had shot a tire on her car.

She ran through the house, followed him outside just in time to see his shadow, cast by the garage light, disappear around the back of the house as he hit a full sprint, gun in hand.

Danica ran to chase him down, to find him. Whatever he was thinking, she was certain her voice could snap him out of this.

In her fog she remembers someone from the neighborhood coming out and asking her what that sound was. Then asking her if she'd called 9-1-1. The neighbor seemed so concerned and engaged, Danica remembered thinking the neighbor would help her, take the initiative and help find Allen. She went back in to call 9-1-1 and the neighbor just went back inside their house.

Danica was on the phone with the 9-1-1 operator when she heard more gunshots out there somewhere. So many shots. But she didn't for one moment think he'd shoot at someone. She was thinking of her Allen, sweet Allen, who would never do that. The only thought in her mind was police would be there soon and he would be arrested, sent to jail. She knew how things could end when an irritable veteran had the cops called on him. They might shoot him. She never thought about his race, of what it meant to call the cops to report a Black man, she said. She only thought about what it meant to call the cops on a man as large as Allen, a man armed and who'd already fired a shot.

She was on the phone and the dispatcher on the line told her to relax. But how could she? She hung up to go find him.

Her thoughts were here and there, jumping to so many places. Was that yelling? What was that? It still didn't occur to her that he could shoot at another person there on that cul-de-sac. Their wonderful Saturday had convinced her he was still, deep down, the man she knew before deployment.

She called Dave, he could help. She told him Allen had left the house. Had a gun. Was shooting.

She hung up, and then like she was in a dream she floated, drifted back outside—running, walking, moving, just trying to find him.

It was quiet now, oddly so. In the silence of that safe cul-de-sac, before the police came roaring up, her thoughts came together for a moment when she realized it wasn't the Allen she had once known who was out there with the gun.

It was a different Allen.

It was the Allen of the here and now.

Someone was there alongside her, told her he had shot at other people, that's all she remembers from this awful dream state. He had shot two of their neighbors, a husband and wife. They were dead. He'd shot their dog, too.

She'd later find out from neighbors that Allen had swept through their house like it was a compound in Afghanistan. He'd shot their dog in the yard first, then charged at the house, and when the neighbors had confronted him he killed the wife, exchanged gunfire with the husband. Allen killed them and came out yelling "Clear!" like he was on some raid in Iraq or Afghanistan.

Afghanistan had ruined Allen, the Taliban IEDs everywhere in the Arghandab Valley, half his Army company blown up and many with Purple Hearts, so many friends maimed, missing legs, his best friend exploded. *Pow!* Legs and intestines pureed by a bomb that had been buried in the dirt. Every step in that valley was torture. When a man knows for certain he's going to eventually be blown up, terror burrows deep into his head. And then Allen was blown up. A suicide bomber collapsed Allen's lungs and ruined his brain.

That deployment and his injuries might have done it, metamorphosed Allen. Or maybe it was trying to deal with the sudden loss of his identity as a paratrooper, trying to navigate the VA system seemingly by himself, not letting Danica really, truly help him. Life did it, it gave rise to this new creation, this Allen, the one Danica couldn't really know because he was always at a distance from her.

Back in her dreamy fog, Danica swept through the neighborhood looking for him. She wondered in that dream of hers, on that Saturday night in the cul-de-sac, if this Allen who could murder people was actually the true essence of Allen. She wondered if this had been someone hiding under a veneer for all these years. No, impossible. Impossible. This had to be someone who'd been created by the war, a monster of some kind. Had to be.

Or was he a monster? Was he still the wonderful Allen she once knew, but damaged by war to allow an anomaly like this to happen? Yet do so many anomalies make a new, unified truth?

On that Saturday night in the sudden quiet before the sheriffs arrived, Danica still had time, a minute, an eternity, to find Allen, to talk to him, to grasp hold of the very essence of him and bring him back to her. She had only a few moments now, so little time, but she could do it. After all, she knew there was no way that Allen, the man she knew and loved, the father of her children, could ever live with himself if he knew that he'd murdered two people. Killed their dog, too.

There was no way he could live with himself, with the aftermath of what he'd done.

She knew, just knew, the real and true Allen had to be thinking the same thing. The Allen she loved must have been wondering how he could live with himself after what he'd done.

Then, close by, a final report from the Glock.

Allen had killed himself.

CHAPTER 24

GOOD DAYS, BAD DAYS

Sergeant J was downright lucky after that IED and his months and months and months at Walter Reed, because, after all, anybody could see plain as day that his legs were gone. Which was great, in its own way.

So many guys take off the uniform and lose all sense of mission and purpose. They lose their identity as a soldier. But a young, fit guy, missing a couple legs, still gets to keep his identity as a soldier. Especially back when the wars were still fresh in people's minds and in the news, a double amputee had a new way of being he could just fold right into. Sergeant J was a bona fide wounded warrior. He had the visible wounds of war and found there was a huge support network right there for him. So on April 6, 2014, when he officially retired from the Army, he was as ready as he could be.

The visible wounds help an old soldier out, they're undeniable and can help a veteran get funding, grants, and all kinds of stuff to help them thrive post-Army. Visible wounds are pretty darn helpful for the people who give all that stuff to veterans, too. It's a simpatico relationship. These groups give assistance, funding, and support to guys like J, and then they get to use pictures of him in brochures. They get to have him hobble up onstage for events.

When they do that, put a photo of him in a brochure, they aren't really using a picture of Sergeant J, per se. They're using a picture of a picture-perfect double amputee.

Guys injured with TBI or PTSD, guys who have a back injury or a bad neck or who are just trying to find meaning in their day-to-day lives after service don't have any of that. They don't have the physical proof, they don't have prosthetics to parade around, to show what they gave. A photo of a regular-looking schmuck with TBI doesn't play so well on a charity's fundraising poster, that's just the God's honest truth about it.

So while it's horrible that he lost his legs, and that one amputation is below the knee and the other is above so he has to walk all crooked and it's messing up his hips and his back, at least he gets something out of it. He knows what it's like for other guys who don't have that community around them thanks to the physical proof of sacrifice.

Yes, of course, there are times he would like for the attention to get turned off, for people not to see his legs and then ask if he lost them in the Army or Marines in Iraq or Afghanistan or something. Happens all the time. But he knows if that attention ever gets turned off, he can't guarantee it will get turned back on again, and having it on is damn sure better than having it off. So whenever J gets frustrated by the attention he just has to think about the guys without it, think about what they don't have. They don't have the clear-cut definition of "disability" upon which everyone can agree. They don't have that readily quantifiable injury.

Sergeant J says he wouldn't trade his service for anything.

"There are obviously the downsides of it," he says in a way that you think should be tongue-in-cheek but it's not. He's so earnest and comfortable with himself that it's not like he says this and gestures with a wink to his legs. No, he says this in a very serious way. He says it because he wants everyone to know that even Sergeant J goes through some shit from time to time.

"Even though I think mentally I'm pretty good, there are times you wake up and you are having a bad day," he says.

A bad day.

He doesn't say he's mentally broken or regretful or despairing. No, he says sometimes he wakes up and is just having a bad day, the way a person who hasn't lost his legs in Afghanistan might say they are having a bad day because they didn't get enough sleep the night before. His wife and kids, though, they always bring him out of it. They are always there for him. He has to be there for them.

* * *

It was a few years after losing his legs that Sergeant J boosted his efforts to stay in touch with the guys from Bravo, started reaching out to guys. The horrible Allen Thomas event was just one part of it. Other guys couldn't extinguish the smoldering embers of the Arghandab and showed signs of strain. Could there be other Allen Thomases among them? He'd call friends, other guys, just to check on them, to make sure things weren't going south.

And he realized that though they were all on the same deployment back in '09, they all had different experiences. Even guys who were right next to him on patrol experienced that particular patrol differently than he did. There are no same experiences, even when it's the same experience.

Similarly, the aftermath of war is different for everyone. He's still trying as best he can to understand that and accept it. "It's so hard to think about other people instead of yourself," he says.

But J remembers that it's easy for him, he's got two missing legs he can point to that explain it all. Guys who came back without visible wounds, it's harder for them. They can't get a custom-made forklift given to them by a veteran charity group. They might not have a wife and kids whom they love, and who love them back just as much. He's learned that and he tries to remember it when he's working to help them out, but sometimes there's so many problems that need fixing at the same time he's got the beehives that need attending and kids that need raising and a damn broken carbon-fiber foot to deal with.

A fellow like Sergeant J feels like he has to do more, but with everything he's going through himself it's hard to find time to reach everyone who might need it. A fellow can only do so much and something has to slip through the cracks. Doesn't it?

* * *

Joey Caron had been blown up in Afghanistan at the same time as Jared Lemon. Nobody was sure if Caron's ghost was visiting his father from beyond the grave and giving him 101 signs. But Jared Lemon remained a man still very much alive. And very much alive without an arm.

After a few years of bumping along, contemplating suicide, and hating how everything seemed to have turned out, Lemon climbed that mountain with those Special Forces guys and realized it was time to get it together. The first step he thought was to go back to college and get a degree. But he had some serious concerns. Along with the lost arm had come accompanying traumatic brain injury from the blast. With his TBI-rattled brain, Lemon had no idea if he could do the hard work of school anymore, so he signed up for what was essentially remedial math at a local community college.

All through high school Lemon had been good at math—it was his subject. English didn't really click for him because it wasn't governed by rules and logic, there wasn't a direct path to the answer, but with math it was different.

A soldier often gets a combo deal when they get blown up. They lose a limb *and* they get traumatic brain injury. It's a twofer. So many of the guys from Bravo who had either been blown up themselves or who were close to bombs when they went off had some kind of shock to their heads. Lemon was no different.

But he aced those first courses and realized he still had it. So he took on more courses: Calculus 1. And Calculus 2. And Calculus 3. He took trig and nailed it. The calculating, thinking part of his brain hadn't been rattled to bits in the explosion—it still worked just fine, thank you very much.

Now he was in a feedback loop, but for the first time since he returned from the Arghandab one arm lighter, it was not a feedback loop of despair and depression. This was a positive feedback loop. The best. The hits just kept on coming for him. He did well, which pushed him to do more.

In the military he used to get positive feedback from physical exertion, from being a soldier. Now he found it, much to his surprise, through school. He thought about all the time he'd wasted not doing a damn thing, just feeling depressed. What a fucking waste! So he decided to make up for it and poured it all into his classes. If he did it right he knew he might be

GOOD DAYS, BAD DAYS   295

able to transfer from community college and enroll in a proper four-year college program.

He'd also found a place where his missing arm didn't interfere with physical activity in any way: scuba diving. He discovered that, when he was in the water, he didn't need an arm, just his legs. And the weightlessness under the water, the quiet, made him forget all about any woes up on dry land. There was an added bonus: Any pain or phantom feelings from his stump magically just went away when he was underwater.

Believe it or not, Lemon went scuba diving with a paraplegic veteran one time and under the water—only under the water, mind you—the paraplegic's legs moved ever so slightly. It was as if the water had magical powers.

He'd also met a girl along the way, she'd been a Marine, and she had decided she liked this one-armed guy pretty well. There *was* a girl who wanted to marry a guy with one arm. How about that!

* * *

After the Arghandab deployment, Lyle Pressley still didn't take his back issues seriously enough. He thought he could tough it out or the problems would just go away. Once he was out of country and back in the United States he was able to rest enough that he could keep the debilitating pain at bay even as he kept soldiering.

In 2011, Lyle deployed again to Diwaniya, Iraq, which was kid stuff compared to the Arghandab. He reenlisted in 2012 and got shuttled off to Italy, but his back problems persisted.

When a guy's badly injured, he might be able to hide it for a while—from himself, from the Army. He can mask the problem if he wants to, deny its pain to himself, avoid questions from his superiors. But at some point, a doctor somewhere is going to get wise to him and actually look into the problem, document it, and send him packing.

Finally in 2016 a doctor recognized what Lyle had long known and the Army medically retired him.

Pain does more than just hurt the body. It causes all sorts of other problems. It wrecks your mind, it wrecks your relationships, it wrecks your sense of self-worth. And without somebody to help you unpack everything that comes with that physical pain, all the emotional pain, well, that just causes more problems.

Even years after the Arghandab, Lyle still goes back there. Sometimes it's the pain, and sometimes there's nothing at all that makes it happen. He doesn't have flashbacks so much as a hole that he falls into. That's how he describes it, as a hole.

"I know I'm not as strong as I think I am," he confessed. "I know that I will have to deal with it one day, but I'm worried about that introspection. There will be a lot of work and pain to get past this stuff."

His wife, though, was that strong and he knew it. She had been there beside him through it all. She was the one there to pull him out of the hole, and he was so unbelievably grateful. But he wasn't able to say it to her, couldn't make it crystal clear how much he depended on her.

Years after the Arghandab, he and his wife were having trouble, and he knew he was the cause. He knew he wasn't talking to her enough, not working through things, not being a good communicator, and it tore him up inside. It tore her up, too, and threatened to tear apart the marriage.

He knew it was so hard on her, on the woman he loved so dearly. He knew on those days when his back hurt something horribly and he couldn't even pull doggone dishes from the dishwasher and put them on shelves that it was she who was really the ever-suffering saint in the relationship. But somewhere between the feelings of deep love and in expressing them, there was some kind of block, and that block might yet cause them irreparable harm.

* * *

Amid all this, Derek died.

Derek Hill of Galax, Virginia.

Hill had changed on his first deployment to Afghanistan, and then the trip to the Arghandab solidified it. The kid who couldn't stop smiling had become a man who didn't seem to want to.

When he came home after that deployment he was short-tempered, carried anger and guilt. His sister told him one time that he wasn't being very patient.

"I don't have patience," he replied. "My patience is gone."

Hill got out of the Army in 2010 and went back to Lowe's to work, just as he had before the Army, because his wife was pregnant with their second child.

"He said he was glad he didn't sign up for another four years," his sister recalls, "but he missed his buddies, his Army brothers."

Hill joined the Virginia state troopers two years later, looking for meaning, purpose, and brotherhood. But the stuff he saw as a trooper bothered him, especially things to do with kids being abused. Then social upheaval across the country started hitting home for him. He was scared to park his patrol car in front of his house, fearing threats to law enforcement. He quit in 2017 because of that strain.

His marriage had been rocky, and he and his wife had separated for a while before getting back together. The Army and the troopers didn't work out, so he became a military contractor and deployed to Iraq in December 2017. When he came home on a break in March he was served with divorce papers. He hadn't expected things to escalate like that, but they did.

He got back home from that deployment in August and went to stay with his sister for a bit, which was a surprising thing for him to do, she remembers. Hill went to a local VA clinic for his health care and had been talking to counselors there, but he didn't seem to be in such a bad place. He didn't talk to many of his old Army friends, and when he did talk to people, he often put on a public face like he was the happiest guy around, his sister remembers.

Then on September 11, 2018, after making some calls to an old Army buddy saying he was going to kill himself, Hill went to a local cemetery.

Hill called his ex-wife and told her to let the state troopers know where he was and to come get him. She did.

He waited until the cops got there and he shot himself.

A note on his phone said he'd waited for the police to show up so that his organs would still be OK to donate.

* * *

Derek died, and so Sergeant J got out the unit flag for the inevitable funeral/reunion.

Old, reliable Sergeant J had become the keeper of the unit flag, the guidon for the veterans of Bravo Company.

And many of the men from Bravo came to the funeral, got together to drink shots of Jameson Irish whiskey and tell old stories. At the end of it, someone said, "See you at the next funeral."

And that was enough for Sarah Verardo. She vowed that there wouldn't be another funeral, not like this.

Sarah Verardo's husband, Mike, had been on the Bravo Company deployment and almost made it to the end. In early April 2010, an IED blew up near him but he was able to soldier on. On April 24 another IED did its job better.

Mike lost a leg and had an arm torn nearly off. He lost so much blood that the medics wrote him off as about to die when he was in the field, but they gave him a battlefield blood transfusion and somehow he made it through. But in the years since the Bravo deployment, he'd slowly gotten worse, enduring more than a hundred procedures and surgeries, with his health declining steadily.

By 2018 and Derek Hill's suicide, Mike needed nearly constant care at home, and Sarah had over the years gotten used to the reality that she had become the caretaker of a wounded husband and mother of three daughters. She had also become an advocate for a range of veterans' issues and the CEO of the Independence Fund, a veteran-service organization with influence in the Trump administration. The fund was best known for giving disabled veterans who couldn't walk something called an Action Trackchair, a wheelchair-like machine that operates on treads rather than wheels to allow men confined to chairs to go off-road to hunt or roll along hiking trails.

The Independence Fund provided Trackchairs to veterans and also managed casework, helping veterans process disability claims and lobbying for changes at the Department of Veterans Affairs.

The Bravo Company deployment had defined Sarah's picture of military service in many ways, with injury and hardship setting the tone for a post-deployment life. In the years since Mike's injury, she used her force of personality to help a handful of Bravo Company veterans keep connected with each other and navigate the vicissitudes of the VA system.

Part of her efforts were to help Bravo Company veterans suffering from mental health issues get plugged into programs available through the VA or through other veteran service organizations.

But those programs treated each veteran as an individual floating through a system, floating through life, trying to find meaning and overcome whatever it was that they'd experienced on their deployments. VA mental health services typically focus on the individual in clinical care settings, such as therapy sessions with professionals and mood-stabilizing drugs. Alternative therapies include yoga sessions, acupuncture, and service animals. But even in group sessions, veterans don't usually get to connect with those they served beside in combat.

Derek Hill's death prompted a wholesale reevaluation of the Independence Fund's approach to helping wounded veterans. The Bravo Company veterans who had stayed in touch with each other were able to talk about their experiences in the Arghandab because they'd lived through it together.

No two persons' experiences are identical and yet, somehow, men who have been on a deployment such as the one Bravo had had congruent experiences. To know a bomb might be underfoot anytime is unfathomable to most people, but for those who have experienced it, it becomes a connection deeper than most anything else could be. The men of Bravo knew and trusted each other. They also had a kinship through service that had with it ineffable bonds.

Bravo Company's final tally from that deployment was three killed in action, a dozen who lost at least one limb, and an untallied number who received Purple Hearts, but nobody's sure of the exact number because the Army didn't keep records of it. The 82nd Airborne Division doesn't have a unit history for Bravo's deployment. The Army used to do a fantastic job in keeping unit histories. After wars they used to produce multivolume bound tomes as comprehensive official accounts. But even as budgets ballooned during the Iraq and Afghanistan Wars, funding for historians deflated. Units were left to their own devices to come up with official histories, and in many cases there wasn't anyone forcing the units to keep those accounts. There is, of course, no unit historian for a group of veterans, so there's no easy way to tally up the problems that Bravo

Company, Charlie Company, or the 2-508 accrued in the years after their service. In the decade since, two men—Allen Thomas and Derek Hill—killed themselves, more than a dozen had made attempts, and others had admitted they seriously considered it.

Suicides, drug problems, spouse problems—the rumors and hints crept around the network of veterans from Bravo already and seemed to be intensifying. One guy kept in touch with another who kept in touch with another, so word spread that men weren't coping well with what had happened in the Arghandab. Some of them had changed, become someone different because of that deployment. Some of them had just found a distilled version of themselves. The crucible might have burned away all but the very essence, and they didn't like what remained.

The men from 2-508, including Bravo, had their own issues related to the pressures of the Arghandab Valley. But they also reflected in many ways the realities facing a generation of veterans who served in Iraq and Afghanistan.

With no active draft since Vietnam, only volunteers served in the military. There were approximately nineteen million veterans in the country, or less than 10 percent of the adult population, according to the VA. Many of the veterans from World War II, Korea, and Vietnam were reaching the end of their lives and, demographically speaking, Gulf War, Iraq, and Afghanistan veterans had come to make up the bulk of the veteran community. Since 2001, suicide numbers among veterans had steadily risen and, in the span of twenty years, had gone up nearly 36 percent.

When Sarah Verardo heard Bravo veterans, at a funeral for one of their own, tell each other they'd meet again after the next suicide, she decided to put an end to that. She had the resources through the Independence Fund to try something new, and she had connections through the VA, Congress, and the White House she could call on to get federal government attention.

Despite lacking any direct connections to her, early on Sarah cold-called Dr. Keita Franklin, then the national director of suicide prevention at the VA, to come up with a way to deal with veterans differently than was common practice.

Dr. Franklin had recently come to the VA from the Department of Defense, where she directed the suicide prevention program. Before that she headed up behavioral health for the Marine Corps. While at DoD she had first seen that the VA could boost its role in helping suicidal veterans by intervening with veterans early and not treating them as free radicals, individuals floating around, seeking care. The VA acted like a big hospital system that treated individual patients. It needed to find a way to create a community to treat scarred veterans who needed their peers, not just admission to a hospital.

Sarah told Dr. Franklin she really didn't understand the fundamental reasons a person dies by suicide but that she had a notion that bringing everyone together would somehow be therapeutic, would do *something* that was very much needed, she remembers. Dr. Franklin told her that it was a fine idea but that such a thing needed a safety net of clinicians to support a group of vulnerable veterans, and since it didn't seem it would cost the VA much money to send staff to a reunion, she said she'd support it, including coming herself to the very first one, a pilot program of sorts. It seemed a perfect opportunity for Dr. Franklin, who felt the VA needed to embrace public-private partnerships like this when it made sense.

Dr. Franklin had seen firsthand the success that comes when troops who have shared combat experience are able to support each other. A few years before, she had helped the Marine Corps change its post-deployment protocols. Instead of sending Marines right to their next unit assignment, the Marines decided to test a system where troops back from combat stayed in their units for three months after they returned. That familiarity and support network dropped suicide rates among active-duty Marines.

She said you can see a snapshot of the strength of combat-forged bonds anytime two veterans who deployed together meet again even years down the road. She saw it in the Pentagon, where she'd worked, when two uniformed service members recognized each other in the hallway having not talked for years, maybe a decade or more. There in the hallowed halls of the Pentagon they laugh and hug like they've found a long-lost brother.

It was the exact stuff the VA needed to tap into, stuff Dr. Franklin had already been thinking about. And it seemed as if Sarah Verardo's idea might do just that.

Besides, Dr. Franklin remembers, at the time suicide numbers among veterans had been essentially stagnant, and the department was facing a clinician shortage and taking flak for its suicide hotline's staggering budget and questionable outcome. Hell, why not try something new?

The Independence Fund would sponsor the reunion to fortify Bravo Company to try and prevent another suicide. Since Sarah's husband, Mike, was part of Bravo Company, it would be the first group to go through the pilot version of the reunion program. They called it Operation Resiliency.

Unit reunions were nothing new. Throughout history and across the world, troops have long gathered to reminisce and mourn their dead. Bringing units back together as a sort of therapeutic process was also not a novel approach. But what Sarah and the Independence Fund sought to do was new.

The Independence Fund came up with a unit reunion that would explicitly focus on mental wellness, and it would pay for lodging, food, and the group events. The trip would be all-inclusive for participants, so even veterans down on their luck would be able to come. Money wouldn't stand in the way.

The group also arranged with the Department of the Army to have Bravo Company veterans who were still on active duty be given special leave in order to attend. And the Department of Veterans Affairs would send counselors and representatives to give classes, facilitate discussion, and make sure everyone who attended the reunion was signed up for VA health care and services.

The Department of Veterans Affairs wasn't solving these veterans' problems. The Department of Defense wasn't, either. When a veteran asks for help, he or she is often treated as an individual, even when sent to group therapy or inpatient treatment. Counselors and therapists have a one-on-one approach, and trust is a hard thing to build. In group therapy people might measure their experiences against the person next to them, trying to figure out who had seen more or was more deserving of trauma. Veterans needed true peer support.

The VA was interested this time in finding out if fellow veterans—soldiers who had been there—could fill in the gaps where the department couldn't. This is what programs like Alcoholics Anonymous are founded on—that one person with a drinking problem trying to help another person with a drinking problem, all supported by a group of people with drinking problems, well, that can help them all get and stay clean. That's how the treatment works. It's not counselors and medication and therapists, it's a bunch of fellow travelers who have all been there and who know that alone they can't find their way out of the darkness.

But together they might.

CHAPTER 25

OPERATION RESILIENCY

In the spring of 2019, ninety-eight Bravo Company veterans mustered in Charlotte, North Carolina, for the first Operation Resiliency reunion. They were all veterans of that Arghandab deployment and they represented a majority of those from the company who had been there.

The men who were still on active duty got special leave from their commands to attend. Still, there were those who couldn't make it because of work or family or whatever other of life's obstacles had been thrown in their way.

Some of them, like Jordan Flake, almost didn't come, sick with the knowledge of what meeting everyone again might mean. Flake did come, though. It was almost hard to believe that such a tall, handsome guy with a bodybuilder's physique could be so scared of facing the past head-on. He was at what he says was the lowest point of his life just then. He was just getting over a horrible relationship and had no real direction. He was totally broke and didn't want to show up to a reunion and not even be able to buy somebody a beer. His sister convinced him to go, that it might do him some good, and his dad slipped him a hundred-dollar bill to have some folding money on him, and so he went ahead.

Even Adam Armstrong, an active-duty major at the time, getting ready to become a battalion commander and lieutenant colonel himself, had some trepidation about meeting men whose fates he had been in such a large way responsible for shaping. Same with Mac.

Jared Lemon came to the reunion from California, where he'd been laboring away with school, trying to prove to himself that he could still do it. Sergeant J was there—how could the keeper of the unit flag not come to a reunion like this? Lyle was there, not making a big to-do about it, all quiet and stoic as usual, but this time with a beard to complement his lumberjack physique.

A picture of Allen Thomas in uniform, back before the cul-de-sac, before Walter Reed, before the suicide bomber, was among photos of the deployment on a poster that was put up outside a conference room they were to use all weekend.

Mike Verardo was there, walking on a prosthetic leg and with his left arm hardly working.

Their old first sergeant, Donald McAlister, stood in front of the men of Bravo Company bleary-eyed and with stubble on his cheeks, still reeling a bit from an extended trip to the bar the night before. Mac was now a retired sergeant major, having remained in the service for a few years after the Arghandab deployment. He had kept pressing on with his career but still said the most taxing and horrible time he ever had was in the Arghandab Valley.

One morning, soon after sunrise, Musil was in formation, in what would pass for Army PT gear, seeing as he was still on active duty. No amount of drink the night before could break him of his ability to fall in and be ready for push-ups or a few miles of running if need be. Matt Hill, a senior NCO now, having continued to rise through the ranks, was exerting his calm influence over things.

The reunion had begun the day before, as men arrived in Charlotte and got together for opening-night pleasantries. Then they headed out to the bar for a few cocktails. That night was a plain old unit reunion, with all the superficial reminiscences of war and of old friendships. And drinks. Lots of drinks.

Next morning, Mac, this former stickler for regulations who had reamed out Jason Johnston for not shaving despite a doctor's note, now stood before the men with a goatee that hung down to his chest and a Mohawk haircut complementing his tattoo-covered arms. He was dressed in a skull T-shirt that bore the motto "Rogue Warrior"—it hugged his barrel chest, but also strained a bit at a stomach that was no longer a washboard.

In front of Mac was a motley mix of mostly civilians. Some men were in shape, some were overweight. Some had sound bodies and some were standing on prosthetics. It was the remaining members of Bravo Company, the men who had all been together in the Arghandab, but it was them ten years later.

A decade had gone by since Mac the now-retired soldier had called this group to attention after their return from that Arghandab deployment.

The last time, they were in formation at Fort Bragg, all still in uniform, still active duty, and had just finished what many remember as one of the worst years of their lives.

It's not quite right to say that all of Bravo had been at that Fort Bragg formation in 2010. Three of them had not made it home alive, and some were still up at Walter Reed recovering from the deployment at the time. So some were in gowns, or in civilian clothes, maybe lying in a bed hundreds of miles from that formation.

The men of Bravo who were there remember that they saw the seeds of PTSD, of combat trauma, at that formation. Some asshole at the 82nd Division headquarters uncorked a ceremonial cannon over at the HQ building, fired a blank artillery round for some formation they were having. When that huge blank round boomed, it took Mac and Bravo Company by surprise, and a bunch of the Bravo guys flinched, some even hit the deck.

A sergeant bellowed out from somewhere in the formation, "PTSD much?" and they laughed nervously. But that should have been sign enough that something had been jarred loose during the deployment.

The ten-year cushion since that last muster and this one in a conference room had provided what seemed like the perfect remove from that singular experience to allow it to be opened up, unpacked, and dissected. This group of paratroopers, many turning gray and thickening in the middle, were no longer fresh-faced young men just back from war. That newly applied veneer of service and sacrifice had worn off.

A decade later, there wasn't the glossy, patriotic gleam that many troops put on a deployment when they get back or the gut-level hatred and anger that other troops immediately apply toward what just happened in-country. For many of these men, the Army was their first experience out of high school. It was the first job they'd ever had, the first commitment to anything bigger than themselves. That deployment had also confronted them with the first serious moral ambiguity that had ever come their way, whether they knew it at the time or not.

Just as these paratroopers weren't gleaming-new vets, neither were they grizzled old men nostalgically reminiscing at the end of life. No, these were men who, like Philip Caputo has said, had passed straight through youth into a premature middle age because of the war.

And now here they were in actual middle age, or approaching it, and in those days since the Arghandab they'd gained families and now had life responsibilities, the dampening of youthful certainty, and the piling on of adulthood. They were in the literal middle of their lives, dealing with the hard work of adult life after they'd already seen and done so much, while still having decades yet to go.

Some things never change, and just as in the old days, it was damn hard to muster every last man this morning in a hotel conference room in downtown Charlotte. Since they were civilians now there were a few they'd been unable to rouse and bring down for formation. Shit, back in the day if someone had showed up late for formation they would have been smoked with push-ups.

One guy back then had the audacity to show up right on time to his first formation, at the exact time Mac had appointed, and as any grunt knows, if you show up on time, you're late. So everybody got smoked, instead of the offender, who had to stand by and watch, dreading his later fate.

But now, a decade on, they could only shrug if someone wasn't on time. They just hoped the missing soldier was in his room sleeping it off and not in jail.

Most of the paratroopers had made it down to the conference room formation, though, even the ones missing legs who came down on prosthetics, but the saddest case of all was a man in perfect physical shape—but who stood barefoot, having lost his shoes sometime between the booze-soaked night before and this morning.

Yet on that April morning in Charlotte as they stood in formation around Mac, the reunion was already working its magic on the men. Some who had refused to talk to each other before this, holding years-long grudges tied to that deployment, tentatively reconnected. Guys who had hated Mac and Armstrong for what had happened on that deployment finally confronted them head-on, and the men found they were ready for the rawness and anger to be gone. Or if they weren't ready for it to be gone, they were ready at least to understand it.

Now that most of them were out of uniform, they felt free to talk honestly to those who once outranked them. They felt free to ask what the hell happened on that deployment in the Arghandab, what did it all mean?

They were freed when they found out that others were hurting and needed help, giving the group permission to admit they were hurting and needed help, too.

And so they unearthed as much of the pain, memory, and confusion about those days as they could.

* * *

Mac's involvement made a huge difference. And he was changing, too.

When Mac was in uniform he never stopped to think about his own pain and trauma, or how it affected the men under his command. He'd first started thinking about it when he came home from the Arghandab on that deployment and visited Walter Reed. There he saw the men from Bravo all convalescing. Hurt.

Mac wasn't scared of anything back then, but he freely admits he was scared of going to see those men in the hospital. He was afraid to face those guys because he was the first sergeant, he was like their dad, and he was supposed to keep them safe. And yet here they were, no legs, no arms, brains that had rattled around like pinballs.

He started thinking to himself on that Walter Reed visit, *twenty years and I'm outta here*. Get to that retirement age and then that's it. He'd done his time in war and now he'd done his time in Walter Reed, visiting all the guys he'd been responsible for. But he still hadn't faced head-on, deep within himself, all the things he'd seen and done.

Then, Mac remembers, one day in—years after all that—when he was getting ready to retire from the Army, going through the paperwork and getting ready for the transition, he went to see a shrink. And an hour into the session that wasn't supposed to be much more than a check-in box on a form, he started bawling. The stress of retirement, the guilt of all those men he had been in charge of getting injured. All of it was too much for him after all these years and he broke down crying. Donald McAlister broke down crying.

Since his retirement, Mac had been working through all the stuff that he'd bottled up for years. He's struck out on a few professional endeavors, a few career changes. He was involved with a clothing company that sold T-shirts with Viking skulls on them and other stuff along the same lines, but that business went under. He also made a go at a burgeoning acting career, trying to break into that industry. And he'd gotten a podcast underway called *Mac's Man Cave*, where he worked through trauma in conversation with other veterans.

During that morning formation at Operation Resiliency, Mac led the men of Bravo Company through their paces with some rudimentary physical training. Guys like Rob Musil, still on active duty, wore Army PT gear and blasted through the push-ups and sit-ups and whatever else came at them. Other men did their best to keep up, and a few just settled back on their haunches to watch the proceedings. Soon enough, Mac cut them loose for a smoke break and to get ready for the day's events.

That day, and that weekend, was filled with activities designed to not let the men have any downtime. Everything was structured and had a purpose.

Sessions at the hotel conference room, with the men sitting around nondescript banquet tables, began with them talking to each other, but then expanded to conversations moderated by mental health professionals brought in from outside organizations and the VA itself. By ensuring events were moderated, the men wouldn't just be able just to tell dick jokes and recount old memories. No, the Operation Resiliency plan was to encourage the men. They'd be forced into a structured environment where they might tell a joke, but then a professional would force them to unpack what was behind that joke. They'd be forced to talk to each other about that deeper meaning. That structured, formal interaction was something that was nearly always missing from a standard-issue reunion.

When the men weren't in sessions at the hotel, they were at planned physical activities. One outing—whitewater rafting at the US National Whitewater Center just outside of Charlotte—was a combination of team building and physical activity. The men took chartered buses to the center, a massive resort area that has the feel of a western lodge. Among ropes courses and climbing walls, the center has an artificial whitewater course, a looping concrete river where kayaks or, in this case, inflatable rafts filled with a half dozen people can shoot the rapids just outside of a metropolitan area.

During the pre-rafting safety brief, the staff joked around with the amputees. They told Sergeant J to make sure he secured his legs because he didn't want to lose them in the bottom of the fake river. He'd have to wait for them to dam the thing up to get a leg back. They tinkered with Lemon's paddle to find the best fit for a guy stroking with one arm, the oar under his armpit for stability.

As in boot camp, it didn't take long for each boat team, randomly assigned, to laugh and talk and joke—just like the old days.

While the men shot the rapids and went under a rustic bridge in the middle of the course, Lyle Pressley stood mid-span watching everyone else having fun. Lyle's back wouldn't let him do something like that, and so, instead of reconnecting and laughing it up, he looked disconsolate as he observed it all.

Lyle's back and legs had been a constant struggle for him since the deployment, and this all reminded him of what he once was and the things that made him what he then had become. He still had hope that the VA would give him the surgery he needed, the last one he could really try—an implant and spinal fusion procedure known as the Tiger Woods surgery, after the famous golfer who'd had it. But at Operation Resiliency, Lyle just watched from the bridge. He'd have to find another way to reconnect with his fellow veterans.

That night there were more meetings, dinner, and then drinks so they could do it all again the next day. The Independence Fund ended up taking heat from some clinicians for allowing, even condoning, drinking during the reunion. But, goddamn, it's a bunch of paratroopers getting together. Sure, booze has been a persistent problem for many of them, along with other dependencies and depression, but if a bunch of combat-hardened soldiers can't have a good old-fashioned booze-up when they all get together, then what's this country coming to, anyway?

The booze the second night took its toll again and made muster the next morning a bleary-eyed endeavor. But the men of Bravo Company had more meetings and made more connections. Perhaps most importantly, they shared their congruent experiences. No matter what other services the VA offered, no matter what inpatient programs might be offered, nothing is the same as talking to people who know exactly, precisely what you've gone through.

At the end of Operation Resiliency, everyone from Bravo Company was signed up for VA services and they were all on a call roster, the exact same thing they had all been on during active duty, where every man could find everyone else's phone number in a moment and it was easy enough to check in on each other regularly.

That reconnection gave some of the men a renewed sense of purpose, or at least it gave them a new feeling of indebtedness to each other. It gave them a new reason to stay around, to work through problems, because they needed to carry on the legacy of that deployment, had to make it mean something and had to not let each other down.

Adam Armstrong was still in the Army, had still been rising through the ranks and still deploying. By the time Operation Resiliency came around he was close to picking up lieutenant colonel, the rank Frank Jenio had when they all deployed to the Arghandab. Armstrong was waiting, hoping, that he would get battalion command and could take all the lessons he'd learned as a lifer and apply them to that command. That would make Bravo's struggles worth something, at least.

Recently he had been doing work to reconnect to the men from that Arghandab deployment, craving something himself, the need to ensure that he did everything he might be able to do to help those men who had fought under his command. But Operation Resiliency made him realize that even once men leave the Army, they still crave some sort of semblance of the discipline and accountability they had while in uniform. Armstrong was convinced that part of the reason men opened up so freely during the sessions was because senior leadership like him and Mac had bought into the program. Other senior enlisted were there, too, so there was a structure by which things operated. Even the men who had been of the lowest ranks on the deployment could see that their leaders were still trying to reach out to them a decade on.

Armstrong had recognized the debt incurred by an officer to his men, but now he recognized the near infinite weight of that debt. He pledged to do his best to work through the Bravo Company call roster, going down the list to call every person when he had time, just to check in on them and talk. Man, but to go down that list takes time. If he called one guy a week, maybe a couple guys, it would take months to get through them all!

But Armstrong pledged to himself he would do just that, work his way down the roster of men who deployed to the Arghandab and check on them. He also pledged to come back for future reunions.

Just to have somebody like that, an active-duty lieutenant colonel, remain so invested in them was worth a fortune to the men. Heck, Armstrong would soon be told that he'd be taking over his own battalion in the Tenth Mountain Division.

Command is a nonstop endeavor, an all-consuming affair, especially as a battalion commander in charge of a thousand people, responsible for multiple companies and all the planning, training, discipline, and headaches that come along with that. But as a major, Armstrong had been an echelon below all that, serving on staffs where he wasn't the head honcho. A guy like Armstrong still worked ungodly hours, devoted to his job, whatever it might be. But battalion command, that would be a whole other level of intensity.

Operation Resiliency had to end, and by the end of the weekend, the men had organized themselves enough to ensure that they could stay connected. Everyone's name was now on that call roster, easy to find and make connections. Some of them had organized ways to get information passed around more efficiently, a call tree of sorts. They'd all filled out a post-conference questionnaire and been given an insulated silver cup with the 2-508 logo on the side as a parting gift.

Like the end of summer camp, there were hugs and promises to always remain connected and to never allow such separations or distance to affect them, ever. On that last day, cabs and cars picked up men one at a time, or in small groups, to ferry them to the airport. But like the end of summer camp, the end of the reunion meant a return to reality. It's all too easy to pledge a new approach to life in the middle of a safe, all-expenses-paid trip. But Lyle had to go back to his aching back. Lemon had to go back to his problems at home. They had to go back.

The experiment had ended. Now Sarah and Dr. Franklin and everyone else had to see if the hypothesis would hold. Could this stanch the bleeding?

CHAPTER 26

CAREFRONTATION

After the resiliency reunion in Charlotte, Jared Lemon was doing pretty well for himself, blasting through his classes and getting fantastic grades. That woman, the Marine, who chose to marry a one-armed dude, well, she was a reason Lemon wanted to succeed and stick around this world. He had his kids from the previous marriage, and his new wife had kids from her marriage. But they wanted children together. The newest member of their crew arrived early in the COVID-19 pandemic, in May 2020, when his wife gave birth to a baby boy.

They named the son after a guy Lemon once knew in combat. He named the boy Joey, after Joseph Caron of Tacoma, Washington.

Lemon was doing great in school, but he was living on just a monthly living stipend from the government. He wanted things to be nice for his family, and while having money doesn't make things good all by itself, it damn sure helps to have a good paycheck as a foundation. All of Lemon's boys and his wife weren't going to feed themselves. He grew up in a household with all brothers and it seemed like the pantry was emptied by those adolescent vultures the day after his parents went to the supermarket.

At the end of summer in 2020, Lemon got the word: He was accepted to the University of California, Riverside. He'd be able to transfer his credits, take about two years of classes, and graduate with a no-shit degree. He could find a great job, get a great paycheck.

Out there in California where he was living, he also got an aboveground pool—some company was selling them at a discount, so he bought one. If he can't go scuba diving, the least he could do was float around in his backyard. Lemon says he was like the Cousin Eddie of the neighborhood, the guy from *National Lampoon's Christmas Vacation*. He floated around back there and it eased his mind. It was no ocean, and it wasn't scuba diving that was for sure, but at least was something.

Still . . .

The family life and school going well still didn't make him whole. First of all, he was missing an arm, so there's that. But there's something else that comes with the loss of the arm, with the death of a friend right there in front of his eyes. Something with the loss of folks around him, all the post-war suicides of soldiers he's known. It made Lemon feel like death follows him. He felt like he could do more about it, always felt that way no matter what he did. It was a constant weight on him, the feeling he could do more to stave off the specter of death.

Bravo Company has been a force of stability for him, and there had been no suicides after Operation Resiliency, but there were other friends from the military or even from Bravo who occasionally posted something on their pages to show they weren't doing so great. The reminder of war was always there in other ways, too, even in the goddamn rash on his shin that he couldn't get rid of no matter what ointments or creams or unguents he tried. The docs thought it might be from exposure to smoke from a burn pit, but there's no way to prove that. It wasn't bad enough the war took away his arm, it also had to give him a fucking rash?

And those feelings constantly bore down on him, that he should do more to fend off that specter of suicide. His closest friend from Walter Reed, Brian, died by suicide in April 2020, just as COVID was shutting down the entire world.

When they could get off campus at Walter Reed for a little while, those long years ago, they used to drag race each other, Brian in his Hummer and Lemon in his Camaro. Lemon would always beat him. But just before he died, Brian got himself a new souped-up pickup truck and said he was just waiting for Lemon to come visit so they could go racing again.

But that didn't happen. Lemon didn't visit his friend. Brian died and Lemon was disappointed that he didn't do more to stay connected. If he could have just made a few more phone calls, it might have made a difference. A few more calls, one visit, then that might have held death at bay.

That got him to thinking: Why didn't he make calls to other buddies from the Army who might be hurting? Lemon knew plenty of them who were showing their hurt, wearing it publicly and who said, clear as day, they needed someone to talk to. As if that weren't enough, he also knew there were other Brians out there, buying new trucks and talking smack with smiles on their faces but then, in private, sinking into an abyss.

Yes, sure, Lemon had his own stuff to deal with. He had a family and school and going to the VA and a therapist, but he was still convinced he could just pick up the phone and give guys a call. Maybe just twenty minutes on the phone to someone he hadn't spoken with for a while.

Maybe just ten minutes?

Lemon tried to call his buddies out of the blue, guys who maybe he hadn't talked to some time, to make sure they knew he wasn't calling for any reason in particular, just to let them know he was their friend. That's the kind of call he wanted to get himself but never did. He desperately wanted to get a call like that, and since he knew how much he wanted a call like that, he tried to call other people because they must have that same desire deep down, too.

But, man, if he called everyone he knew he should check in on, if he called a person a day, he'd not be able to get through his Rolodex in a year. And if he couldn't get through to everyone, then the one person he actually needed to call would probably slip through the cracks. The next Brian is the guy he didn't get around to calling, that's the way it would be. It was daunting to think about all the calls he needed to make, that cumulative effort that's needed to really check in on everyone. But he could still do it, twenty minutes a day to keep death at bay.

Twenty minutes.

Maybe ten.

By the time he realized he needed to make time for others, those minutes were harder to come by because he finally had so much else going on. School took up time. He was a real student at a four-year school, which meant it was a no-kidding full-time job. That's the way school's supposed to be. His kids, his wife, his family, they took up time, too. It's a big job to have a well-functioning family. But that's the way family is supposed to be.

Yet sometimes the family seems to not function. He and the wife get into arguments with each other, normal stuff. But she's a Marine and he's him, so things can escalate quickly.

In the middle of all this he had to try and leave time to take care of himself, to have some kind of therapy. Some of that came from a therapist, an actual shrink he went to regularly or, during COVID times, just saw on Zoom, the video teleconference program that became ubiquitous during the pandemic. But finding a decent therapist also seems like a full-time job sometimes. He never could just jump headlong into a confidential relationship with a therapist on the first appointment. He had to get to know the person, figure out their quirks and how to talk to them, how to tell them things. A therapist is a person, too, not some widget. Though it sometimes felt like the VA figured any therapist can do the trick: plug and play.

By late 2020, Lemon had been seeing a new therapist for about two months and wasn't sure if he liked the guy. Lemon moved all around since getting out of the Army, so he had a few different therapists and each time he had to start a relationship over again. It went like this: He'd move someplace and start to feel really shitty, so he'd call the VA to get a therapist. Some scheduler would call him back and start asking whether he wanted to come to the VA hospital for sessions or to find someone near where he lived.

They'd take down his preferences for a therapist, a basic one, for example, did he want a male or a female clinician? Some case worker would jot down his order like he was at the deli ordering a sandwich. Then the VA would go off and find someone near him who treated veterans and ticked off the boxes he was looking for and call him back to say, "Hey, here's what we've got, sound good?" And then a couple weeks after he'd made that first call, he'd have a new therapist with all the trimmings. The only problem with all this mixing and matching and moving to new towns and ordering up doctors with all the attributes he was looking for was how was he ever going to be truly satisfied. When you're at the deli you regret not getting horseradish rather than mustard or you realize you want rye instead of whole wheat, and sometimes you forget that, despite regrets, it's still a fine sandwich.

And Lemon never had a therapist he was really happy to go see.

* * *

In early 2021, Lemon was so busy with school and family that he hadn't gone to see the therapist in months. Sure, he hated the therapist, hated most of the ones that he's had, but he talked all the time about not being able to go see them.

Kids and school, and the realities of living through a pandemic, prevented Lemon from going to a therapist. He and his wife ended up taking it out on each other, he said.

She was a Marine. It's one of those things that brought them together, and one of those things that allowed her to be attracted to a one-armed slot-machine former soldier. But that means she was in the service, too. So much to wade through for both of them.

And when they fought, it was bad. They knew each other's cracks, their broken places. It's one of the byproducts of loving each other. And they went for those cracks.

There was so much stress in the marriage. She had two preteen sons from another marriage. Lemon had kids from his first marriage. And then they had the baby who's all theirs. That's a lot of kids, and a lot of overlapping concerns about parenting styles and who gets to tell which kids how to do what.

And when they started arguing, it was like an explosion was inevitable. He'd see it coming but felt like he couldn't do anything about it. It was almost like he was watching it from the outside, a spectator to the unstoppable.

That was what he felt sometimes thinking about the past, snapping back into it so quickly and seamlessly, as if transported there by an alien force, for there is no way such a rip in time could happen by his own accord. There must be some force outside himself that made it happen, because it was so immediate and total.

He couldn't stop it, he just watched the whole thing. But Lemon wanted his agency back. He didn't want the timeline for all eternity to be imprinted and unchangeable. So he was working to find a way to say no, this fight isn't inevitable, and what he was about to say to his wife wasn't foreordained.

Yet, it was like he was watching from the outside, from above himself, like an out-of-body experience all over again. Was this a different kind of out-of-body episode? But he knew—just knew—that it wasn't predetermined, not mapped out, and it was not something he just had to watch. With mastery over his demons he should have been able to master these moments and prove they could be changed. That's one of the reasons he asked for techniques, for help in halting the odd sensation of observing his own life.

It was the men of Bravo Company whom Jared Lemon turned to for help, not as much to the so-so therapist or anyone else. Instead, a group of five others, all men of Bravo, all who had been with him there—they were his new support team.

He found his way to talk to a small group of Bravo Company friends. They served as ersatz therapists for each other thanks to a scheme cooked up by fellow Bravo Company veterans Dave Huff and William Yeske in the wake of Operation Resiliency. Preventing suicide, curing loneliness, working to better oneself—there are all sorts of reasons he started these meetings meant to intervene in one another's lives with care. Dave said it was for betterment of the person. It was for realization of goals and self-improvement or any other way of using CEO self-help lingo that might describe what they were doing.

Dave found success since leaving the Army. He married a strong-willed spouse who matched him one-for-one with cocktails, cuss words, and ambition, and one-ups him when it comes to smoking cigarettes. He began a contracting company, wrote bid proposals for a living, and made a nice life for himself. So sure, he was going to say it's about self-help rather than self-preservation.

Dave admitted, though, that there's some self-preservation in the midst of it all.

Back around the time when COVID-19 hit the United States full force in mid-2020, Dave started thinking about a way to bring people together.

He was concerned about the already pervasive loneliness and separation guys felt and how that would only intensify in a pandemic-provoked quarantine. He arrived at his idea in the wake of Operation Resiliency, after he was shown what can be accomplished by bringing everyone together to form an organic support network.

Then there was another suicide, not from Bravo but from Charlie Company, a guy whom a lot of men from Bravo knew. The guy was active-duty Special Forces, he should have been the last person to die by suicide. Dave knew that guy had a lot more support than many of the guys in Bravo, so he realized he ought to do something.

So many of the guys have connected through social media. The best thing Facebook brings is the ease of keeping tabs on people and giving you a quick ability to see if a guy is falling apart. Facebook posts can be the same as running a gigantic red flag up a pole for all to see. But beyond providing an SOS, the connections Facebook offers are often superficial. Maybe a comment on a post here and there, but no in-depth discussions. Dave wanted to break them out of Facebook, to create an active support network that allowed for real conversation and regular, preventative contact.

It wasn't the same as Operation Resiliency, where the entire group got together, but it grew out of that event, as has so much of Bravo's recent efforts. After Operation Resiliency they had a call list, they had a new Facebook group, they had a way to check on one another, and they had that tangible knowledge of what it felt like to have that in-person, one-on-one connection. They knew what it felt like to have accountability. They had begun what the clinicians call "longitudinal peer support."

So Dave pulled together some ideas from a business support group he'd taken part in. Modeling his new group on that group's structure and inspirational messaging, Dave cobbled together a Bravo Company–focused small-group support system.

The idea was to get about a dozen guys together on a regular basis over Zoom. Over a three-hour meeting everyone checked in, gave an update on how they were doing, and presented some issue they were facing. The others asked the guy questions, and the person who organized the meeting kept things moving and on track so it didn't devolve into telling war stories and making dick jokes. Without an authority figure, all Army gatherings devolve into the telling of dick jokes. The point of the thing wasn't to give people advice; no, it was to probe deeper and to ask questions that matter.

Besides, nobody there was a goddamn licensed therapist, and they had their own fuck-ups and problems, so maybe their advice on how to actually fix things wouldn't be the greatest. But they could ask questions. And they could focus on the person talking, really focus on him. That small group of friends really cared and really listened, and they were all there on Zoom, as together as possible. They could be honest without worrying about getting a lecture. It was a simulacrum of family.

If a guy brought some dark shit, if he was in a place that was real bad, the moderator could jump in to say, Brother, maybe you need to get some professional help. And then, in the days following, they could all check on the guy with texts and phone calls to make sure he'd done something about it.

Sometimes they could just be honest and say, Man you need to get off your ass and go for a walk, go for a run, get out of that bedroom you're sitting in all day long. Man, just do something, anything, to not be lonely and moping around the house.

Some of the guys would even tell Dave, the moderator, Man you look like shit, you been hitting the bottle or something?

It's "carefrontational," Dave said with a laugh.

Dave, the consummate CEO type, saw this thing as a franchise operation. It's not to make a ton of money or anything but to have growth while balancing quality control and whatnot. You know the spiel if you've read a Form 10-K filing and annual investor report.

The key to making it work was in keeping the group relatively small. It had to be a squad and not a platoon. And it had to have good moderators. It's those moderators who keep the trains running on time. And since it was his model, he wanted to make sure he was grooming moderators properly. Proper moderators. That's key. He wanted to train the trainer, just like they did in the Army, but he wasn't dopey enough to think everyone could do it well. He was back on a training mission.

First of all, prior rank in the service doesn't matter for shit when it comes to moderating well. The Army doesn't exactly pick the best managers to begin with, despite claims to the contrary. Everyone knows the dipshit officer they had once upon a time whom they wouldn't trust to shovel snow properly in the civilian world. And once that type of jerk is back in civilian garb, all bets are off. Sure, some guys always retain respect and leadership gravitas, but some of those supposed leaders are just duds.

For the guys in the group, some of them would rather frag their former officers than give them the time of day. If it had been a decade since they've had to take orders or feign respect, well, then fuck off. And some of those lowly enlisted guys who were always shat upon really hit their stride once out of the Army, like that guy from high school who was a late bloomer.

The moderators had to have the respect of the group, you can't fake that, and you can't force that. The sessions had to have a whiff of formality to them, some structure. The moderator had to know when to cut someone off and when to let things flow organically. It was an art as much as a science.

Dave figured out the import of these types of meetings, but he hadn't broken out the philosophy and psychology books to explain how it all works.

Maybe that's some of the power here: that it's not some VA shrink steeped in degrees and case studies, it's guys who cared about each other making it work, building the plane as they flew it, as Dave said.

* * *

It's on one of Dave Huff's support group sessions where Jared Lemon admitted he felt stuck in a predestined timeline when fighting with his wife, a true testament to how free the men feel to talk. For Lemon, it was only in a situation like this, where he could trust that people are really listening and care, that he said the things he wouldn't to some crappy therapist. The other members listened. They asked some questions. And they suggested a simple solution: Take a beat.

It's on a Zoom call that Lemon pledged to take a few moments, a split second, to process what he was about to say during that next fight. He said he would take that moment to think through what he was about to say to her and to change the very fabric of time, disrupt the inevitable certainty of its progression.

If he could change the trajectory of one fight with his wife, if he could change one moment in time, standing there in his kitchen, if he could prove the master of the moment then, by God, he could prove that he had the power to shape the destiny of the universe. Because if Lemon could show himself that the course of the next fight isn't inevitable, that it can be changed by merely taking a split second to think through the next word that he speaks, well, then what else could be changed?

Maybe not much.

Just months after that session, Lemon and his wife were getting ready to file for divorce. It was all over.

For a spell there, Lemon had gotten COVID-19 and was living without his wife, taking care of his kids, and wondering how in the hell was he going to be able to keep going to school and his family going. How could he keep himself going? It seemed out of control and crazy. But that had been his pace for years now, speeding along at a breakneck tempo through life, never knowing if he'd be able to hang on, hoping for some reprieve that always happened to show up at just the right time.

And thanks to Mac, he had that reprieve. They'd really connected during the pandemic and Mac had even taken Lemon along with him to Las Vegas in early 2022 for the SHOT Show, the huge annual gun trade show. Who'd have ever thought that some hard-ass first sergeant would be pals with one of his soldiers so many years later? Who ever thought he could provide that needed reprieve to a man hurting and in need of it?

Man, the Army must be getting soft.

CHAPTER 27

EXTERMINATING

When Tyler Koller got back from the Arghandab he kept going to church, but he soon lost faith in the Army and in the God of Pentecost. He soon started saying the word "fuck" and reveling in it. That and drinking Stag beer.

The majority of his time in uniform was spent deployed. He was in the Army for fifty-four months total and was deployed twenty-nine or twenty-nine and a half months of that, depending on how you count things.

The Arghandab wasn't literally the Valley of Death, but Koller felt like he'd done his time walking through Psalm 23. That second deployment ruined it all for him, and he decided it was time to get out of the Army. He still had faith in one thing, the desire to start a family, to have kids. So he got out.

And getting out, that turned out to be the biggest reason of all for him to wallow. He saw the combat, the death, the injuries. But he also knew all too well what might be the most painful part of being a veteran of combat: He knew the bone-deep regret at not being part of it anymore and of having given it up voluntarily.

Every soldier in every unit on every base in Uncle Sam's Army is getting out as soon as his contract is up. At least, that's what every soldier professes and will swear to up and down from sunrise to sunset. From the lowliest PFC to a West Point graduate, everyone in uniform, be they Army, Navy, Marine Corps, Air Force, or Coast Guard, every sonofabitch in the military says they're getting out as soon as they can, as soon as that reenlistment contract is up—which is, at most, a few years away. Even generals and admirals think to themselves, *Shit, is this really worth it? Maybe I should get out and not try for that next star.*

Granted, there are the occasional perverts and masochists who always know they're going to re-up, but they are rare and little seen in the wild. Even guys who set themselves up to be lifers tell themselves that they might be better off getting out after their contract's up. It's a truth universally acknowledged that an enlisted man in possession of an Army contract must be in want of getting the hell out.

But the time to get out actually rolls around and the Army offers a bonus, or a chance at going to scuba school, or something fancy like that as an enlistment sweetener. Or some first sergeant reminds his guys who are about to get out that the civilian world is scary and awful. Or they get a whiff of what it'd be like to find meaning and purpose in life without having it handed to them on a silver platter—and back they go.

But there're guys like Koller who do their time and then really do say, No, Sir, I am out of here. And many then regret it for the rest of their lives.

"When I was in, I knew I was making a difference, that I had a purpose," Koller said. "Since I got out, I don't feel like I did anything."

He got out because he was tired of the Army and ready to get on with things, with real life—whatever that is. He found out too late that real life is whatever you are doing right now. Too often a fellow lets life slip though his fingers while waiting for it. After the Army it was a string of failed relationships and bad jobs, nothing that made him want to jump out of bed in the morning.

The biggest reason Koller got out was to start a family, the thing he wanted more than anything else in life. He even had boys' and girls' names picked out for when the kids get here. But he hadn't found anyone he wanted to have kids with. All of a sudden he was worried it just wasn't going to happen, and the years just started rolling by.

"Every time that clock ticks I feel like I'm worsening my name," he said.

Koller had a playlist he could turn to when he needed to wallow, when he was feeling the way he sometimes felt. The way he often felt. That playlist was where he knew he could find refuge, where he could find solace.

One of the songs on that list was Nathan Fair's "Fallen Soldier." Fair was actually a soldier himself and he and his Ibanez guitar gave Koller the perfect song for when he was down deep in a dark place.

"This is for the ones who ain't coming back," Fair sings.

That playlist was the best consolation sometimes. Movies sometimes also let Koller sink down into it. They could be the catalyst. And, oddly enough, sometimes he chose to watch a movie that kicked off the whole wallowing chain reaction. It seemed like a weird thing to do, to purposefully pick at a scab that's healing over. But sometimes he had to.

Adam Armstrong was talking to Koller one time, on one of Armstrong's check-in calls, and Koller said he'll sometimes watch the movie *The Outpost*, an action flick about an Army base in Afghanistan that gets just about overrun by Taliban fighters.

Koller's girlfriend at the time asked him why he wanted to watch that kind of thing, because all it did was make him sink into a dark spot it seemed he hated going to.

Koller really couldn't answer her. He was telling Armstrong about it, and Armstrong gave him some perspective. He said to Koller, "Maybe you like to go to that place, maybe you want to go to that place?"

And Koller said, "Goddamn, Sir, you're right." He knew where to go to wallow, the direct route to get there and how to revel in it.

There's bowling, too, that could serve as a refuge for him. It was probably his favorite pastime. He's got his name in the Bowling Hall of Fame in Milwaukee, for Chrissake. When a guy rolls an honest-to-God 300 perfect game, they put his name in the hall of fame. Koller's done it three times at sanctioned events, no shit.

But bowling's a fickle mistress, and sometimes she scorned him. She'd given him three perfect games, yes, but on days when she wanted him to suffer, he might roll a 190 or something and it just pissed him off. It made him mad and depressed in a way that wallowing doesn't. He knew he should have mastery over the alley and damn it all when he didn't.

Bowling is unpredictable. A depressing playlist isn't.

So when things got bad, on anniversaries of deaths or at whatever moment the melancholy welled up in him, he'd turn on those songs that didn't require him to keep his wrist locked just so and to mind his follow-through.

Koller thought about trying to go back into the reserves or the National Guard, but he couldn't imagine serving with a lesser unit than the 82nd. Why would he want to join a unit, maybe deploy, and know that he's not serving with the best? He'd just be worried and annoyed the whole time. And there's no going back to the 82nd, Big Army, after cutting ties. That ship has sailed, there was no way to go back full-time in uniform.

By 2020 Koller had become an exterminator, doing pest control in crawl spaces and blasting vermin in god-awful government housing. Sometimes he'd go out on an extermination call where he just couldn't do anything—the apartment he was called to was just too filled with trash and rats or roaches for him to attempt anything. In those cases, he called the landlord and reported the nightmare scene. It was the best he could offer.

He traded the Army for this?

His Army experience was the highlight of his life so far, he said. A decade later, he said he didn't have any really good days. He only had days that weren't so shitty.

Koller knew he could call some of the Bravo guys anytime he needed to talk, but he wasn't geographically close to them. The COVID pandemic prevented gatherings for so long there right after the reunion, and he was stuck out in the middle of Illinois.

The Army wasn't an option anymore, but maybe, just maybe, one of these days he'd pick up and move to North Carolina, where he could be close to many of the Bravo guys, close to where he could see and touch and feel the presence of his Army buddies. That would be more comforting than church to him now.

* * *

J was a natural leader, an outgoing guy and just plain nice. Even though he lost his legs on a different trip to Afghanistan, the men from the 2009–2010 Bravo Company deployment unit were the ones he felt a true kinship with—the ones who truly appreciated the full scope of what he'd been through, the loss he experienced—so he stayed connected with them. He was kind of a hub, connected to people.

He reached out to his fellow Bravo guys pretty regularly for years and noticed some of the pain and dislocation they were feeling. J was in a good place, content with life and family and his war wounds, confident among his hives, a rock-solid foundation for Bravo on those prosthetics.

Sergeant J also was the keeper of the unit flag that started making its way to every funeral for someone close to Bravo Company, whether by suicide or overdose or death from illness, sickness sometimes triggered by Army service. The unit flag made its appearance and then went back to J.

Those suicides started happening to people around them, people in the orbit of Bravo, and that flag started coming out with some regularity. Some guys can't get beyond that deployment and what they saw, what they did. Combat. Life after. Operation Resiliency came about after that. But what about the rock-solid Sergeant J?

J still slipped into those dark times, too. Maybe for a week he won't want to do anything. It wasn't PTSD or memories of the combat or even the loss of his legs that got to him, he said. He wasn't mad, he just got in a bad mood. Maybe it was the combat trauma or the regret for decisions made and that can't be changed. Most likely, he says, it was because he probably would have stayed in twenty years, made a career of it. For about a decade he got to do cool shit like shoot guns and jump out of airplanes, hang out with his best friends all day every day. And all that disappeared in the flash of an IED.

But when those dark days came over him, he remembered his obligations and the things he truly loved: his wife, his three kids, and most of the time that snapped him out of it. Real life is the one that's here and now and J knew he had to be thankful for it and to live it. That wonderful family of his, they depended on him, loved him. If he gave up on life, what would happen to them? How would it affect his mom? She didn't bust her hump to bring him to the United States, hoeing those fields all day long so he could give up. To give up, to give in to some depression, is just selfish. That's shirking. And to know he couldn't give up, that it wasn't not an option, is what got him through.

He probably met only two guys in the civilian world since leaving the Army that he felt as close to as the guys he served with. His relationships with the men he shared a uniform with weren't really nostalgia for him, some harkening back to an imaginary perfect time that didn't really exist. Lots of soldiers get misty-eyed about the perfection of an Army they hated at the time. Nope, J knew his time in the Army was the imperfect time it was, but because of that imperfection, it was perfect.

The sheer shittiness of training in horrible weather and deploying to Afghanistan—that was what made it so good for him.

"It's the hardships, the training. Going through all the hard stuff together," he says. "You don't do that kind of stuff in everyday life. You can't replace it."

Now that was gone, and that was worse than losing some legs. When he talked to old Army buddies, they reminisced, talked about the Army like some people talk about high school. He was happy to talk about those old Army days as long as they'd want to talk about it. If they wanted to talk about the past, they should do just that. Guys got so mad about politics or the news—why ruin a relationship that's a decade old with that nonsense?

And sometimes those guys got mad, got all worked up about the Taliban. Sergeant J was never mad at the Taliban, even when he was in the middle of fighting them. No reason to be angry, even though he was 99.99 percent sure one of their IEDs blew off his legs. "It was a bad day at the office," he says.

They did their job. He did his. They were fighting for their cause. He was fighting for his. He never hated them. That doesn't mean he had mercy for them. He sure as shit wanted to kill the enemy whenever and wherever they presented themselves. But that was the job. Well, that was his job a few years back.

What did they accomplish in Afghanistan? They dominated their area of operations as best they could, and they were part of something much bigger. They had to have been part of something bigger, he said. That's what he wanted to believe.

They were a piece in a bigger puzzle, one tiny doll nested inside a larger doll, and on and on. He's happy to have done his job. In mid-2020, as the war finally drew to a close in Afghanistan, he was fine with it. Peace has to come sometime, after all, doesn't it?

* * *

A decade after that deployment to the Arghandab, Rob Musil was coming up on a career's worth of time in the Army, nearly twenty years, and was still trying to find a reason for all that he'd done and what he continued to do. All those years of violence and of trying to make meaning of all the deployments and all this shit he'd waded through. All the death he'd seen. All the death he'd caused.

Thanks to his philosophical turn, Musil was able to keep competing ideas in his head, have them spar with each other, have them exist in lively tension. The inside of his head was like a philosophical debate team, all trying to defeat the logic of a proposition with outlandish what-ifs.

That gave Musil's philosophical meanderings a disjointed and unfinished sense as he let all these concepts play out in his mind, trying to edge out each other for primacy. It means he was never able to settle on an Answer. But he's found a few small-*a* answers.

There's no higher power or some religious imperative to it all, he figured that much out. He certainly wasn't taming the heathen or doing God's work out there on the battlefield.

So there must be some sort of a temporal reason for all this, a this-wordly ultimate purpose to the wars he's fought in, right? At the very least it's got to be championing human rights, or making life better for people who'd otherwise be living under horrible dictatorships or theocracies. Or maybe it's making the world safe for democracy. Something. Anything?

No.

There doesn't seem to be any good reason for it all, no reason a general or a statesman might give that would have satisfied him. The paycheck wasn't even a reason. Hoping for some lasting diplomatic and geo-strategic gains for the good old US of A wasn't even a reason.

The 2009 deployment to the Arghandab with Bravo Company is exactly the case in point: Sure, the United States and the Afghan government controlled the territory for a little while. But who controlled it a decade later? The Taliban, that's who.

In the waning days of the Donald Trump administration and in the first year of Joe Biden's presidency, the United States got busy withdrawing from the Afghan War, and the Taliban got busy retaking everything they'd, on paper, lost over the past two decades.

It would probably be better to say the Taliban were again asserting power over areas they'd temporarily neglected for a decade or two.

The rush for the exits began when Donald Trump made clear in February 2020 that his administration was ready to leave Afghanistan and was not going to insist on any real conditions that the Taliban would have to follow other than an agreement that the Taliban would reduce violence. They proved to not abide by that agreement. Instead of cracking down on the Taliban, Trump agreed to release thousands of Taliban fighters who had been held prisoner by the Afghan government. In October 2020, the former president said in a Twitter post that he wanted all US troops home by Christmas. He didn't accomplish that, but the message was clear.

The drawdown sped up to breakneck speed in February 2021 under Joe Biden, who said he was going to carry through with the withdrawal. He later said he wasn't going to pass the buck in the same breath that he passed the buck, saying he was hamstrung and nearly forced to continue the course set by his predecessor. Besides, the Biden administration said, the Afghan military and government would be able to stand on its own for a while after the American departure.

In July of 2021 the Biden administration signaled an imminent withdrawal of US forces by pulling troops from Bagram Airfield, the major base for US troops and the one so close to Kabul. The Taliban showed an imminent ability to sweep through the entire country and resume exercising power. In the course of a few weeks later that summer, the Taliban took provincial centers and towns, barreling through the country and eventually grabbing all but Kabul and a few scattered pockets of the country.

Hamid Karzai International Airport became an unmitigated shitshow in August of that year as Afghans hoping to flee the country and the Taliban takeover flocked to the airport to try and get on any flight to anywhere. The American government was caught unprepared and couldn't even airlift all the US citizens who wanted to leave the country. It took a motley coalition of foreign governments, aid groups, former commandos, and the remaining might of the US military, now humbled, to get desperate Afghans out of the country. One young Afghan man, so despairing of his plight, clung to the outside of an American military plane as it trundled down the runway and into the air. He fell from the plane after it took off, dying once he hit the ground.

Within days the Taliban was in charge. The old Afghan government with women in positions of power and progressive intentions was gone. The Afghan National Army dissolved. Afghan Air Force officers flew what aircraft they could out of the country.

The mullahs had won. The twenty-year project had failed. In the winter of 2022, Afghans across the country were starving, their government helping little. Taliban funds were frozen by Western nations and the United States government. Then, Joe Biden's administration turned to American domestic affairs and all but ignored Afghanistan. Many Afghans who had made it to the United States for resettlement languished on military bases awaiting processing. After billions spent on decades of war, the US government couldn't provide winter coats for children housed on US Army bases and left it to aid agencies to fill the gaps. Menstruating Afghan women resorted to using paper towels because they didn't have adequate sanitary napkins.

President Joe Biden and Chairman of the Joint Chiefs General Mark Milley were ready to move on to focus on threats from China and Russia. The Afghanistan War was over, after all.

Then came Russia's assault on Ukraine, the next big war. Any military focus shifted there. Afghanistan was suddenly, definitively, a war of the past.

So what if Musil was part of a unit that won and (technically) controlled that battlespace for a little while? So what? The Taliban got it back.

It's not like the Taliban are a bunch of morons who stumbled into success. No, Musil lauded and respected the Taliban commanders. He didn't respect their religious or moral values—those fundamentalist assholes had always been hypocrites as far as he was concerned. But damned if he didn't respect them as fellow combatants in the profession of arms. Damned if he didn't respect them as statesmen for winning in the end, for beating the US military at its own game.

Every time Musil went to Afghanistan he gained more respect for the

Taliban. They kicked the shit out of the Russians a few decades earlier and then they beat the most technologically advanced military on the planet. They ripped America a new one.

Good for them, man. Let the Afghans do their Afghan thing and work things out among themselves, he thought. Why did Musil need to fight there for so many deployments if that was what was going to happen anyway?

Musil sort of felt that, after the Arghandab, he'd gone a decade with no big win. And after Operation Resiliency, after the reunion, he started thinking about the future and about his past. Thinking like that takes away from a fella's ability to win glory. No, he decided to focus that passion for war on something different. He opted to head into the Ranger schoolhouse to teach the next generation of soldiers the awful and beautiful profession of arms.

Musil went down to Florida to be an instructor at the Ranger School, eschewing deployment and instead chasing the Platonic form of war. At the same time, he decided he'd better go talk to a counselor—a first for him—to figure out what the hell was going on inside of him way down in the depths.

After all, all those guys who had died by their own hands, all those guys whose lives had fallen apart since deployment . . . why not him? There but for the grace of God and all that.

He's read his Søren Kierkegaard, he knew it took a leap of faith into the darkness, into the void, to have an existential reckoning. And he was trying that now by going back to the schoolhouse, by seeking some counseling—he really was trying to find out how to make it all make sense.

Even as he recognized the need to fill the void, he knew he was doing it, filling the void, with war and booze. He'd tell you straight up that the booze was a problem and a little out of control. But what the hell, it's silly to pretend every soldier's a gentleman with an ascot and monocle. No, guys like him drink too much and cuss. They're supposed to. They were built like that. Or at least, they turned into that.

But even at Ranger School as an instructor, Musil tried to short-circuit his own plan. He signed up surreptitiously, a few months into his new position, to jump on a deployment to Syria. His command found out about it and said "Hell no," he made his bed to be an instructor and now he's lying in it.

And he was still filling that void with booze.

One night, in the fall of 2020, he was zooming around in his car after drinking and got a flat tire. What bad luck. Some Good Samaritan stopped to help him change the tire and thought Musil was drunk, so they called the cops. What bad luck. When the cops showed up there was a standoff and old Musil ended up in a bad way.

Then he was en route to Texas, to a drunk tank for inpatient treatment. A helluva way for him to go. It's one thing for a guy to realize he's got problems, and another to deal with them. But there's an advantage in knowing you're fucked up, even if it's hard—seemingly impossible, even—to deal with. Musil has what former SecDef Donald Rumsfeld would call "known unknowns"—problems that he was sure were there but wasn't sure what they were.

After he finished drying out—somehow blessedly avoiding getting busted by his command for the effort—the upheaval in Afghanistan began. Taliban takeover. Panicked evacuation. It was all over the news, everywhere he turned, a subject of every conversation. Musil drank too many beers again and rolled his BMW over into a ditch. He almost killed himself.

The woman he was dating called him that night and didn't get an answer (he always answered). She imagined the worst. She called around to every hospital in the area until she found him. She went to the ER and got there, by sheer stupid luck, right as the doctors were contemplating what to do about this unconscious guy in the ER.

She told the doctors he was a soldier, had brain trauma from the war. They decided to hold off on major surgery. They didn't crack open his skull or anything. He came back around, regained consciousness, and maybe finally figured out he should slow down a bit and not constantly taunt fate. Well, he figured it out yet again.

He dried out after the accident. Musil had long said he should know better, but it took the accident for him to take his own counsel. At work he was formally reprimanded, but thanks to his extensive record of excellence—the tangible benefits of being among the high priesthood—his command didn't smash him to bits.

They did take him out of the rotation at Ranger School, though, wouldn't let him teach students anymore, which very much hurt him. He knew his time deploying and fighting was coming to an end, or maybe had already ended, but he wanted to pass along so many lessons to the next generation, seminarians training for their own investiture.

* * *

For Lyle Pressley, the summer of 2020 was when he was finally able to have the Big Surgery, that back procedure known as the Tiger Woods.

But having that surgery, the Big One, means that things either would get better for his back or they wouldn't. There would be no more wondering about his body's future, it would be determined. It was a last-chance thing.

All his chips were on this one, and if the pain was still there after everything healed up, then he didn't know what he was going to do. He imagined his only option might be just to live the rest of his days in a dark, dark place. He'd fall into that hole again and his wife might not even be able to get him out.

By the fall of 2020, he'd had the surgery and it seemed a success, even though he was still in a lot of pain. There was still some healing that had to happen, so there was hope yet.

Thank God for his wife, who had been there by his side for all of this.

But it was still so hard to talk to her. There was always something behind every conversation, or rather in the middle of it, blocking things, and he worried whether there would always be the promise of future conversations. It was almost like she was too close to him to have these conversations he so desperately wanted to have.

And the counselor at the VA, and the shrink, they were no good, either. They were too far away and didn't know enough about him and about what he'd gone through. The behavioral health counselor at the VA just kept giving him these stupid worksheets to look at and work through. Printouts, like some middle school teacher. How the hell was Lyle supposed to connect with a guy who's never been there in combat and who gives him damn printouts?

The shrink was a different problem. She just wanted to give him more meds or adjust the dosages of the ones he was on. She seemed only to be interested in tinkering with his scripts like a DJ fooling around with an equalizer. He wasn't a science experiment. But in that way she was no different from any of the docs he'd gone to at the VA—they all seemed to be constantly tweaking and playing around with his meds. Some for his moods, some for his PTSD, some for his back pain.

After the Tiger Woods surgery, he had to go back on oxycodone, there was no two ways about it, even though he'd rather have not been on it. He had such a high tolerance for the stuff, but he needed to heal up, and it was so damn painful all the time still.

But the oxy made him clam up even worse than usual, made the communication that much harder. And it's just another medication added to the mix.

During the COVID period, after the surgery, he was on a dozen medications, so many he didn't know himself anymore, and he asked, please, couldn't he just get off some of them to find a baseline and then reassess and represcribe? He didn't even know what the real him felt anymore.

But the shrink wouldn't do it, and he didn't dare try and mess with the dosages or the number of scripts himself. How can you do something like that on your own? And anyway, if he didn't follow their prescriptions, he might be identified as an uncooperative patient. What if that led to a drop in his VA rating, how much he got for his disabilities? That would have hurt his wife, who he cares about so deeply, and his kids, the emergency escape he could always depend on to bring him out of the hole when he finds himself in it.

But time went by and healing happened. After a few months the surgery seemed to have really worked. The physical therapy seemed to be working. Yes, he needed a pill to get the day started, but he no longer worried that the wrong twist of his hips or tilt of his head would send him spiraling into misery. He could play with his kids, he could unload the dishwasher. He could do his schoolwork. He could do it.

So many questions resolved themselves as his back began to recover, as he dug out from under the weight of chronic pain and immobility.

His engineering degree was so close by early 2022, and he'd lined up a good-paying job upon graduation.

His back had been rescued, pulled back from the brink, it seemed. He still had the memories of the Arghandab and all the darkness that brought, but the place no longer had a physical hold on him. He'd broken free of it in that way, so perhaps he could break free of its memory, too.

Most important, he still had his wife after all this. They had each other. They had their kids. He found himself talking with her. They had a future that made him smile and wonder in awe at her endurance and love.

Wonder at her ability to shoulder any load, like Paul Bunyan.

* * *

Amid the upheaval and horrors of withdrawal from Afghanistan, Bravo Company's old interpreter, Johnny, wanted to get out.

After his time interpreting for Bravo Company, he had bounced around to other US military units. But he was very, very tired. That Bravo deployment was enough in its own right. After all, he still talked about the fact that nearly half the interpreters on that deployment quit because it was so dangerous and scary. They didn't get replacements. Instead guys like Johnny had to pick up the slack and do more work.

He got married and in 2014 quit interpreting. His parents told him that he'd been flirting with danger for too long, that everyone in their town knew he'd been working for the Americans, and that one day that résumé of his would get them all killed. They knew the Americans would eventually leave, while Johnny and his family would remain in Afghanistan. So he quit.

He took jobs at a gas station, at a supermarket, just the sort of jobs he'd avoided when he became an interpreter in the first place. But he had a wife, and they started having children. And he was happy to finally settle down. In 2020 he applied for a Special Immigrant Visa, a US government provision for Afghans who had served the Americans in roles like interpreters. But the process, like any bureaucratic process, took forever. There were interviews and documents and testimonies. He had to take advantage of that résumé his parents were so worried about.

Then Trump started making deals with the Taliban, and Biden kept going with it. The situation seemed to suddenly unravel, get worse day by day, with the Taliban slowly creeping into districts and provinces and getting closer to his hometown of Lashkar Gah. Johnny fled to Kabul, like so many others, as the Taliban sped to power in the summer of 2021. That résumé of his was suddenly very, very worrisome. If the Taliban took over, if the Taliban found out about his past, what would happen to him, his wife, his three daughters, the rest of his family?

So he deleted all the photos on his phone and on his computer, all the images of him alongside Americans. He burned his documents, destroyed the résumé he'd worked years to build, and hoped beyond hope that the copies he'd sent for his visa were safe. He'd gotten to Kabul early enough to get passports for his family, arrived before the full collapse of the Afghan government that he'd help fight for.

As other Afghans pulled whatever strings they could to get out, many of them unsuccessfully, Johnny reached out to his Bravo Company brothers. He reached out to Sarah Verardo. With the Bravo Company family fighting for him, using military and government connections, Johnny and his family got a flight out of Afghanistan in August of 2021, in the middle of the fall of his country. In a whirlwind they left the country, came to the United States, and spent a few days at Fort Lee in Virginia, warehoused with so many others before he and his wife and children could settle in North Carolina, in Charlotte, where Sarah Verardo and Mike Verardo and other Bravo brethren lived.

A local family had space in a rental property, so Johnny's family had a house. The kids were enrolled in a local school. They went to the Verardos for dinner. His children played soccer on a team with Mike and Sarah's kids. At one soccer practice, as Mike sat next to Johnny in the placid sun of a peaceful suburb, they heard the soccer coach tell the children they needed to stand shoulder to shoulder if they wanted to win. Johnny leaned over to Mike and reminded him that "shoulder to shoulder," or *shona ba shona,* was the mantra US forces always used when working with Afghans. It was a pledge that soldiers and defense officials repeated again and again as a guarantee the Americans could always be trusted to stand with their Afghan counterparts no matter what might happen. If the US government forgot about that pledge, Mike and Sarah Verardo had not.

* * *

And after it all, what could the men of Bravo Company look back on and glory in? Had they done anything worthwhile in the Arghandab or had they just gotten blown up for no reason? Yes, sure, there is always the notion that soldiers, once in the trenches, aren't fighting for some strategic goal but rather for the men right next to them. That much is true, and will always be true, but it's far too simple an explanation to be any explanation at all.

Every man or woman who's served takes pride in the immediacy of what they did, but for a company ravaged by war and haunted by it a decade later, there has to be something more, doesn't there? Looking at a microscopic view of a deployment really doesn't give great satisfaction that a grander mission was accomplished.

Likewise, to look at the big picture doesn't do much, either. The Arghandab and the rest of the country reverted to Taliban control, so in the grand cosmic sense, it seems like nobody did their mission in a way that was worth it. It's foolish to look at the grandest of grand schemes and hope to glean real purpose. Everything falls apart in the end.

So where does a soldier look to determine if what he or she did was ultimately worth it? Seems that there's a spot that's not too close and not too far away where a soldier can hope to find some answers. Somewhere between what happened on a single patrol and the final outcome of the war.

That spot is where the sweat and blood and sacrifice may have created a worthy accomplishment of some sort, allows the next unit that comes in to have an easier time of things, lets generals plan a follow-on effort.

Lieutenant General Dan Bolger said, in a short and paradoxical compliment, what might be the best thing that the men of Bravo Company and the 2-508 could ever have said about them. In one sentence he said something that might just mean the world to these men.

He said of their time in the Arghandab:

"They accomplished a task that was beyond their capability."

* * *

In February of 2021, Lieutenant Colonel Adam Armstrong talked on the phone as he drove to Fort Drum in upstate New York. His wife, Kim, was in the car ahead of him, her vehicle burdened with a car-top carrier: yet another move to yet another base.

Since leaving Bravo, Armstrong had a new job every few years, as is typical in the Army. An officer isn't always commanding troops, contrary to what many might think. In fact, an officer rarely gets the opportunity to command troops himself, and since being a captain and spending that time in the Arghandab, he hadn't been in command of a combat unit. He hadn't had that onerous burden, the kind that he had only recently begun to feel the full weight of from Bravo Company.

The Armstrongs were on their way up to Fort Drum because he was taking command of a battalion from the Tenth Mountain Division. He was about to assume the same spot in the Army's hierarchy that Frank Jenio had occupied at the beginning of that 2009 deployment. Armstrong was to become a battalion commander.

He and Kim had been married fifteen and a half years at that point. And he'd spent more than five of those years deployed in some manner or fashion. Now he was about to take on battalion command, which was like a deployment even while living in the United States. A battalion commander's job is round-the-clock. They would be living in a house on base, so he'd be just minutes away from the office.

The burdens of the forthcoming job worried him in ways they worry every new battalion commander who's about to take charge of millions of dollars' worth of equipment and be responsible for some one thousand souls under his command, liable for everything they do or fail to do. But he was also worried about his existing commitments, the pledges of fidelity and responsibility he'd made to the men of Bravo Company.

Armstrong confessed that another soldier, a man who'd once commanded a battalion himself, said Adam was crazy to think that he had any further ties to Bravo beyond what he'd already done. He was moving on to a new command and had those men, and himself, to consider. But Armstrong had told that officer that he was going to do it, he was going to stretch himself as much as he had to in order to do the right thing. He'd done it before, so why not try?

And, goddammit, look how much they'd been able to do since he really started making the effort. Since Operation Resiliency there had been zero suicides among Bravo Company veterans. Zero. He was talking to men when he could, and he was always keeping tabs on them through

Sarah Verardo, who often enlisted Armstrong to make a call or intervene with a guy in crisis, sometimes at a moment's notice.

About a month after his arrival at Fort Drum, the boys from Bravo Company held a little virtual ceremony for Armstrong over Zoom. A number of them turned up, men who had laughed at him years before, called him Captain America. Men who had hated him for what had happened on that Arghandab deployment and who had blamed him personally for the deaths of friends, for their own grievous injuries. They turned up to pay their respects and well-wishes to this man who had proven his fidelity and devotion to them long after he had any bureaucratically dictated reason to do so.

"You're 100 percent the best commander I ever had," Mac, his old first sergeant, told him. "You always made the hard call over the easy one because that's what a good officer does. What means so much to all of us is that you're still here."

A few other men expressed their gratitude. Danica thanked him for his dedication to her and her family.

Armstrong wiped away a tear and told the men that he had to be honest, time would be at a premium at his new command, but he reiterated his pledge to them—his Army family—that he'd always be there and always be available if needed.

And they believed him. They knew it was true. They were his family. And they had each other.

* * *

Weeks later, at Fort Drum, Armstrong sat on a plastic chair in a nondescript hall, the Army's version of a massive conference room. He was waiting to formally take over command of the Second Battalion of the Twenty-Second Infantry Regiment, part of the Tenth Mountain Division.

The troops from the battalion had seen this shit before. A new commander taking over, charging in like he was some sort of big shot.

Armstrong got his chance to speak and stood up, that tall, lean runner's build bulked up by loose-fitting Army combat fatigues. He looked serious. He didn't uncork that enduring smile of his.

He spoke to the men of the battalion, the officers and enlisted. The speech wasn't anything grand, nothing that will ever be placed under glass in the National Archives or anything. In that way, it was like so many other forgettable speeches that have been given since time immemorial by officers trying to say the right thing in front of their troops. *Rote bullshit*, a salty cynic in the crowd may have thought.

But for anyone who knows Adam Armstrong, the shopworn platitudes meant something that they don't mean when a typical officer spouts them off. And as he concluded, he told these men, most of whom he'd not yet been able to talk to personally, that he now considered them family.

And they couldn't possibly know what a vow of that kind meant from Lieutenant Colonel Adam Armstrong.

To many of them, such a seemingly preposterous claim made him seem like a lifer trying to say something to impress the generals. He was clearly just in it to win it.

To the salty troops of his new battalion, he was just another goddamn Captain America.

AUTHOR'S NOTE

I first met Bravo Company in the writing of a *Wall Street Journal* article about them in April 2019. I went down to Charlotte, North Carolina, for their suicide-prevention retreat called Operation Resiliency and spent a few days talking with those who became central characters of this book. One evening they headed off as a group to a private event, and I was left with nothing to do other than think through my notes.

I walked to a brew pub, and amid seersucker-clad Carolinians who laughed and watched college basketball on massive televisions, the enormity of Bravo Company's story hit me—as did the immense responsibility of what it meant to write about them. There was no way I could do them justice. I broke down and cried there at the bar, wept into my pilsner. It was the first time in nearly a decade of reporting that such a thing had happened.

It was also the first time since my deployments as a Marine to Iraq and Afghanistan—the very same war in which Bravo served—that such a thing had happened. Somewhere down deep, I reckoned that in telling their story I would somehow tell a version of my own.

The resulting *Wall Street Journal* story came out in July 2019. With little fanfare, I moved on to other stories. I liked how the feature turned out, but I also felt I'd been given a chance to tell Bravo's story and hadn't done them justice. I'd brought neither these men nor myself any resolution. I'd squandered my chance.

Jamison Stoltz of Abrams Press wrote me soon after the *Journal* article came out, urging me to do more with the story of Bravo Company, their war, and its aftermath. Afghanistan had again receded from headlines by this time, and even moved to the back of my mind as I was more recently focused on reporting from the front lines in Iraq, where Islamic State demanded attention. Over the course of a few months, Jamison applied ever-increasing pressure. The cosmos, via a New York publisher, demanded resolution. I relented. I still felt unworthy of writing Bravo's story, but I was now bound by a contract and deadlines.

Before becoming a reporter I served as a Marine Corps infantry officer. I had combat deployments to both Iraq and Afghanistan. I had never taken the time to unpack those deployments, to talk through what they meant to me. In the decade since I'd left the Marine Corps, I'd barreled forward in life. I attended Northwestern University's graduate journalism school thanks to my GI Bill benefits, then rushed off to join the *Journal*. As a reporter I covered the Pentagon and the Department of Veterans Affairs. I was a foreign correspondent and combat correspondent, and I covered presidential elections. My wife and I also began a family. We had four children amid it all. That's a lot of kids. In other words, since taking off the uniform things were hectic, and that maelstrom gave my life meaning. One of the many things I learned from Bravo Company is that you have to slow down and make an effort in order to properly reflect back on such matters.

People don't often ask me about my experience, how being in and reporting about war has affected me as a Marine, a journalist, a father, a person. It's not that I've put aside my experiences as a veteran or tried to avoid them, it's just that amid multiple children, last-minute reporting trips, and the ever-increasing pace of family life, I never reflected systematically about the enormity of the experience. And, frankly, it doesn't seem that most people care. Yet, in conversations with family, over that one extra drink with friends, or while just lying in bed in the stillness of night, I'd sometimes grab on to a single thought, an isolated moment, or one theme. I'd tarry with that thing for a moment. But, as in the parable of blind men who can't comprehend an entire elephant in feeling only its trunk or leg or tusk, I never made sense of all the pieces at the same time.

Some smart friends told me this book needed an author's note to explain the "so what" of the book. They wanted to know how I fit into it. More important: What does all this reporting and writing mean in the end? In writing about Bravo for years and in unpacking my own story and my own relationship to war I have come up with just a few things I'm willing to put stock in. The most important: Every person's story in this book remains unfinished. Many men and women mentioned are still alive as I write this and are thus themselves still works in progress with unfinished legacies. Their free will is still electric in its power to make change. What they've done previously, if bad, can be yet redeemed. And if they've lived a noble life so far, it can yet be despoiled and tarnished. What's more, for those no longer alive, their legacies aren't etched permanently in history. Even soldiers from Bravo Company who are long-dead and buried have stories that remain ever-changing. The seemingly hard facts of their lives and deaths are still open to interpretation and reinterpretation, even up to the very time you read these words. And beyond.

Even facts themselves might be subject to change as memories shift, as events are forgotten or misremembered. They are subject even to the vicissitudes of ever-changing interpretations of history. Certainties get questioned.

In writing this book, I learned that no veteran's service is ever finished. Our responsibilities to one another don't cease. Hard to believe it took a bunch of Army paratroopers to help a Marine better understand *Semper Fidelis,* but such is the nature of things. I hope, in turn, that some soldiers find meaning in what this Marine gleaned after a few years of talking with them. We owe that to each other, don't we?

This reporting made plain to me the futility of one-upmanship when it comes to trauma. If you want to prove your PTSD is worse than the next person's, you've got it all wrong. Many combat-hardened veterans welcome others to talk about their traumas, their problems, their crosses to bear, so we can all do the same. Yes, certain traumas may seem objectively greater than others, but we can't know the suffering borne in the hearts of our fellow human beings.

Through years of interviewing others about their experiences I addressed my own feelings, many yet unspoken, as if I had been on a therapist's couch. I hope my sincerity of effort comes through in these pages, and that when others read this they gain solace by it and use their resolution to comfort others. I hope the book is like a batch of sourdough, the original version fermenting away as parts of it are taken for future batches. Better batches, I hope.

Writing this book made me—and there's a sadness in what I'm about to say, so bear with me—more deeply realize all the things I could have done better in my life. It laid bare all the mistakes, misgivings, and errors I need to atone for, and my need for redemption. I think we'd be better off in our lives and as a species if we all were honest about such matters. But recognizing those many past failings—and, ah!, here's a great happiness— opened the door to true redemption, to making a better future, beginning right now.

There's no telos in war or society, no definite end state everything moves toward. But perhaps there's a telos for each and every one of us. Perhaps there's a Good Life we're supposed to move toward, like flowing water finding its way to where it ought to be. After all these long conversations with Bravo Company veterans I know one thing for certain: The deepest existential truths only can be revealed through genuine interaction with other people. God evinces the divine in our fellow humans and we'd better pay attention to such power wherever it manifests. It takes other people to let us look more deeply at ourselves. It takes others to help us interpret and understand what we've gone through and what we're going through. In other words, we need other people in our lives in order to call us out on our bullshit. Likewise, we need others to praise us for that which we do well but don't give ourselves credit for.

My greatest hope is that this book is written so that even the people who were at the events described herein and who described to me their firsthand experiences might be taken to a place they previously didn't know existed and to which they hadn't any access before. What more can any author hope for?

So, in the end, what is it all about? What does the experience of war mean? If you think you really know, then you're either a fool or you're full of shit.

Well, that's not true. You may say, simply, that you are certain it demands you to walk more humbly before your god and fellow man.

Ben Kesling
Chicago
Summer 2022

ACKNOWLEDGMENTS

I owe many people thanks for inspiration, help, and forbearance in undertaking the telling of Bravo Company's story, and I apologize in advance that this list cannot be longer.

Thanks to those who read early versions of the manuscript, including Tom Bolin and Doug Belkin who read it in its messiest form and gave me hope it could come together. Phil Klay's read of this book as it neared the finish was invaluable and I thank him for showing us all how we might approach writing, thinking, faith, and family. Wes Morgan shared his time and Afghanistan expertise at the beginning of this endeavor and, as always, set an example of how journalism serves humanity, that reporters ought to help one another in the collective effort to document and understand war. And Dr. Mark Huffman ruined a passel of his green felt-tip pens, marking in the margins of an early manuscript a greater number of suggestions than there are stars in the sky. Thanks to everyone for catching errors, it goes without saying that any remaining are mine alone.

I can't say how much I have benefited from the teaching of Marcel Pacatte, Karen Springen, Joe Mathewson, and Jim Miller at the Medill School of Journalism. Posthumous thanks to Bill Placher, the most humane theologian and wonderful man Wabash College could ever hope to produce. Much of my thought on life—and the divine—come from his description of the vulnerability of God. I miss him. Thank you to the great editors

I've had, especially Jason Dean, Joe Barrett, and Bob Ourlian at the *Wall Street Journal*. Thanks to my agent, Rafe Sagalyn, and to Del Quentin Wilber and Brett Forrest for giving me a gentle shove into the deep end of book writing. Mike Phillips has been a wonderful mentor at the *Journal* and he came up with a great lede for the original newspaper story about Bravo Company: the story that got this whole process rolling. Michael R. Gordon has been a wonderful colleague. Thank you to Jon Eig for his encouragement, friendship, and example.

During the process I had support at home on a weekly basis from Andy Mitchell, Darren Szrom, Scott Thomson, John Wyman, and Mark Huffman who listened to a writer's woes and seldom complained. Many cocktails probably contributed to their magnanimity. Rob, Stella, and Beck Hansen were never far whenever I needed support—or if home-improvement assistance was required. Added thanks to Rob for his excellent photography.

Lisa Katona gave me early insight into the profession of therapy and the power of truly, and deeply, listening to someone tell their story. If someone speaks, we ought to listen. John Ravizza, Bridget Burke Ravizza, and Clare have always provided steadfast friendship and remain exemplars of hospitality and lived faith. Alas, their collective euchre skill is wanting.

Thanks to Graeme Smith, Sarah Chayes, Beth Cole, Marine Nitze, Carter Malkasian, Neamat Njoumi, Art Kandarian, Andrew Bacevich, Leon Panetta, Admiral Mike Mullen, Scott Gratian, Army Secretary Pete Green, General Peter Chiarelli, Kevin Carroll, and others who graciously gave their time as I researched and worked on this project.

David and Glenda Kesling have been ever supportive of all endeavors I've undertaken, and I appreciate it more than they can ever know. Parents can always have done better, I reckon. But these two certainly could have done a damn sight worse. Tim and Mary Jo Brecht have likewise been wonderful to me, despite myself.

I thank Sergeant Major Don Reynolds, USMC, for being the platoon sergeant every second lieutenant ought to have, and for all the invaluable lessons he taught me when I was a young Marine Corps officer with no idea of everything that goes into being a professional soldier. I am still trying to understand it. Thank you, Reynolds.

Everybody's got to thank their editor. I mean, you need know which side your bread's buttered on. But in my case the gratitude is genuine. Without Jamison Stoltz of Abrams Press this book would never have happened. He read my newspaper story of less than one thousand words about Bravo Company and reached out to ask if there might be a book in there somewhere. There was. For his editing and vision I remain thankful.

Thank you to Bravo Company and all their families and friends who have been willing to open up to me and tell their stories. I remain amazed when people open up and make themselves vulnerable and then trust me to do justice to them. I hope they realize I take this duty seriously and that fear of misrepresenting or fumbling their stories keeps me up at night.

Thank you, Mara, for everything you've done to encourage this book and to encourage me. You are an exemplar as a scholar, a mother, and a partner. Finally, to Kate, Gus, Lewis, and Alice: The fundamental issues addressed in this book will remain very much relevant by the time you're able to read and understand them. I hope this book might help you to make sense of some of them. Please know your arrival in this world has made my life much richer and meaningful. I love you all.